JAPANESE RURAL SOCIETY

ELECTION CANVASSING IN A VILLAGE

JAPANESE RURAL SOCIETY

BY

TADASHI FUKUTAKE

*Professor of Sociology
University of Tokyo*

TRANSLATED BY

R. P. DORE

Cornell Paperbacks

CORNELL UNIVERSITY PRESS

ITHACA AND LONDON

$2.95

First printing, Cornell Paperbacks, 1972

Published in the United Kingdom by Cornell University Press Ltd., 2-4 Brook Street, London W1Y 1AA.

International Standard Book Number 0-8014-9127-4
Library of Congress Catalog Card Number 72-4314
Printed in the United States of America by Vail-Ballou Press, Inc.
Librarians: Library of Congress cataloging information appears on the last page of the book.

CONTENTS

vi

LIST OF PLATES

PREFACE TO THE ENGLISH EDITION

I HAVE attempted in this book to give a general systematic survey of every aspect of Japanese rural society. It was first published in Japanese in 1964, but the idea of making it available in English was already present in my mind when I began to write the Japanese original. It was an idea which had occurred to me during a year of foreign travel in 1960-1, when I was frequently asked by my Indian and American friends to recommend to them a good general introductory book dealing with Japanese villages. It was, in fact, my intention to write such a book as soon as I returned, but the intention was temporarily thwarted by a survey trip to India and the preparation of reports on that trip, first in Japanese and then in English.

The Japanese manuscript was eventually written chiefly in the summer of 1963. It has been translated into English by Professor Ronald Dore, my closest friend among foreign scholars since the days, fifteen years ago, when we first went together on field trips to Japanese villages then still bearing the scars of the recent war. I am grateful to him indeed for the trouble he has taken over this translation when he was busy with so many other things, particularly since, as he makes clear in his introduction, he disagrees with some of my judgements and conclusions. In his more polemical moments he accuses me of 'neo-agrarian fundamentalism'. I think he is wrong, of course, though the stimulus of his criticism has helped me to rethink some of my own assumptions. I am looking forward to continuing our friendly disagreements when we visit Japanese villages together again this summer.

Tokyo, April 1965   TADASHI FUKUTAKE

TRANSLATOR'S INTRODUCTION

THE rise of modern Japanese industry is well known. It is also well known in general terms that the growth of manufacturing was accompanied by—indeed made possible by—a steady rise in the efficiency of Japanese agriculture. Most people with some knowledge of Japan are also generally aware both of the material cost of this progress and of its material rewards. They have read of the plight of the villagers in the thirties who could not even afford the proverbial bowl of rice a day that Japanese were supposed to be able to live on, and they read now of the villages of the present where four out of five farmers have a television set, and a washing machine is as much taken for granted as a cooking pot. Much less is known in the West, however, of the subtler social changes which have accompanied these material transformations—of the changing balance between individual self-assertiveness and loyalty to the corporate family on the one hand and to the corporate hamlet on the other; of the adaptation of traditional hamlet communities to modern associational forms, and of the balance between expressive solidarity and instrumental association which they now display; of the ramifying economic and political links which tie the villages to the outside world and the way those links have affected their structure.

Professor Fukutake is concerned precisely with these matters, and it is difficult to think of anyone better qualified to fill this gap in Western literature. For more than a quarter of a century he has been visiting villages; chiefly in Japan, but also in China and more recently in India, Europe and America. In his two weeks in this village and three weeks in that, he has acquired an unrivalled store of personal knowledge of the variety of structural forms and of cultural patterns to be found in Japanese villages. Consequently, the generalizations he makes are no off-hand extrapolations from a few examples. Many of the changes he records in his discussion of the transition from the traditional to the modern are changes he himself has witnessed. For earlier periods, his picture of the villages of the Meiji era derives not only from contemporary writings, and documents preserved in village offices and hamlet archive-boxes, but also from the personal reminiscences of countless farmers. And no one who has seen Professor Fukutake squatting at a smoky farm-house hearth chewing a fly-blown slice of pickled egg-plant and drawing out a farmer's story with sympathy and humour, can doubt his capacity for empathy, for getting at the heart of a man's memories, his anxieties and hopes, his hates and loves.

Rural sociology in some parts of the world is an arid subject, largely concerned with elaborate statistical measurements of such things as the rate of diffusion of innovations or participation in organizations which townsmen believe promote the farmer's welfare. The tradition which Professor Fukutake represents differs in two respects. Firstly, his work is firmly placed within the framework, if not of a hard-and-fast theory of social development, at least of the intellectual concerns of social development theorists. The changing weight of primary and secondary relationships, the transition from community to association, from status to contract, are among his central interests.

Secondly, Professor Fukutake's sociology is both a committed and a politically conscious sociology. When he looks at a village he is always concerned that it should become a better village and always keen to trace the responsibility for it not being better than it is in the political and economic system in which the village is enmeshed.

The reader will quickly perceive that Professor Fukutake's intellectual concern with development and his ameliorative commitment are related. His description of the contemporary village is always juxtaposed firstly with the picture of what it was, but secondly, also, with an ideal picture, sometimes implicit, sometimes made explicit, of what it ought to become. If it is the gap between the past and the present which engages his scientific attention, it is the gap between the present reality and the ideal which chiefly exercises his social conscience. And the ideal is often an extrapolation of trends—to greater individualism, greater equality, greater class-consciousness—which he sees in the past.

On some points—on the basis of a much more limited experience of Japanese villages and hence with some tentativeness —I would take issue with Professor Fukutake, both as a theorist and as a social critic. I am doubtful, for instance, of his theoretical assumption that the cohesive solidarity of hamlet communities usually depended on the relations of personal dependency involved in the authoritarian status structure, and that the narrowing of differences of economic power and social prestige has therefore itself led, *pari passu*, to a decline in community solidarity. To be sure the bonds that tie individuals to their community have been weakened, as he points out, by economic differentiation, the growth of part-time farming and the influences of urban culture. But it does not seem to me that greater economic equality is itself a weakening factor, nor, *vice versa*, that the continued existence of strong ties of group solidarity is *prima facie* evidence that a hamlet is dominated by 'bosses'. In other words, the emphasis on 'hamlet harmony' is not always a weapon for the repression of the poor. There can be egalitarian as well as authoritarian solidarity, and I think Professor Fukutake underestimates the frequency with which, in part thanks to a sense of hamlet loyalty, leaders exercise authority by real and rationally given consent, not by virtue of their lineage or superior economic power, and exercise it with a sense of responsibility, and with more regard for the welfare of the poorer members of the community than one finds in most societies.

As a critic of government policy, too, I suspect that professor Fukutake overstates his case and overestimates the extent to which farmers are being, or have been, exploited by governments wholly subservient to business interests. When the Meiji government 'forced' heavy educational expenditures on rural local governments, it surely did so at least partly in the belief (and a belief by our present standards surely justified) that it was promoting rural welfare. And equally at the present day I

xiii

think it has to be admitted that, however dubious the vote-catching motives which inspire it, budgetary support of agriculture already contains a large element of income redistribution in the farmer's favour which can neither be justified on the grounds that it represents the most productive investment of national resources, nor interpreted as a service to industry.

But these are matters very much open to debate. And however one might wish to modify some of Professor Fukutake's judgements it is impossible to doubt the generosity of the sympathies which underlie them, or the accuracy of the general picture he presents. Fifteen years ago my first trips to Japanese villages were with Professor Fukutake. One could not have wished for a better guide to the intricacies of Japanese rural social relations. He is just as good a guide on paper, and the clarity and comprehensiveness of this book make it an excellent introduction for those who wish to learn something of the past and the present of Japanese villages.

R. P. Dore

PART ONE

JAPANESE AGRICULTURE AND JAPANESE VILLAGES

CHAPTER I

AGRICULTURE AND THE VILLAGES BEFORE WORLD WAR II

Agriculture and the Development of Capitalism

THE modern history of Japan begins less than one hundred years ago. It was in 1868, with the Meiji Restoration, that she set out on the road of development which was to make her a modern capitalist state.

For the preceding two and a half centuries Japan had been a feudal society, a society whose pattern had been evolved by the Tokugawa Shogunate, the government of the ruling family which seized control of the country at the beginning of the seventeenth century. The farmers had been peasants subject to the restrictions of a rigid system of social barriers between 'estates'—between the 'four orders' of society defined, in order of social honour, as: the samurai, the peasants, the artisans and the merchants. They were forbidden to sell their land; their right to sub-divide it was limited; they had no freedom to change their place of residence, and even the crops they could grow were restricted in order that they should be able to pay their taxes in rice. Practically forced into a self-sufficient subsistence economy in small villages, and bearing collective responsibility for the annual payment of their rice taxes, the individual was submerged in an isolated and exclusive community.

There was, however, in the latter half of the period, though only in certain districts, an increasing production of cash crops and an increasing penetration of the monetary economy into the villages. There were some new developments in agricultural implements, and fish manure came to be used as fertilizer. With this penetration of the commercial economy, some farmers expanded their production or entered trading activities themselves, thereby accumulating wealth, while others, on the other hand, declined into poverty, mortgaged their land, and eventually lost it to the landlords whose tenants they became. With this process of class division among the peasants the stability of feudal society came to be threatened.[1]

However, it would be wrong to say that in the century before the Meiji Restoration conditions had matured for the spontaneous dissolution of feudalism and for the internal development of a capitalist economy. There were, indeed, by the end of the Tokugawa period, what can properly be described as manufacturing establishments, but these were by no means common. As far as internal factors are concerned, Japanese feudalism, while losing its stability, was still capable of survival. The fact that feudalism was brought to an end nevertheless with the Meiji Restoration must be attributed to the stimulus of foreign powers. England, the pioneer capitalist country, had already begun her industrial revolution a century before, and the shock waves of expanding capitalism spread from England and the other European powers to Japan's Pacific islands, threatening the security of her two centuries of dreamy seclusion as demands became more insistent that she should open her doors for trade. As Japanese history and world history came together, the disparities in their stages of development became obvious, and it was equally obvious that unless this gap were bridged Japan was in danger of becoming a colony of the advanced capitalist powers.

Thus it was that, after the Restoration, as well as re-ordering her political structure on modern lines, Japan pursued the policy of—to quote the contemporary slogan—'enriching the country and strengthening the army', and set about the process of forced-draft capital accumulation. As a result Japanese capitalism developed at great speed, and she achieved a rate of economic development which has attracted world-wide attention. By the 1890's, capitalism was firmly established and from then until the development of monopoly capital in the

[1] For the history of agriculture in the Tokugawa period, see Furushima Toshio, *Nihon-nōgyō-shi*, 1956 (Iwanami Shoten).

second decade of this century she showed an astonishing rate of growth. At the same time, along with this economic development, went development as a military power. By the First World War, Japan had become one of the world's five great powers, and soon, in their vainer moments, the Japanese counted their country along with America and England as one of the Big Three.

Such rapid development necessarily created great strains and distortions and on no section of the economy did they press more heavily than on agriculture. It would be no exaggeration to say that the Japanese economy developed at the expense of agriculture.

To start with, in the period immediately after the Meiji Restoration the peasants, who made up 80 per cent. of the population, paid in land taxes some 80 per cent. of the total revenue of the Meiji government, and it was this which provided the basis for the construction of a capitalist state. At a time when Japan had little industry to speak of, it was only by converting the feudal revenues (formerly paid in kind to local lords) into land taxes paid in cash to the central government, without any reduction in the level of taxation, that it was possible for the state to pursue its policies of protecting and developing the mining and manufacturing industries.

Secondly, because—as is generally the case in late-developing capitalist countries—Japanese industry was from the very beginning of a relatively modern and highly capitalized kind, it was unable to absorb a great deal of labour from agriculture. Since Japan did not pass through the period of simple manufactures but began industrial production with the import of advanced machines from abroad, labour requirements were not especially heavy. In the light industries, in particular, young female labour was adequate to satisfy all requirements. Hence, although industry developed it did not exert a sufficient pull to reduce the agricultural population. Agriculture always held a reservoir of surplus population and it was this which made possible the low wage rates of world-wide fame and which gave Japan the strength to compete with the advanced capitalist powers.[2]

[2] Moreover agriculture, as well as aiding the development of industry by

In these circumstances there was no remedy for the great defect of Japanese agriculture—the small size of holdings. Despite the rapid development of a capitalist economy, the number of farm families in Japan remained throughout at around the 5½ million mark. And in a country which had for so long been under cultivation there was very little possibility of expanding the total cultivated area. Consequently the average size of a holding was never much greater than 1 hectare and Japanese agriculture continued to be characterized by the minute size of family holdings. As we shall see, in the economic disruptions of the early Meiji period a good deal of land passed into the hands of landlords, but as long as there was an abundance of farm families unable to move out of agriculture it was always more profitable for the landlord to lease his land to tenants than to cultivate it himself on an extensive scale. Thus it was that capitalist agriculture never became of any importance in Japan.

TABLE I

Farm Households by Size of Operated Holding (Percentages): 1908–40

	Size of Holding (has.)					
Year	*−0.5*	*−1.0*	*−2.0*	*−3.0*	*−5.0*	*5.0+*
1908	*37.3*	*32.6*	*19.5*	*6.4*	*3.0*	*1.2*
1910	*37.6*	*33.0*	*19.3*	*5.9*	*2.9*	*1.3*
1920	*35.3*	*33.3*	*20.7*	*6.1*	*2.8*	*1.6*
1930	*34.3*	*34.3*	*22.1*	*5.7*	*2.3*	*1.3*
1940	*33.4*	*32.8*	*24.5*	*5.7*	*2.2*	*1.4*

It will be seen from Table I just how few big holdings there were—never as many as 2 per cent. containing 5 hectares and with nearly 70 per cent. of farmers cultivating less than a single hectare. There was a slight increase in the proportion cultivat-

supplying labour, also bore the social policy costs for mining and manufacturing. It is often said that Japanese workers were migrant workers. The patriarchal family system of the peasant family preserved social bonds which in some sense linked these industrial workers to their native families. The fact that in times of depression unemployment could be absorbed without too much disorganization was largely due to these familial ties; workers could return to their native village or at least call on their families for assistance.

ing between 1 and 2 hectares and some decrease in the proportion with less than half and more than 2 hectares, so that one can speak of a tendency towards concentration in the medium size class, but these trends are slight ones and broadly speaking the picture is one of stability.

Inevitably such small holdings meant poverty. It was impossible to make a living from less than half a hectare, and in consequence, these farmers were forced to supplement their income by additional work outside agriculture. Even the inadequate agricultural statistics which are available show the proportion of part-time farmers as never less than 30 per cent.[3] According to a farm household survey in 1938, 24 per cent. of farm households relied less on agriculture than on other occupations and another 31 per cent. received some income from non-agricultural work. Thus less than half of Japanese farm households could be called full-time farmers.

Certainly it is possible for the farmers' level of living to rise even without an expansion in the size of holdings if there is an increase in agricultural productivity. And it is true, if we take for instance rice, the main staple of Japanese agriculture, that in the second decade of the century production per acre was already 50 per cent. higher than in the early years of the Meiji period and by about 1930 some 70 per cent. higher. However, these increases in yield were all but cancelled out by the relative fall in agricultural prices and by the rise in the general standard of living. Clinging desperately to their land for lack of any opportunity to find a job in industry, the farmers continued to produce as long as there was any possibility of scraping a bare living out of agriculture. Consequently it was easy to keep agricultural prices at a low level. With the self-sufficiency of their economy destroyed, now fully involved in the commercial economy, they were unable, even though they achieved some increase in income, to catch up with the increase in living levels in Japanese society as a whole.

Since they had no capital with which to buy machines and so

[3] Agricultural statistics before 1938 were compiled from reports made by officials of village agricultural associations. For more information on agricultural statistics, see Kondō Yasuo, *Nihon nōgyō no tōkeiteki bunseki*, 1953 (Tōyō Keizai Shimpōsha).

raise the productivity of their labour, farmers' attempts to raise their level of living were directed towards increasing the productivity of their land. The increase in agricultural production was achieved chiefly by the use of improved crop strains and by increased fertilization. By the third decade of this century, admittedly, there was already a certain amount of mechanical power in use, but there was still no machine tillage, and agriculture was still predominantly at the stage of reliance on the labour of bare human hands.

Thus developed the image of Japanese farmers as doomed to perpetual poverty however hard they might work. There was, of course, in the slums of the cities a stratum of population even poorer than the farmers and the income of a farmer of middling to upper status made him by no means poor in the context of the general Japanese situation. However, that income was achieved only by using the total labour of the whole family, and the level of income per worker was still extremely low. Japanese agriculture was left behind in the development of the Japanese economy and seemed unable to escape from its depressed position.[4]

Being unable to escape from this poverty, and practising an agriculture which was still essentially no different from that of the feudal period, it is hardly surprising that the farmers who made agriculture their livelihood, and the rural society which those farmers created, should have been of an old-fashioned character. The astonishing development of Japanese capitalism was supported by the mechanism of cheap rice and cheap wages but it did not confer any fringe benefits on the villages. Rather, its development depended on keeping Japanese agriculture and Japanese villages firmly entrenched in their old-fashioned mould. It was as if Japan could not afford the time or the energy to think of modernizing her villages.

Landlords and Village Society

Approximately two-thirds of Japanese farmers before the war were tenants. Hence, not only were they never liberated from

[4] For the historical development of Japanese agriculture since the Meiji period, see Ouchi Tsutomu, *Nōgyōshi*, 1960 (Tōyō Keizai Shimpōsha).

the poverty caused by lack of sufficient land; they were also tormented by the burden of rents. The relation between landlord and tenant was the most important single social relationship in the pre-war Japanese village, and no account of Japanese village society can ignore the landlord system.

In the Tokugawa period the majority of the peasants were *honbyakushō*, that is, peasants who had registered cultivating rights to certain pieces of land and the duty of paying feudal dues for that land to the lord of their fief. In very general terms what happened in the transition to the Tokugawa form of feudalism was that, by the separation of the farmers from the warrior class, the former landed squire became a samurai living in the castle town, while the actual cultivators, who had until then rendered him serf-like labour dues, became the *honbyakushō*. However, in the more remote districts of Japan and particularly in mountainous areas, some of these landed knights did not become samurai but instead became themselves *honbyakushō*, their serfs remaining serfs. Later in the period this system changed and the serfs, instead of cultivating their master's land under his direction, became independent tenants. Here was one of the origins of the landlord system. However, there were other routes to landlordism too. As the monetary economy began to penetrate the villages in the latter half of the Tokugawa period some merchants and moneylenders managed to acquire fairly considerable holdings of land. In some districts such merchants acquired land through the financing of land reclamation operations. And generally throughout the country it happened that some among the small farmers subject to the harsh exactions of their feudal lords and to the vagaries of uncertain harvests, mortgaged and sold their independent cultivating rights as *honbyakushō*. They became what were known as 'water-drinking farmers' (*mizunomi-byakushō*), while others more fortunate than they acquired their land and became their landlords. In these various ways one can consider the landlord system to have been already fairly well established by the end of the Tokugawa period.[5]

By the beginning of the Meiji period already more than a

[5] For the history of the landlord system, see Furushima Toshio, *Nihon jinushi-sei-shi kenkyū*, 1958 (Iwanami Shoten).

quarter of the arable area was tenanted land. And this proportion rapidly increased after the Meiji Restoration. The reasons
lay in the reform of the land tax system which began in 1873
and in the economic fluctuations which followed it. As a result
of the new tax system farmers who until then had paid their
feudal dues in rice were now required to pay, in cash, a fixed
annual tax calculated on the basis of the value of their land.
Since they now had to sell their crops in order to acquire the
money to pay their taxes, they were to that extent drawn more
closely into the monetary economy. Too many farmers found
themselves unable to adjust to the successive waves of inflation
and deflation which followed. As the price of rice became
inflated while their taxes remained fixed their standards of
living rose, but when the reverse process set in, in the 1880's,
their income fell rapidly. A large number of farmers lost their
land in the process. The area under tenancy, estimated to be
about 29 per cent. in 1872 before the new land tax was insti-
tuted, approached 40 per cent. only fifteen years later. This
percentage continued to increase gradually, and at its peak in
1930 reached 46.7 per cent.—nearly half of the total area.

TABLE II

*Farm Households by Ownership Status
(Percentages): 1888–1940*

Year	Owner-farmers	Part-owners, part-tenants	Tenants
1888	33.4	46.0	20.6
1910	32.8	39.5	27.8
1920	30.7	40.9	28.4
1930	30.6	42.6	26.8
1940	30.5	42.4	27.1

This tenanted land was shared between about 70 per cent. of
the total number of farmers, 30 per cent. of them classified in the
official figures shown in Table II as 'tenants' (i.e., those who
owned less than one-tenth of the land they cultivated) and some
40 per cent. as 'part-tenants' (those who owned less than 90 per
cent. but more than 10 per cent. of the land they cultivated).
In detail the figures show that during the Meiji period there
was an increase in the number of tenants, while after about 1920

a bigger increase came in part-tenants, but it remains true for the whole period since the late nineteenth century that owner-farmers made up less than a third of the total. The landlord-tenant relationship was a crucial one for village society, not simply because of the high proportion of tenanted land, but because of the very high proportion of farm households which were involved.

There were, however, among the landlords thus involved with such a large proportion of the farmers, a variety of types. There were the local magnates of long standing, descended from the medieval squires mentioned above. There were the merchant-moneylender landlords. And then there were the peasant landlords, the owner-farmers who by their own efforts had managed to secure extra land which they leased to tenants. Some among them, particularly the merchant-moneylender type, owned very large estates (by Japanese standards), but for the most part landlords of whatever type held modest holdings. There were no more than about 3,000 in the whole of Japan who owned more than fifty hectares of land, and about 50,000 with more than ten. Even the number holding five or more hectares of leased-out land was only about 100,000; which means, if we assume a total number of about 150,000 hamlet settlements, that there was less than one per hamlet. However, if we include the small landlords owning between one and five hectares of tenanted land, the total number of landlords becomes 380,000 of whom more than 160,000 were themselves cultivating farmers. If one takes into account the fact that the owners of very large tracts of territory appointed managers of their land in hamlets in which they did not themselves live—the manager in this case performing much the same kind of social role as the landlord—it is a fairly safe assertion that there was hardly a single hamlet in Japan from which landlord domination was absent.[6]

The concrete nature of this landlord dominance varied, of course, according to the type of landlord, but certain common characteristics were shared in all cases and may be considered

[6] For the number of landlords, see Ouchi Tsutomu, *Nōgyō Mondai*, rev. ed., 1961 (Iwanami Shoten). His fourth chapter on the structure of land ownership presents a clear and neat analysis of the available data.

typical of Japanese landlord-tenant relations. They are as follows.[7]

In the first place, rents for rice land were usually fixed in kind at so much per unit area and they were fixed at the same high level as the feudal dues of the Tokugawa period. From around 1930 rent rates began to show a slight decline, and since yields were improving there was an additional slight decline in the proportion of the crop paid in rent, but even so it would be no exaggeration to say that rents generally amounted to as much as half the crop.

Secondly, tenancy contracts were for the most part verbal, and written contracts were rare except in the case of very large landlords and in districts where there had been tenancy disputes. Moreover, except for a small number of cases where rights of permanent occupancy were recognized by custom, the term of the contract was rarely specified. This did not mean that the tenant was able to stay indefinitely on the land; it meant rather that his cultivating rights were insecure since the landlord could always evict him at his own convenience. For a tenant family the prospect of being forced off its land meant immediate privation, and in a situation of surplus population with consequent keen competition for tenancy rights, this further strengthened the position of the landlord.[8]

Then, thirdly, the agreed rent rate though expressed in terms of a fixed amount of rice, was by general custom open to reduction in years of bad harvest. The usual procedure was for the tenant to ask the landlord for a reduction, and for the latter then to inspect the crop and grant relief according to the degree to which it fell below the normal yield. But whether such a reduction was granted or not, and if so by how much, was entirely left to the discretionary benevolence of the landlord.

For these various reasons, the tenant-farmer was in a weak position *vis-à-vis* the landlord. If he offended his landlord he

[7] There is a good deal of material on tenancy practices of which a convenient summary appears in Koike Motoyuki, *Nihon nōgyō kōzō-ron*, rev. ed., 1958 (Jichō-sha). For more comprehensive material, see Tsuchiya Takao, *Taishō-jūnen fuken-betsu kosaku-kankō chōsa-shūsei*, 2 vols., 1942–3 (Kurita Shoten).

[8] For a description of permanent tenancy rights, see Ono Takeo, *Eikosaku-ron*, 1924 (Ganshōdō).

might be evicted from his land; at the very least it would become difficult for him to ask for a rent reduction if his crop failed. Except for tenants of the local magnates of feudal origin, or of other large landlords who held something like monopoly rights over land in certain districts, it was usual for tenant-farmers to rent parcels of land not from a single landlord but from several. In other words, tenants who depended on a single landlord were in a minority. But despite this diffusion of dependency the tenant was still unable to treat on equal terms with his landlords because of those characteristics of the landlord-tenant relationship outlined above. The patron-client relationships typically found in districts where there were old-style local magnates with tenants who had only in recent centuries evolved from a more direct form of serfdom, represent only a more exaggerated form of the landlord-tenant relationships typical of the whole of Japan.[9]

However, the pattern of landlord control in the villages changed slowly. The big and medium landlords who accumulated land after the Meiji Restoration gradually, around the turn of the century when the foundations of Japanese capitalism were established, reduced the size of their own cultivated holdings or gave up agriculture altogether, thus becoming purely parasitical landlords. Even among those with smaller holdings there were a number whose children were sent away to receive higher education, often coming back to become school teachers or village officials and give up farming. These tendencies weakened the authority of the landlords in the villages. As a consequence—and as a result, too, of changing attitudes on the part of tenants caused by the spread of literacy, their military experience as conscripts, and the proselytizing activities of left-wing intellectuals—from around 1920 there were frequent outbreaks of tenancy disputes. There developed an organized tenants' movement which gradually gathered strength as the tenants' demands increased—from rent reductions for a particular bad harvest to permanent reductions in rental rates and the guarantee of secure tenure.[10]

[9] On this point, see Ariga Kizaemon, *Nihon kazoku-seido to kosaku-seido*, 1943 (Kawade Shobō).

[10] A useful source on the tenants' movement, despite its bulk, is Aoki Keiichirō, *Nihon nōmin-undō-shi*, 5 vols., 1958–60 (Nihon Hyōron Shinsha).

This tenants' movement, however, never succeeded in destroying the landlord system. Even at the peak of its activity it did not extend over the whole country. Even if the larger and medium landlords did come to play a purely parasitical role, and even if a number of the smaller landlords did move out of farming, the majority still continued to be peasant landlords cultivating a holding of their own. They continued to function as the ruling stratum of the village.

Thus, despite changes in the landlord system *pari passu* with the social and economic development of Japanese society after the Meiji Restoration, the landlord remained the dominant element in rural society. One should, however, distinguish between those who were responsible for progress in agricultural technology and for the creation of Agricultural Associations in the Meiji period or who played a major role in developing local self-government after the system was founded in 1888, and on the other hand, those who, in the 1930's, carried through the remoulding and strengthening of the traditional village social order and so prepared a firm basis for putting the country on a war footing—the landlords, that is, who were active in the producers' co-operatives and organized the new Farmers' Associations. Though both types bear the name landlords, their character was different. As the former ceased to farm and gradually lost their control of the villages, the latter, as farming landlords, came to play the major role in dominating them. These changes over time in the ruling stratum necessarily brought, of course, simultaneous changes among the tenants and part-tenants—the stratum of the ruled. But for these changes to take any conclusive form it was not enough simply for the landlord system to change; it had to be entirely destroyed. This was postponed until after the war. The landlord system, though changing in character, continued until the defeat in World War II to be the main determinant of the structure of Japanese village society.

FURTHER READING[1]

There are a number of general works in English which cover topics treated in various parts of the book, studies either of particular villages or of modern rural society as a whole. The most important are listed in full below and will be cited in abbreviated references henceforth.

R. K. Beardsley, J. W. Hall and R. E. Ward, *Village Japan*, Chicago, 1959.

J. B. Cornell, 'Matsunagi; the life and social organisation of a Japanese mountain community', in University of Michigan, Center for Japanese Studies, *Occasional Papers*, 5, 1956. (This is half of the work sometimes cited as R. J. Smith and J. B. Cornell, *Two Japanese villages*.)

R. P. Dore, *Land reform in Japan*, London, 1959.

J. F. Embree, *A Japanese village: Suyemura*, Chicago, 1940, London, 1946, Chicago (paperback), 1964.

A. J. Grad, *Land and peasant in Japan*, New York, 1952.

E. Norbeck, *Takashima: a Japanese fishing community*, Salt Lake City, 1954.

A. F. Raper, *The Japanese village in transition*, SCAP, Natural Resources Division, Report No. 136, 1950.

R. J. Smith, 'Kurusu; a Japanese agricultural community', in University of Michigan, Center for Japanese Studies, *Occasional Papers*, 5, 1956. (The other half of the work sometimes cited as R. J. Smith and J. B. Cornell, *Two Japanese villages*.)

R. J. Smith and R. K. Beardsley, eds., *Japanese culture: its development and characteristics*, Chicago, 1962.

On the history and pre-war development of Japanese agriculture, see, for the Tokugawa period:

T. C. Smith, *The agrarian origins of modern Japan*, Stanford, 1959.

For later periods:

R. P. Dore, 'Agricultural improvement in Japan, 1870–1900', *Economic Development and Cultural Change*, 9, i, pt. 2, October 1960.

Dore, *Land reform*.

Grad, *Land and peasant*.

B. F. Johnson, 'Agricultural development and economic transformation: a comparative study of the Japanese experience', *Food Research Institute Studies* (Stanford), 3, iii, November 1962.

M. D. Morris, 'The problem of the peasant agriculturalist in Meiji Japan', *Far Eastern Quarterly*, 15, May 1956.

E. H. Norman, *Japan's emergence as a modern state*, New York, 1941.

T. Ogura, ed., *Agricultural development in modern Japan*, Tokyo, Japan FAO Association, 1963.

J. W. Robertson-Scott, *The foundation of Japan*, London, 1922.

H. Rosovsky and K. Ohkawa, 'The role of agriculture in modern Japanese economic development', *Economic Development and Cultural Change*, 9, i, pt. 2, October 1960.

[1] These notes have been prepared by the translator.

CHAPTER II

THE PRESENT STATE OF AGRICULTURE AND THE VILLAGES

The Land Reform and the Development of Agriculture

WE have seen how the relation between landlord and tenant which played such an important part in the structure of Japanese rural society began gradually to change in character from about the time of the First World War. As Japanese capitalism approached the monopoly stage the national political power of the landlords began to decline. Indeed, those landlords who had become most purely parasitic began to lose direct control even in their own villages, and it was the average and small cultivating landlords—those who were themselves farmers— who inherited their position of dominance.

There was a concomitant change in the tenants. As their productivity increased and they became ever more deeply involved in the marketing process, they became increasingly conscious of the burden of their high rents. We have already seen that from about 1920 tenancy disputes occurred with increasing frequency and ferocity; Farmers' Unions were organized and a farmers' movement (predominantly a tenants' movement) spread rapidly through the country, paralleling the growth of the labour movement in the towns. This was especially the case in the late twenties and early thirties when the conditions created by the depression gave the movement even greater impetus. This represented a great crisis for the Japanese capitalist system.

The Government responded to this situation by strong repressive measures against both the farmers' movement and the labour movement. At the same time, in order to prevent a worsening of the situation in the villages, it attempted to adjust rents and establish schemes whereby tenants could purchase their land. But in the last analysis these policies had very little effect; they certainly did not amount to a solution for the tenancy problem. Later, however, as Japan moved into a state of war-mobilization, the situation was changed by a series of wartime control measures involving the protection of the tenants' right to cultivate, the control of rents and finally a system for the compulsory requisitioning of food crops. Thus the unrest which the land problem had caused within village society was stilled by superior force.

This did not, of course, mean that the problem was solved. As soon as the war was over the contradictions of the landlord system inevitably came once more to the surface. Apart from anything else, it was necessary, in order to reconstruct industry destroyed by the devastating bombing raids and re-establish the capitalist economy, to break through the inflationary spiral exacerbated by the shortage of food. This meant ensuring compulsory deliveries of rice at low prices, and this in turn made it necessary to reduce the burden of rents on the cultivating farmers.

In this way the Government recognized that a reform of the land system was absolutely essential and attempted to carry through such a reform on its own initiative. In December 1945, soon after the defeat, the Government placed before the Diet a Bill to amend the Agricultural Land Adjustment Law. This is generally known as the first land reform. The measure allowed landlords to keep up to five hectares of their property, and envisaged the freeing of some 40 per cent. of the tenanted area in the course of five years.

However, the Headquarters of the Occupation Forces had already in a 'Memorandum on Land Reform' instructed the Japanese Government to 'break the economic bondage which has enslaved Japanese farmers through centuries of feudal oppression' and soon after the passage of the law it halted the execution of this first land reform and required the Government to prepare a more thoroughgoing measure. The result was the 'second land reform' which began the following year, 1946.

It was a drastic reform, the like of which could hardly have been contemplated in pre-war Japan.

Under the reform laws, all the land of absentee landlords and all leased-out land of village landlords in excess of one hectare was purchased by the State and resold to tenants. The practice, until then general, of paying rents in kind was forbidden, and cash payment was required. Moreover, rents were controlled; landlords could no longer demand rents at a level which had justly been described as feudal. This reform was practically completed within the short space of a little over two years and as a result the area of tenanted land, which before the war had been approximately 53 per cent. for rice land and 40 per cent. for dry land, fell to below 10 per cent.

TABLE III

*Farm Households by Ownership Status:
(Percentages): 1946–60*

Year	Owner-farmers	Part-owners, part-tenants	Part-tenants, part-owners	Tenants
1946	32.8	19.8	18.6	28.7
1950	61.9	25.8	6.6	5.1
1955	69.5	21.6	4.7	4.0
1960	75.2	18.0	3.6	2.9

Note: The distinction between the centre two columns depends on the proportion of the total holding owned. Some farmers have no land (apiarists, etc.); hence the total is less than 100 per cent.

Again, as Table III shows, whereas only about 30 per cent. of farmers were owner-cultivators before the war, the figure is now 75 per cent., and the proportion of farmers who rent all their land has fallen from around 30 per cent. to a mere 3 per cent. In this way the dominance of the landlords in village society lost its material economic basis. The land reform may be considered, on the whole, to have succeeded in liberating Japanese farmers from 'feudal oppression'.[1]

[1] There have been many assessments of the land reform. Considering only those works which have the land reform as their chief or sole subject, there are: Kondō Yasuo, *Nōchi-kaikaku no shomondai*, 1951 (Yūhikaku); Ishiwata Sadao, *Nōchi-kaikaku no kihon-kōzō*, 1954 (Tōkyō-daigaku Shuppankai); Yamazaki Harushige, *Nōchi-kaikaku to Nihon-nōgyō*, 1957 (Otsuki Shoten);

AN AERIAL VIEW OF SETTLEMENT PATTERNS

AGRICULTURAL HAMLETS

RICE PLANTING

SPRAYING PADDIES WITH INSECTICIDES

As a result of this reform, the productivity of Japanese agriculture began to increase. As what had been rented land became their own, farmers' incentives were heightened. In the past, when their tenure had been insecure, there was always the danger that if they improved the land, the landlord might reclaim it for his own cultivation, and in any case tenants did not have the capital to carry out improvements. Again, if yields improved there was always the possibility of rents being raised too. It is not surprising that the tenant-farmers lacked any positive incentives to improve their productivity. After the reform, on the other hand, any increase in yields meant an immediate increase in income. Farmers showed a keen interest in adopting new techniques and agricultural study groups were organized in villages throughout the country. Schemes to rationalize field patterns, improve drainage and irrigation and consolidate holdings, schemes which before the war had been carried out in some districts on the initiative of landlords, were now carried through by the farmers themselves and problems of land improvement were tackled with great vigour. The Government, too, through the Agricultural Extension Service newly established after the war, sought to diffuse new techniques among the farmers.

As a result, the yield of rice, the main crop of Japanese agriculture, increased with every succeeding year as cultivating techniques improved. At present it is more than double the level of the early years of the Meiji period. Before the war anything over 3,000 kg. per ha. was looked on as a bumper crop, but by 1950 this had become a normal yield and in recent years the figure has been around 3,700–3,800 kg. Production of the other important grain crop, wheat, has remained stagnant and the planted area has decreased, but in compensation there has been a big increase in the production of fruit, especially in recent years when it has reached more than double the pre-war level. Even compared with 1955 the production of mandarin

Oshima Kiyoshi, *Nōchi-kaikaku to Nōgyō-mondai*, 1958 (Nihon Hyōron Shinsha), etc. Other important sources are: Nōchi-kaikaku Kiroku-iinkai, *Nōchi-kaikaku tenmatsu gaiyō*, 1951 (Nōsei Chōsakai); Nōsei Chōsa-kai, *Nōchi-kaikaku Jiken-kiroku*, 1956 (Nōsei Chōsakai).

oranges has increased by 2.8 times and of apples by 1.8 times. Equally marked has been the growth of the livestock industry. Whereas in the 1930's there were about 20,000 dairy cows in Japan, that figure had reached 200,000 by 1950, 420,000 by 1955, and 820,000 by 1960, since when the same rapid growth has continued until now there are more than one million. These improvements in yield and development of new types of agriculture have gone hand in hand with greater mechanization. Farmers who once willingly did everything by hand because they looked on family labour as a free resource, have now come to use machines of every sort. For example, in 1935 there were fewer than 50,000 electric motors on Japanese farms whereas the figure today is more than one million and if one adds gasoline engines there are nearly three million general-purpose motors on Japanese farms.

TABLE IV

The Diffusion of Farm Machinery
(Thousands of machines): 1936–60

Year	Electric Motors	Gasoline Motors	Powered Cultivating Machines	Powered Threshers	Powered Hullers
1935	47	96	0.2	91	104
1945	152	262	0.7	352	177
1950	601	383	13.2	827	378
1955	956	1,134	82.3	2,038	689
1960	1,124	1,696	517.0	2,477	843

Table IV shows similar great increases in threshing machines and hullers. Most striking of all is the mechanization of the cultivation process. Whereas before the war there was an insignificant number of mechanical tillers and ploughing was almost exclusively by animal power, the number of small garden tractors rapidly increased during the fifties to over half a million in 1960, since when the rate of increase has accelerated until today there are more than 1.8 million of these machines.[2]

However, despite this progress in agricultural production,

[2] Although it is now somewhat out-of-date a good description of these post-war developments can be found in Nōrinshō, Nōrin-keizai-kyoku, Tōkei-chōsabu, Chōsei-ka, ed., *Nihon no nōgyō-keizai—Sengo no seichō to kōzō-henka*, 1957 (Tōyō Keizai Shimpōsha).

the problems of Japanese agriculture were by no means solved. The kind of development symbolized in the rapid diffusion of mechanical cultivators does not hold out a bright future for Japanese agriculture; rather, it indicates a deepening of its inherent contradictions.

The story of the post-war development of Japanese agriculture begins from the land reform, but the reform was a reform which in one sense brought no change. It transferred the ownership of land, but had no effect on the size of holdings. In fact the situation was worse than stable. Those who had lost their jobs and were squeezed out of industry and commerce by wartime destruction, and those who were returned from the ex-colonies, flocked back to the post-war villages. The number of farm households, which since the beginning of the Meiji period had fluctuated around 5½ million, rose to over 6 million, and the average size of holding fell from the pre-war average of about 1 ha. to 0.8 ha.

TABLE V

Farm Households by Size of Operated Holdings (Percentages): 1946–60

	Size of Holding (has.)					
Year	−0.5	−1.0	−2.0	−3.0	−5.0	5.0+
1946	39.2	31.2	23.5	3.7	1.4	1.0
1950	40.9	31.9	21.7	3.4	1.2	0.9
1955	38.4	32.7	22.9	3.5	1.4	1.1
1960	38.0	31.8	23.6	3.8	1.6	1.0

Table v shows the distribution of holdings by size for the post-war period, and a comparison with Table i will show that the increase has taken place in the smaller holdings. The problem of atomized holdings, the cancer of Japanese agriculture, was not cured by the post-war land reform. It had, in fact, become even more serious.

However much agricultural productivity expands and yields increase the shortage of land remains decisive for Japanese farmers. Moreover, although the improvement in yields has increased farmers' gross income, there has been a marked rise in their expenditure on fertilizer and agricultural chemicals, while increased purchases of machinery have added a further large burden of costs. In addition the living standards of farmers have risen considerably compared with before the war. A good proportion of farm households find it impossible to maintain these living standards simply from their agricultural income. This tendency has become particularly noticeable in the last few years when the Japanese economy has been developing at a very high rate of growth. It is not surprising that for some years there has been talk of Japanese agriculture reaching a turning point.

Structural Change in Rural Society

If the development of agriculture was thus running into a blind alley, and failing to maintain farmers' standards of living despite the increase in productivity, industry showed a marked contrast. From about 1955 it began to make a rapid recovery from the thorough destruction of the war years. The growth of manufacturing industry was particularly marked and its development formed the spearhead of an astonishing growth in the Japanese economy as a whole. With 1955 as 100, the index of the gross national product in real terms for 1961 stood at 182; in other words there was almost a doubling of production in these years. But while the overall rate of growth was maintained at this very high figure of more than 10 per cent. per annum agriculture barely managed to maintain a growth rate of about 3 per cent. per annum. Thus the weight of agriculture's contribution to national income rapidly fell from nearly 20 per cent. in 1955 to not much more than 10 per cent. in 1960. This growing disparity between agriculture and other sectors of the economy has been a growing cause of concern.

The result has been a marked tendency for the agricultural population to decline and for employment to increase in other sectors, particularly in manufacturing industry. Whereas in 1950 there were 6.2 million farm households and about 16 million agricultural workers, in 1960 the latter figure had fallen below pre-war levels to 13.7 million, and a continued decrease since that date has brought the figure below the 13 million mark. The proportion of agricultural workers in the total employed population fell from 45 per cent. to less than 30 per cent. be-

TABLE VI
Farm Households as Percentage of all Households:
Agricultural labour force as
a percentage of total labour force.
Agricultural income as percentage
of total national income: 1930–60

Year	Farm Households	Agricultural Labour Force	Agricultural Income
1930	44.2	47.0	16.2
1940	38.3	41.7	14.9
1950	37.6	45.5	21.2
1955	34.8	39.7	18.0
1960	29.6	29.8	11.2

tween 1950 and 1960. Even more striking is the fact that whereas, in 1950, some 25 per cent. of all those leaving school entered agriculture, this figure fell by 1960 to about 10 per cent. and in recent years has been below 6 per cent.[3]

Thus there seems every danger of agriculture being left behind the main stream of Japanese economic development, for with the continued decrease in the number of workers in agriculture, the agricultural labour force is coming to consist increasingly of women and old men. True, if a decline in the agricultural population means a decrease in the number of farms and an expansion in the average size of holdings this is something very much to be desired from the point of view of agricultural development. However, a decrease in the agricultural population does not necessarily automatically imply a decrease in the number of farm households. Even in 1960 the number of households stood at 6.06 million, not very different from the figure for 1955. In the last two or three years there has been a slightly more rapid decrease to about 5.8 million, but it seems unlikely that there will be a rapid decrease in the near future. This disparity between the trend in the agricultural population and that in the number of agricultural households

[3] On these recent rapid changes in the population situation see Namiki Masayoshi, Nōson wa kawaru, 1960 (Iwanami Shoten). Also, for a general view of various aspects of rural population problems see Nojiri Shigeo, Nōson no jinkō—atarashii kadai to sono taisaku, 1959 (Chūō Keizai-sha).

derives from the fact that it is the young men who are leaving agriculture for other industries while the women and older men continue to cultivate the family holdings. One of the major reasons for the very sharp increase in the number of mechanical tillers in recent years is because farmers are seeking to raise the productivity of their labour to adapt to these new conditions. It is a sign, in other words, of the fact that Japanese farm households are moving rapidly along the path towards part-time farming.

The post-war rise in farmers' standards of consumption was greater than the rise in agricultural productivity. Hence, as we have already pointed out, a good many farmers were unable to maintain this standard of living simply out of their agricultural income. They had to seek part-time earnings outside agriculture. Even before the war, as was mentioned earlier, some 40 per cent. of farm households derived part of their income from part-time employment, but by 1950 this proportion of part-time farmers had risen to one half. Thereafter there was a rapid increase until in 1955 the figure was 65 per cent. In the next five years there was very little increase in the total figure though the proportion deriving more income from outside agriculture than from within it increased by 5 per cent. The more rapid population movements of the last few years seem to have brought further changes, and according to a sample survey at the end of 1963 the number of full-time farmers had then fallen to a mere 24 per cent. while as many as 42 per cent. got more than half of their income from outside agriculture.

TABLE VII
Farm Households: Full-time and Part-time
(Percentages): 1941–60

Year	Full-time	Part-time	
		Primarily farmers	Primarily not
1941	41.5	37.3	21.2
1950	50.0	28.4	21.6
1955	34.8	37.7	27.5
1960	34.3	33.6	32.1

It is obvious that the term 'farm households' in Japan now covers a multitude of families which are far from farmer-like.

The available figures, however, require a certain amount of interpretation, since they normally include as part-time farm households all cases where, for instance, a daughter or a non-inheriting younger son commute to some other employment. Hence the number of part-time farmers in the stricter sense of the word—namely, families in which the head of the household or his heir are engaged in some other part-time employment—is smaller than the above figures suggest. However, if one takes into account the volume of farm sales in making the distinction between full-time and part-time, one arrives roughly at the following classification: farmers in the true sense of the word, a little less than 40 per cent; farm households with income both from agriculture and other employment, a little over 20 per cent; households best looked on as not farm households at all, a little under 30 per cent; farm households living in poverty, unable to secure opportunities for alternative employment, somewhat over 10 per cent. One thing is certain, that the differentiation between full-time farmers and part-time farmers, each with their several and different characteristics, is proceeding rapidly and that this division is bringing structural changes to village society. The change is in the direction of greater complexity.[4]

In the pre-war villages, too, there was stratification according to land-owning status—there were landlords, owner-farmers, part-owner-farmers, part-tenants, tenants and so on. These divisions were interwoven with differentiation according to size of holdings, and there were a number of part-time farmers. There was no single straightforward category of 'farm households', and the structure of village society was by no means simple. In the post-war period, by contrast, stratification by ownership status has ceased to mean very much; in this sense there has been a large measure of equalization. On the other hand, as the modern village becomes increasingly differentiated into a group of commercial farmers who concentrate on agriculture and depend on it for their income, and a group of part-time farmers who farm for little more than their subsistence rice, the result—particularly since the latter category have much more

[4] On these points see Nōrinshō Tōkei-chōsabu, ed., *Nihon no nōgyō—1960-nen sekai nōrin-gyō sensasu*, 1961 (Nōrin-tōkei Kyōkai), pp. 11–13.

complex links with society outside the villages than did their pre-war predecessors—is a structural picture of greater complexity.

In the first place, in the field of family relations, the increase in contacts with outside society consequent on economic change was bound to exert various influences on personal relations within the family, on marriage and on inheritance. The rural family which used to be looked to as the ideal typical model of the 'Japanese family system' has come to show very marked changes indeed.

Secondly, there has been a change in the structure of social relations within the village. Before the war, even if there was stratification by ownership status and by the degree of part-time work, there was, nevertheless, a general tendency for the villagers to be united, under the leadership of the landlords, in a shared concern for agricultural production. Now, however, with the landlord system destroyed and with the villagers divided between the full-time farmers concerned with developing commercial production on the one hand, and on the other the subsistence farmers who are concerned with supplementing an income from other sources or simply with preserving some source of income for their old age, it is hard for a common and united sense of purpose to develop in the villages. In addition, the villages contain many people who commute to industrial work and live in the villages simply because they cannot afford a house in the town. It has thus become difficult to integrate all the inhabitants of a village within the framework of a single village community.

Thirdly, it is not only that the social and economic changes have brought greater internal differentiation by linking the villages much more closely with the outside world, they have also meant that the sphere of daily life of all farm families has been greatly expanded. The increased commercialization of agriculture and the rise in standards of living have drawn the villagers ever closer to the towns. The daily movement of workers, for instance, from the villages to the city areas, provides continuous links. Then again, the amalgamation of local government units, which began with the Law to Promote the Amalgamation of Towns and Villages of 1953, reshuffled the local administrative system established in 1889, and created local government areas several times bigger than the existing ones. In this way villages were incorporated in the same large administrative areas as town centres, and the ties between town and village were consequently strengthened. It is now quite out of the question to consider the villages as self-contained communities devoted to agriculture as a way of life.

Finally—although this does not of course apply to every village—when plans for regional development are carried through, involving the attempt to create new industrial towns and so break up the present excessive concentration of industry, village society undergoes a further decisive structural change. Given the present wide difference between industrial and agricultural incomes most local authorities are pinning their hopes for economic development on plans to entice industry into their area. In modern Japan this tendency is too strong to be ignored, and it presents a grave problem inasmuch as it implies the possibility that agriculture will be allowed simply to run down.

In order to avoid this and contribute to the development of agriculture it is essential to reform the structure of agriculture itself and rescue it from the blind-alley dangers mentioned above. The first step in this direction, though a theoretical one, was the Basic Law of Agriculture of 1961. It was followed the next year by the beginning of the Agrarian Structure Improvement Programme. On present showing, however, it seems unlikely that this Programme will suffice to bring about any fundamental improvement in the agricultural structure.

Thus Japanese village society is undergoing a rapid—one might even say violent—change, but it is change which is not solving the contradictions of village society; it is rather making those contradictions wider and deeper. At present one cannot hold out bright prospects for Japanese agriculture and Japanese villages. And that is a matter for considerable concern. Unless Japanese villages can somehow, in the course of their transition, move towards a solution of these contradictions, Japanese village society will never become a truly democratic society. And, unless the villages become better places to live in, however much the growth of the Japanese economy continues henceforth, Japanese society will never become a stable democratic society.

FURTHER READING

On the land reform, see:

Dore, *Land reform.*

Grad, *Land and peasant.*

L. I. Hewes, *Japan: land and men*, Iowa, 1955.

W. Ladejinsky, 'Agrarian revolution in Japan', *Foreign Affairs*, 38, i, October 1959.

K. Sakamoto, 'Marxian studies in agricultural problems of post-war Japan', *Japan Science Review: Economic Sciences*, 4, 1957.

On recent developments, see:

Agriculture, Forestry and Fisheries Productivity Conference, *Agricultural Development Series*, Tokyo, International Trade Service Bureau, 15 vols., 1959–60.

(The fifteen volumes, each of 50 to 100 pages, deal respectively with: 1. Agricultural extension. 2. Land reform. 3. Land improvement. 4. Home living improvement. 5. Credit. 6. Co-operatives. 7. Food controls. 8. The national budget. 9. Productivity. 10. Machinery. 11. Rice-growing. 12. Land utilization. 13. The farm household economy survey. 14. Marketing. 15. Statistical surveys.)

Ministry of Agriculture and Forestry, *Annual report on the state of agriculture, 1961*, Tokyo, 1963. Ibid., for subsequent years.

E. Norbeck, 'Postwar cultural change and continuity in northeastern Japan' *American Anthropologist*, 63, 1961.

S. Tobata, *An introduction to agriculture of Japan*, Tokyo, Agriculture, Forestry and Fisheries Productivity Conference, 1958.

PART TWO

KINSHIP AND
FAMILY LIFE

CHAPTER III

THE STRUCTURE OF THE RURAL FAMILY

General Characteristics of Farm Families

AGRICULTURE in Japan is carried on by family labour. In a country where holdings bigger than five hectares were so rare that they could be virtually ignored, capitalist farm management by means of hired agricultural labourers never developed. As we have already indicated, even when landlords gathered a good deal of land into their own possession, since they could command such high rents they always found it more profitable to lease their land to tenants than to cultivate it themselves by means of hired labour. Thus Japanese farmers, owner-occupiers and tenants alike, continued an agriculture of smallholdings depending on manual operations and the labour of the household members.

Hired labour was not, of course, entirely absent. At the peak periods of labour demand, particularly at rice planting, a good many farm households were unable to manage with family labour alone. They commonly filled the breach with day labourers. Alternatively, to some extent they made use of the *yui* system of exchanging labour between families. However, farmers with relatively small holdings who might in this way use hired labour, at other times offered their own services for hire, and even the farmers with relatively big holdings used hired labour only to supplement the labour of the family.

Again, in the more backward districts where holdings were relatively large it was common for upper class farmers to employ living-in help on an annual basis. Also, one should not forget that until the end of the Meiji period there were some large landlords who cultivated their land themselves and used labour hired by annual contract to do so. However, the former were characteristic of rather limited areas, and even in these cases family labour was still the main stand-by. As for the latter, this form was found only among a few of the local-magnate type of landlord in backward districts, and by the turn of the century it was of insignificant proportions.[1]

In other words, since the beginning of the modern period the self-sufficient family holding has been the dominant form and hired labour has been only of an emergency supplementary character. It was, moreover, labour which, apart from a very limited degree of mechanization of the threshing and hulling process, was chiefly direct manual labour intensively applied. Consequently, although the holdings were of a size which seems incredibly small by international standards, a holding which was sufficient to provide a livelihood for a full-time farm family required more than the work of two persons. A husband and wife could not manage by themselves; it was necessary at least to make sure of the help of an inheriting son. In the case of some of the bigger holdings, it was necessary even to keep younger sons tied to the home until the eldest son should marry and so bring a bride as a new worker into the family, even if this did mean an excess of labour in the slack periods of the agricultural cycle. Despite the development of Japanese capitalism a labour market capable of absorbing this surplus labour never developed, and consequently there was very little pressure in Japanese agriculture to promote mechanization and reduce the labour burden. In this way Japanese farm families required a relatively large amount of labour and consequently the average size of farm family remained at a fairly high level.

Farm management at such low levels of labour productivity

---

[1] In the early part of the Tokugawa period it was fairly common for large holdings to rely chiefly on servant labour, but towards the end of the period, as the servants became independent, the family smallholding system came to predominate, and by the Meiji period the present operational pattern was pretty well established. For a description of agriculture and family patterns up to the Meiji period see Furushima Toshio, *Kazoku-keitai to nōgyō no hattatsu*, 1947 (Gakusei Shobō).

required that every member in the family, young and old, man and woman, should work to the very limits of his capabilities. Leaving aside the part-time farmers with tiny holdings, for the full-time farm family agricultural production was an activity of the whole family, and as such was inseparably linked with the family's life as consumers. For every member of the family, family life was literally a complete whole. Agriculture was not thought of as an enterprise designed to produce profit, it was a vocation which produced a livelihood. It was not an occupation of single individuals; it was the 'family business' of a whole family.

The family was not only large and united, it was also more complicated in structure than the simple nuclear family of a married couple and their unmarried children. Farmers lacked the economic resources to establish married children in separate households, and the idea of doing so did not occur to them. It was considered natural that the eldest son should continue to live with his parents after marriage. At the same time, since the Tokugawa ban on the division of holdings officially limited the possibility of setting up younger sons on separate holdings as branch families and so led to the adoption by the farmers of samurai-type patterns of unitary inheritance, and since in any case the division of tiny holdings would have led to mutual disaster, it was necessary to send younger sons off into other industries and into the towns. Consequently, although it sometimes happened in the more backward districts, where agricultural productivity was low and the urban labour markets distant, that younger sons continued to reside with their parents for some considerable time after marriage, this was generally a very rare phenomenon and the very large household was quite exceptional.

Hence, the Japanese farm family, as compared with the typical Western farm family—the 'modern' family of a married couple and their unmarried children—was both large in size and more complex of structure. At the same time, whereas in China and India there were strong moral objections to dividing the family property during the lifetime of the parents even if the children were already married, Japan had no such tradition and so lacked the complex joint family structure of those countries.[2] To draw comparisons within Japan itself, the farm family was more complex and larger than the urban family. It was, certainly, a principle of the Japanese type of family structure common to both urban and rural families that the inheriting son should continue to live with his parents after marriage, but in practice, in the towns, it was very common for married children to be living apart from parents who still lived in the country. Again, there was a difference in birth rates, which were generally higher in the countryside, so that for this reason too the urban family was smaller than the rural family.

These conditions continued to hold good until after the war. Since in the difficult economic conditions of the post-war period it was not easy to establish separate households, the average size of families in Japan as a whole remained for some time at the pre-war level, and even showed a slight increase. However, from about 1955, as the pace of economic growth began to accelerate the average size of family began to decrease—among farming as well as among other households. Progress in the mechanization of the cultivating process led to certain economies in the use of labour, and there was an increasing out-flow of population into other industries. The formerly high rural birth rates, too, kept pace with the declining birth rate in Japan as a whole.

However, this certainly does not mean that there has been any basic change in the characteristics of the Japanese rural family. As families operating smallholdings by family labour their basic character remains unchanged, and the practice of the eldest son setting up a separate house from his parents on marriage has still not developed even at the present day.

The Demographic Structure of Farm Families

These general characteristics of farm households can in fact be statistically demonstrated. It is true, of course, that strictly speaking most of the statistical information concerns 'house-

[2] At the same time, in practice, neither in China nor India was the average family particularly large, and the complex joint families were on the whole rare. For a comparison of the Chinese with the Japanese family, see my *Nihon nōson no shakaiteki seikaku*, 1949 (Tōkyō-daigaku Shuppankai).

holds', not family groups, and the two are not necessarily the same. However, as we have already seen, the number of households which contained non-related hired servants represents a negligible proportion of the total, so that in the discussion which follows this distinction need not bother us too much.[3]

The fact that the pre-war farm household was generally bigger than the Japanese average can be seen from the result of the first census held in 1920. The average farm household then contained 5.44 members, compared with 4.26 for families whose househead was engaged in mining, 4.40 for manufacturing, 4.60 for commerce and 4.16 for professional and public service occupations. Again the fact that the farm family had a much more complex structure than other families can be seen from the results of a 0.1 per cent. sample drawn from the same census. Table VIII shows this from the point of view of the number of generations contained in the family. It will be seen that there

TABLE VIII

Number of Generations in a Single Household, by Occupation of Househead: (Percentage): 1920

| Occupation | Number of Generations | | | | |
	1	2	3	4	5
Agriculture and Forestry	9.48	48.07	37.80	4.44	0.05
Commerce and Manufacture	22.40	60.13	16.64	0.83	–
Public Service and Professional	32.52	49.99	16.67	0.82	–

TABLE IX

Average Household Size and Proportion of Rural in Total Population: 1946–60

| | No. of Persons per Household | | Population in Farm Households |
Year	All Japanese Households	Rural Households	as Percentage of Total Population
1946	4.9	6.0	46.8
1950	5.0	6.1	45.4
1955	5.0	6.0	40.8
1960	4.6	5.7	37.0

[3] For a more detailed consideration of the distinction between families and households see Matsushima Shizuo and Nakano Takashi, *Nihon shakai yōron*, 1958 (Tōkyō-daigaku Shuppankai), Chapter 1.

were a good many farm families containing three generations and nearly 5 per cent. with four or more.[4]

We have already seen that this situation continued with very little change after the war; in fact there was rather an increase in the total number of family members. As Table IX shows, throughout the post-war period the farm household has contained at least one person more than the average Japanese household. It should be pointed out however that this national figure conceals a considerable difference between north-eastern Japan and the south-west. In the north-east there are a number of prefectures where the average size of household is nearly 7 persons, while for most of the south-western prefectures the average is below 6. These differences reflect a difference in the average size of holdings and in the degree of industrialization. The relationship between size of holding and size of family is quite clear from the figures yielded by the agricultural censuses which are shown in Table X.

However, the important thing to be noted here is the difference between the figures for 1955 and for 1960. Ever since the first census of 1920 the average size of Japanese families had been between 4.9 and 5.0 persons but in 1955 it fell to 4.56 persons and the fall, it will be noticed, was very much the same for farm households too—from 6.0 to 5.7 persons.

TABLE X

Size of Household by Size of Holding: 1955 and 1960

Year	Number of Persons in Households of Farmers Farming (in has.)					
	−0.3	−0.5	−1.0	−1.5	−2.0	2.0+
1955	4.8	5.4	6.1	6.9	7.6	8.3
1960	4.7	5.1	5.7	6.4	7.0	7.6

And as Table X shows, with the exception of those with the smallest holdings who are really no longer farmers at all, there has been a decline in family size at every level of holding. These figures reflect the migration of the youthful population to other

[4] For this analysis see Toda Teizō, *Kazoku-kōsei*, 1937 (Kōbundō). Table VIII has been constructed from the information contained therein by Koyama Takashi; see Koyama Takashi 'Nihon kindai kazoku' in *Shakaigaku-taikei*, Volume 1, *Kazoku*, 1948 (Kunitachi Shoin).

industries, a migration which is also reflected in the age structure of the farm household population shown in Table XI. The ages below 39 are the ones which show a declining proportion, and in the period 1955–60 there was a particularly marked decline in the population aged 20–29.

TABLE XI
*Age Structure of Population
in Farm Families: 1947–60*

Year	Percentage of Population Aged			
	−15	16–39	40–59	60+
1947	34.8	37.3	18.1	9.8
1955	36.4	34.4	18.5	10.7
1960	34.6	33.8	19.4	12.2

Again, before the war, except in households of part-time farmers with very little land, it was the rule for the eldest son, as soon as he left school, to work on the family farm. Today, however, as we have already seen, only a small proportion of eldest sons take up farming on leaving school, and no more than a quarter of farm families are succeeding in keeping an heir on the farm—not more than a half even of the households cultivating more than $1\frac{1}{2}$ hectares. To be sure, not all of these children who have not taken up agriculture have left home. Some of them commute to other employments from the farm, but nevertheless this is a change of considerable significance for the structure of the farm household.[5]

However, these changes still do not mean that the farm household has now become typically the nuclear family of husband, wife and unmarried children. This will be clear if we divide households according to family type into the following categories:

A Nuclear family households.
B Stem family households (i.e. containing at least three generations).
C Households which additionally include collateral relatives.

[5] On this point see the sections on farm management in *Zusetsu nōgyō nenji-hōkoku*—Shōwa-37-nendo, 1963 (Nōrin-tōkei Kyōkai), pp. 32–127.

According to a 0.1 per cent. sample of the 1960 Census analysed by the Ministry of Welfare, in farm families cultivating more than 0.3 hectares of land, type A makes up 35 per cent., type B 55 per cent., and type C 10 per cent., of the total number of households.[6]

TABLE XII

Type of Household by Region: 1920 and 1960

Year	Type of Family	All Japan	Six large Cities	Smaller Cities	Towns and Villages
		Percentage of each Type in			
1920	Nuclear Families	60.0	73.5	72.6	56.9
	Extended Families	40.0	26.5	27.4	43.1
1960	Nuclear Families	65.1	78.2	67.8	55.0
	Extended Families	34.9	21.8	32.2	45.0

Table XII does not make a distinction between farm and non-farm families though one can assume that the small town and village column reflects the farm situation. The greater predominance of complex families in this category is obvious. What is more, although there has been a general overall increase in the proportion of nuclear families between 1920 and 1960, both in the medium and small cities and in the town and village categories there has in fact been a decrease. It is not possible to draw any precise conclusions from this since the actual areas designated by the different categories have changed as a result of the amalgamation of local administrative districts following 1953; large rural areas have been incorporated into cities leaving only the most remotely rural areas in the village category. However, it is safe to say that there are no clear signs of a modernization of the formal structure of the farm family. This has still to begin. We may conclude that the *ie* system which has so long survived in Japanese villages remains a dominant force.

[6] This Ministry of Welfare survey was conducted under the direction of Professor Koyama Takashi. The results have not been published, though they are partially available in Koyama Takashi, 'Kazoku-kōsei no henka', *Jimbun Gakuhō* (Tōkyō-toritsu-daigaku), No. 29, 1962. Table XII derives from this source.

CHAPTER IV

THE *IE* SYSTEM AND FAMILY LIFE

The Ie *System in the Farm Family*

In peasant societies where small holdings are farmed on a family basis it is not individuals but families which form the constituent units of society. As a general rule such families are not newly created by each new marriage; instead they are formed by 'splitting off' from existing families. The central relation within the family is not the relationship between husband and wife, but the relationship between parents and children, and rural families of this kind tend commonly towards a strongly patriarchal form. Japanese farm families are no exception. Individuals have little independence from their family and it is families which are the constituent units of village society.

Moreover, the family is not thought of simply as a family group but as an *ie*—the continuing entity, perpetuated, in principle by patrilineal descent, from ancestors to descendants, an entity of which the family group at any one time is only the current concrete manifestation. The *ie*[1] in this sense is the embodiment of a direct genealogical continuity, and as such, on the one hand it is possible for a single individual to represent the *ie* without forming a family group, and on the other it is possible for servants of a family enterprise to be incorporated in the group by the creation of fictive kinship ties. New families are created by sub-division of such *ie*, but the new *ie* which are so

[1] For the concept of the *ie*, see Kawashima Takeyoshi, *ɪdeorogii to shite no kazoku-seido*, 1957 (Iwanami Shoten), Chapter I.

created—the *bunke*, or 'branch families'— will themselves, in exactly the same way as the *ie* which gave them birth (spoken of as their *honke*, or 'stem family'), be continued directly through the generations from ancestor to descendant.

Hence, it is impossible to understand the family in Japanese rural society apart from the concept of the *ie* considered as a continuing entity transcending individuals. This concept of the *ie* included not only those members of the family who made up the family group at any particular time, but also the 'house' in which the family lived (like the English word 'house' the Japanese *'ie'* means both the physical house as well as the continuing family— as in 'the House of Windsor'), the family possessions, the grave-yard where the ancestors are buried, its fields and its forest land, its oxen and its agricultural implements—everything was included in the concept. And as a continuing entity of this kind the *ie* occupied a certain fixed position in the society of the village. It was also far more important than the individuals who at any one time composed it, and hence if 'for the sake of the *ie*' the personal wishes and desires of those individuals had to be ignored or sacrificed, this was looked on as only natural. People talked less about individual personalities (*hitogara* or *jinkaku*) and spoke rather of *iegara* or *kakaku*—words meaning something like the 'reputation' or 'standing' of the family. Family members were expected to try to improve the 'family reputation'; they were expected to conform to 'the ways of the family'. Especially in old and wealthy landlord families there would be a set of 'family precepts' and everyone was enjoined to their obedience in the name of the ancestor who formulated them, so that the *ie* should for ever be preserved and flourish. In short, the idea of the *ie* with the emphasis on continuity of descent was central to the traditional Japanese family system. It is, also, a feature very much bound up with the establishment of feudalism in Japan.

Since the *ie* received so much emphasis, it was natural that a great deal of authority should attach to the position of the househead who controlled it. The strong powers of the house-head, that is to say, derived from the fact that he controlled the disposition of the family property (and note that it was con-ceived of as *family* property, the property of the *ie*, not as individual property); from the fact that he played the central part in rites for the ancestors, and directed the family business and the participation of the family members in it. Members of the family were expected to submit obediently to his authoritarian control, for his management of the family business was based on his firm possession of the family property. One might almost say that the relationship between family head and family members was in many ways similar to a feudal type of master-servant relation. It is for this reason that actual servants of the family have been able, through the creation of fictive kinship ties, to become members of the family. Moreover, since the powers of the househead were superior to the parental power, the head of the family was able to exercise over his grandchildren a stronger authority than the children's parents themselves, and he also had strong powers *vis-à-vis* his own younger brothers. The authority of the househead was much more marked the higher the family's position in the social scale, and among the middling and poor farmers—and certainly among the very poor—this authoritarian direction by the househead never developed. Families of this stratum, as families with a low 'family standing', simply did not have the material basis for a strong '*ie*-consciousness'. However, the poverty of such families inevitably required continuous solidary co-operation on the part of every family member, so that even here individuals were forced to take second place to the *ie*, and when grave decisions had to be taken the wishes and opinions of the househead carried a very great deal of weight.[2]

Inheritance patterns conformed to these other characteristics. Inheritance was primarily a matter of 'succeeding to the house' as one might say one 'succeeds to the throne'. Generally speaking it was the eldest son who succeeded to the position of head of the family, but if there were no sons then the husband

[2] If the *ie* is considered as something which *normally* includes servants then one cannot speak of the creation of 'fictive pseudo-kinship ties'. This, for instance, is the view taken by Ariga Kizaemon (*Nihon kazoku-seido to kosaku-seido*, 1943 (Kawade Shobō), p. 250). The nature of the *ie*, of course, varied according to social stratum. On this point the differences between the samurai-type Confucian family system and the popular family system is discussed in Kawashima Takeyoshi, *Nihon-shakai no kazokuteki-kōsei*, 1948 (Gakusei Shobō, and later Nihon Hyōronsha).

of a daughter (known as a *muko-yōshi*) might take over instead. In succeeding to the headship the eldest son would also either take over the family property as a whole or at least have a prior claim on it. This is not to say that his brothers and sisters received no portion of the family property. If, because their labour was necessary for operating the family's holding, younger sons had stayed for some considerable time working with their parental family they would normally receive a portion of the property when they eventually established a *bunke* branch family. Even then, however, since the maintenance and continuity of the main *ie*—the 'stem family'—always was a prior consideration, their portion was never a very large fraction of the whole. Again, if younger sons found themselves occupations outside of agriculture the family would give them some initial support, and likewise when daughters left the family to marry they would be given a dowry which may be considered as their share of the family property. These apportionments, too, were never such as to endanger the continuity of the main *ie*. If, in fact, the main *ie* was too poor to offer any assistance or any share of the property it was considered natural for the younger sons and daughters who had gone elsewhere to send home money to contribute to current living expenses.

This system of primogeniture inheritance is the quintessential characteristic of the *ie* system and may be considered a product of the feudal social order. As Max Weber has pointed out, feudal systems in the very strictest sense of the term were established only in Europe and in Japan and the development of feudalism in Japan is responsible for the formation of an *ie* system different from other eastern societies such as China and India. Whereas these latter countries adopted a system of inheritance by equal division among all agnatic relatives, in Japan the samurai type of family system spread down to the common people, and was eventually reinforced by the inheritance provisions of the Civil Code enacted towards the end of the nineteenth century. Of course, in the case of farm families, primogeniture inheritance was not the invariable rule, and in the Tokugawa period, despite the authorities' ban on the division of holdings, *bunke* branch families were in fact sometimes created and apportioned part of the stem family's land.

Again in districts where productivity was low it was fairly common to get a husband for the eldest daughter as soon as possible and pass on to him the headship of the house—a practice institutionalized in some districts and called by the name *ane-katoku*. In yet other districts—where, for instance, holdings were generally small—ultimogeniture was instead the rule. The eldest son and his brothers moved out of the parental family as they reached maturity until only the youngest son was left at home to inherit. However, after the nineteenth-century Civil Code gave legal sanction to the samurai form of inheritance, primogeniture became the system throughout Japan and was even more rigidly institutionalized in those farming districts where holdings were in any case far too small to be divided.[3]

Finally, marriage under such an *ie* system is a matter not so much for the two marriage partners themselves as for the two *ie* to which they belong. As a bond which establishes a relationship between two families the agreement between their respective househeads is the decisive factor, and above all else it is important that there should be a reasonable match between the 'family standing' of the two families. As a result we find in the villages that the very top stratum and the very bottom stratum of families tend to take their marriage partners from some considerable distance because they suffer from a shortage of suitable candidates near at hand. Families in the middle strata were able to make alliances with families of fairly equal standing living not far away, but since the last quarter of the nineteenth century the degree of village endogamy has considerably declined. Thus, for instance, in some districts it was formerly common for age groups—the so-called *wakamono-gumi*, or young men's groups— to exercise some control over marriages within the village. But even in such districts the *wakamono-gumi* have gradually lost this function and the go-between marriage has become the standard form—relatives or friends of the family taking it upon themselves to search out a suitable partner for a young man or woman. This go-between whose function is to

[3] Nakagawa Zennosuke, 'Basshi-sōzoku', Nakagawa Zennosuke and Shioda Teiichi, 'Ane-katoku-sōzoku', *Kazoku-seido-zenshū, Shiron-hen*, 5, 1938 (Kawade Shobō).

bring the two parties together is not always necessarily the same person as plays the role of go-between at the wedding ceremony. The system of appointing a separate ceremonial go-between (known as a *nakōdo-oya*) was institutionalized in some districts as a form of patron-client relation, and will be discussed in that connexion below.[4]

In such a marriage system, the personal character of the bride was of secondary importance. First of all it was necessary that the families should be of roughly equal 'standing', though it was also often considered an advantage to take a bride from a family a little less well off than one's own. This was thought to make the daughter-in-law easier to handle. The second consideration, of next importance to family standing, especially in the middle and lower strata, was whether or not the bride was 'a good worker'. The young bride in a farm family was in a quite literal sense 'the bride of the house'. She entered an already existing *ie*, with, to put the matter in the crudest terms, the dual function of providing an heir to make possible the continuance of the family and at the same time adding her energies to the family labour force.

As a consequence it was by no means a necessary condition for marriage that there should be any loving affection between the two partners themselves. It was enough if the househeads or parents considered the marriage to be suitable. It is true that as time passed, the wishes of the partners came to be given some consideration with the development of the practice known as the *miai* or 'mutual viewing', the carefully arranged meeting at which the prospective bride and groom were allowed to 'inspect' each other. But even this was by no means a fully mutual affair; the girl's function was simply to be seen and she had almost no opportunity at all to express her own personal wishes regarding her own marriage. 'Love' was considered to be on the same level as the casual mating of animals, and marriages based on it were generally considered to lead to unhappiness— witness the proverbial expression: 'those who come together in passion stay together in tears'. In the Meiji Civil Code of 1897, there was a clause which required parental consent for marriage

[4] For a description of 'patron-taking' marriages see Ariga Kizaemon, *Nihon kon'in-shi-ron*, 1948 (Nikkō Shoin).

up to the age of 30 for men and 25 for women, thus reinforcing the social custom which gave the power of decision over marriage to parents. One can say, in brief, that the young bride owed a duty of obedience more to the househead than to her husband; it was primarily as a daughter-in-law, rather than as a wife, that she had to adapt herself to 'the ways of the family'. And, if she failed to adapt, it was at the whim of the househead or parents-in-law that she was divorced.

Such, in outline, was the *ie* system. It was a system supported by the characteristics of the Japanese agricultural structure, and at the same time the ideological conditions for its maintenance were provided by a code of specifically Japanese family morality. The *ie* system extended to all Japanese families, but it was particularly deep-rooted in farm families.[5]

Since the war, however, with the change in the Civil Code and the collapse of the ideology of the *ie* system, even in the villages these institutions have changed. The *ie* system is in process of dissolution, and the farm family of the present day differs considerably from the foregoing description. But this is not to say that the modern farm family has been entirely liberated from the institutions of the *ie*. Before we go into this question, however, we might first elaborate a little more concretely on the characteristics of personal relationships within the farm family in the heyday of the *ie* system.

Personal Relations within the Farm Family

It was said above that the position of the househead was given its authority by virtue of his functions as the director of the family ritual, as the trustee of the family property and as the manager of the family business. What does this mean in more concrete terms?

The househead was also designated by the nineteenth-century Civil Code as the owner of the family property, and thus in legal terms had control over the family's farming operations, directing the labour of the family members. One might expect, given the intensive manual labour common in

[5] For a study of various problems connected with the rural family see Suzuki Eitaro, *Nihon nōson-shakai-gaku genri*, 1940 (Jichōsha). Chapter IV is devoted to the question of the family as the unit of village social structure.

Japanese agriculture, that as the househead grew older and as his physical work capacity became inferior to that of his children his say in the management of the farm would decline, but this was not in fact the case. In a traditional agriculture whose cultivating practices depended not on scientific techniques but on empirical skills the househead with his longer years of experience was able to retain the directing power. On tiny holdings there was little chance of setting aside a few fields for an enterprising son who wanted to try out new ideas of his own. Too much was at stake to afford the risk of failure. And in any case, under such conditions the young heir to the family had little positive incentive to seek to acquire new techniques. Until the time should come when he in turn should succeed to the headship of the family, he worked away diligently in obedience to his father's direction. And if this was true even of the eldest son, the future head of the family, it was true *a fortiori* of the househead's wife and his daughter-in-law who were even more passive participants in the family's work.

The income which was received as a result of these labours all went into the househead's pocket. The individual work contribution of family members would in any case have been difficult to calculate separately from the total labour of the family as a whole, but in this case there was no question of anyone ever making the attempt, for this was income from agriculture carried on as the *family* occupation, on land which was the *family* property. The result was that the househead, since he kept a tight grip on the family's agricultural income, also had complete control over its pattern of consumption. For small everyday expenses the househead's wife, as mistress of the household, would be granted a small sum of money for use at her discretion, but for large items of expenditure the money had to come from the househead's purse and could not be used without his permission. For their own pocket money, too, members of the family had to ask the househead whenever they were in need.

In this way the position of househead was always a strongly authoritative one in both fields, of production and consumption, although if one excepts the old established families of big land-lords, there was no especially exaggerated symbolic emphasis on the authority of the househead. The practice of giving him special privileges in everyday matters, for instance, was hardly a general one. At the most he would have the right to be the first in the family bath, or he might be given a bottle of *sake* with his evening meal and an extra side dish of pickles to go with it. But, as is symbolized in those districts which use the open hearth by the fact that one side of it, known as the *yokoza*, was reserved as his special seat, whether or not the househead had any special privileges, he occupied the central position of authority in the family.

Such being the position of the househead, it was natural that the eldest son, as his heir, should also enjoy high status. There is a phrase which aptly describes the position of the children in the farm family: 'One to sell, one to follow and one in reserve.' In the ideal family a girl should be born first. She was the 'one to sell'—to be given away in marriage. Then should come a son, the heir of the family. Finally, since no family could feel secure with only one son, another son was necessary in case the eldest should die young. It was fairly general for the eldest son to be given clearly different treatment from his younger brothers, as a more important person. This was most clearly marked in the less developed areas, especially of the north-east, where the eldest son was referred to as *ani* and younger sons as *onji*. In such districts younger sons really were mere 'understudies'. There is no reason to believe that the intrinsic appeal of children to their parents depends on the order of their birth; it was, rather, a categorical imperative of the *ie* system that the heir should be given a higher status than his younger brothers. This was not only because he was destined to take on the headship of the family, but also because it was he who would have the responsibility of caring for his parents when they were old and helpless.[6]

By contrast, younger sons—except in those richer farm families which could afford to send them to middle schools— would be expected, if the family had a sufficiently large holding, to work on the family farm as soon as they left the primary

[6] For the character of rural eldest sons, see Matsumaru Shimazō, *Nōson ni ikiru seinen*, 1953 (Shin-hyōronsha). The author also considers the typical personalities of daughters and younger sons.

school. This was known as 'thank you service'. Then, after they had done their army service as conscripts, they would normally find some way of making themselves independent. In poorer farm families, which did not have enough land to use their labour, they would as soon as possible become shop assistants or factory workers or craftsmen's apprentices, in the hope that they would not only become independent, but also capable of contributing to the support of their parents. In the less developed districts where holdings were large, these younger sons might continue to live in and work for the main family even after marriage. A married younger son who did this was usually spoken of as 'doing service' to the family which his elder brother was going to inherit. The phrase aptly indicates the position of the younger son in the institutional system developed in the Tokugawa period.

Daughters, on the other hand, were not necessary for the continuance of the *ie*, and since considerable expense was involved in marrying them off it was no cause for congratulation if too many daughters were born. The reason for wanting 'first a girl' was only that, assuming that half the children are likely to be girls anyway, the sooner one had a daughter who could help with the housework and with younger children the better. The fact that girls were apt to be spoken of, since they were destined to be married off, as 'things to sell' is an indication of the low status they enjoyed. In an *ie* system in which men were all-important, it was necessary when a daughter was married to give her away with a 'premium' in the shape of a reasonable dowry, and even after marriage one might have to supplement her supply of clothing and pocket money. Hence the proverb to the effect that the birth of three daughters can mean the ruin of a family's fortune. However, among the poorest farmers a daughter had little hope of having this much money spent on her. For such families daughters were workers who might bring in some money for the family from the pittance they earned as factory girls, or else they were quite literally 'to be sold'—into prostitution for the sake of their parents.[7]

---

[7] The need to spend large sums of money on weddings remains unchanged. For a post-war survey of such expenditure, see Norinshō, Tōkei-chōsabu, eds., *Nōson no konrei to sōgi—sono hiyō no jittai to shakai-keizaiteki kōsatsu*, 1954.

THE HOUSE OF A FORMER SMALL LANDLORD WITH,
ON THE LEFT, A FIREPROOF STOREHOUSE

THE HOUSE OF AN OWNER-FARMER WITH
GARDEN AND WORKING SPACE

PLOUGHING WITH A POWER-CULTIVATOR

A CART-LOAD OF FALLEN LEAVES BEING PULLED
BY A HAND-TRACTOR

And when a girl gave up the status of daughter for the status of bride the marital relationship which she entered was always subordinated to her husband's relation with his parents. The bride in the farm family has been described as 'a hornless work-and-milch-cow'; her function was both to have children and to work in the fields. And the way she was treated is illustrated in the proverbial expressions: 'Parents are irreplaceable but brides can be changed at will,' or: 'Brothers and sisters are like hands and feet, but wives are like a kimono—one can change them.' Unless she served her mother-in-law and was careful not to upset her husband's sisters (known as *ko-jūto*; literally 'little mothers-in-law') her status as bride might be hard to maintain. It was fairly rare for a marriage to be registered by transferring the bride into the family register of her husband as soon as the marriage took place. Only after she had passed the test and shown that she could fit into the 'ways of the family' and serve her parents-in-law, or perhaps only after she had become pregnant, would her common-law status be exchanged for a regular legalized marriage. For a girl entering a new family as a bride, the birth of a child was the first step towards achieving security of position in her new family.

Since the bride had no opportunity to be with her husband before marriage there was no question of their entering on marriage in a spirit of loving intimacy. So it was very difficult after marriage for her to talk to her husband freely and without reserve. Even if, in their life together, intimacy did gradually develop there were severe restraints to prevent them from giving it overt expression. Her mother-in-law who had once in her turn been a daughter-in-law and given patient and arduous service to her own husband's parents was likely to demand the same stoic restraint from her own daughter-in-law. Her relation with her mother-in-law was thus a source of great frustration for the young bride. And her husband was unable to provide any solace for her frustrations, for, given the enormous weight attached to the parent-child relationship, it was hard for him to side with his wife or to protect her *vis-à-vis* his parents. Even without such protection, if there had been the consolation that the young couple could escape into a private world all of their own, life might still have been more easy to bear, but the open structure of a typical farm house did not offer any island of privacy to the young couple. In a situation in which one could not even talk privately in bed, the bride's mental suffering was bound to be of no mean order.

Nor was her suffering only mental; the bride was the first to get up in the morning and the last to go to bed at night. In every aspect of daily life—at mealtimes, in the order of taking baths—the lowly status of the bride was always made explicit. Physically, too, she was liable to be exhausted. This was especially so in the agricultural busy season. Consequently her visit to her parental home, customary during the holiday at the end of the busy season, was the one bright spot of the bride's existence. It was not only an opportunity physically to recoup her energies, it was also a chance to relax with her own parents and brothers and sisters and so, freed from the psychological pressures of her normal existence, to unwind the knot of her mental tensions. It also provided an occasion for her parents to supplement her pocket money or to help her out with new clothing. Without such help from her own family the bride's position would have been even harder to bear.

The pleasure of these visits home was bound to diminish as the bride bore children and as she became accustomed to life in her husband's family. Eventually her days as a 'young bride' would be over. As her husband became househead she too would become the mistress of the household and her position would be secure. In some districts there was a special ceremony, known as *hera-watashi* (literally 'handing over the paddle'—the flat wooden spoon with which rice is served) to mark this transfer of authority to the new mistress of the household, but in most districts there was a gradual and natural transition as the parents-in-law became old and unable any longer to work. Parallel to the patriarchal authority of the househead was what might be called the matriarchal authority of the mistress of the household. All household matters were within her sphere of competence; her long years of backbreaking toil in the fields as well as in the home had earned her a status of some importance. She was still very much subordinated to her husband, however, and although one speaks of the authority of the mistress of the household, it was an authority far inferior to that of the househead. Finally, as she grew older and reached the status of retired grandmother, or when her husband died and her son became househead, her position in the family once again declined. Now she had to take orders from the new househead, her son, and from his wife, formerly the young bride whom she had under her control.[8]

It was natural enough, given the kind of marital relationship in which she was involved, that the young bride should concentrate on her children all the affection which she could not feel for her husband. It was fairly general for the Japanese mother, not only in farm families, to lavish excessive affection on her children, and this had the incidental effect of making even more difficult her relationship with her son's wife. But the young mother was not the person solely responsible for disciplining and training the children. The children were not only her children, they were also the grandchildren of her parents-in-law, and this was a source of inconsistency in child training, for children were very frequently spoiled by their grandparents. As the child grew older however, and as the position of househead passed from his indulgent grandfather to his stricter father he was required to give implicit obedience. To obey was the first and primary meaning of filial piety. And so the child, indulged when he was young, was, as it were, increasingly repressed as he grew older.

In these ways members of the family observed, each according to his separate status, the patterns of behaviour which tended to maintain harmony in an *ie* of which the househead was the central focus. This harmony was considered to be a matter of emotional unity; there was no sense of suppressed individuality. It would be much more accurate to say, not that harmony was maintained at the cost of brutal sacrifice of the individual ego, but rather that the system did not permit the development of any egos to be sacrificed.

---

[8] The position of women in Japanese villages is discussed in my essay, 'Nōson shakai ni okeru fujin no chii', *Nihon no nōson-shakai*, 1953 (Tōkyō-daigaku Shuppankai). See also Maruoka Hideko, *Onna no isshō*, 1953 (Iwanami Shoten), and Kumagai Motoichi, *Mura no fujin-seikatsu*, 1954 (Shin-hyōronsha).

The Dissolution and Survival of the Ie

The post-war Constitution, accepting the principle of the essential equality of the sexes, specified in Article 24 that marriage was only to be based on the freely given consent of both man and woman. Subsequently the Civil˙ Code was revised to conform with the principles of the modern Western family, and the *ie* system was legally discarded. The concept of succession to the headship of the family disappeared, and sons and daughters received the same rights to equal inheritance shares. It was feared, as a result, that the already small holdings of Japanese farms would be subjected to even further subdivision, and there were frequent moves to enact special legislation to deal with the inheritance of agricultural property. These failed, however, and the provisions of the revised Civil Code were applied to farm families as to any others. This in itself marked a big change from the days of the former Civil Code modelled as it was on the Confucian family system of the samurai class.

Admittedly, as long as the actual conditions of daily life remained remote from those envisaged by the law, a mere change in the latter did not bring about the disappearance of the *ie* system as a social custom. Farmers' ideas about the *ie* were not immediately altered. Among the wage and salary workers of the towns who were already in no position to maintain the traditional customs of the *ie*, the provisions of the new Civil Code were fairly easily accepted, but in the villages where the *ie* system really was adapted to the actual conditions of family life, there was no possibility of a sudden transition to the new patterns which the law specified.

A survey carried out by the Family Problems Study Group provides some illustration of this point. It is based on a somewhat limited sample, but it shows the differences in ideas between wage or salary workers living in an apartment area in Tokyo, and farmers in a mountain village not far from the city. Table XIII shows the answers to two questions, and it will be obvious that there was far more support for the old system in the villages.

TABLE XIII

Opinions of the Ie *System: City and Village*[9]

Question	Answer	Percentage giving each Answer in	
		Village Sample	City Sample
Which do you think was better: the old Civil Code or the new?	The old.	42.6	16.0
	The new.	27.4	51.4
	Both have their points.	6.7	24.4
	Don't know.	23.3	8.2
When an eldest son marries, do you think it better for him to live with his parents or not?	Better.	72.2	18.7
	Better not.	17.5	58.8
	Depends on circumstances.	8.5	20.8
	Don't know.	1.8	1.7

However, as the judgement that the traditional *ie* system was a 'feudal' family system gradually became firmly established in the general value system of post-war Japan, and in particular as the idea that the rural family was the most feudal of all slowly penetrated even into farm families, the grip of the *ie* system on the villages began to weaken. The process was naturally hastened by the development of agriculture in the post-war period and by the rapid growth of the Japanese economy.

In the first place, even in farm families there was a diminution of what one might call '*ie* consciousness'. Compared with the pre-war period when the *ie* as a whole, including ancestors and descendants, was looked on as much more important than individuals, individuals became more self-assertive. It gradually came to seem less reasonable that the individual should be sacrificed for the sake of the *ie*. The kind of '*ie* consciousness' which emphasized the careful preservation of the property handed down from the ancestors and which made it a man's prime duty to guard the ancestral graves and maintain or even raise the 'standing' of the family in the village received a powerful blow from the land reform. And the idea that perhaps

[9] From Koyama Takashi, ed., *Gendai kazoku no kenkyū—Jittai to chōsei*, 1960 (Kōbundō), pp. 77 and 86. For other field surveys which describe family life in relative detail, see Furushima Toshio, ed., *Sanson no kōzō*, 1949 (Nihon Hyōronsha, and later, Ochanomizu Shobō) and Isoda Susumu, ed., *Sonraku-kōzō no kenkyū*, 1955 (Tōkyō-daigaku Shuppankai).

the ancestors were less important than still-living individuals began to penetrate even into the villages.

The declining importance of the *ie* also weakened the power of the household. Even in the families of full-time farmers the swift developments of post-war agriculture have prompted a shift of managing authority from the household to his youthful heir. The use of farm machinery, of new techniques and new agricultural chemicals, is often too much for an aged household, and as the traditional empirical agriculture lost its prestige and long years of experience ceased to count for very much, the household was forced to relinquish his central position in the family enterprise. Again, in part-time farming families, as soon as sons began to bring home their own pay packets for their non-agricultural work, not only did the household lose control over his sons' working life, it also became unrealistic for him to expect that their wages would always be pooled in the central family purse under his control. If, further, it should be the household himself who took some non-agricultural job, the inevitable result was to enhance the status of his wife who looked after the farm in his absence, and correspondingly to weaken his own authority. And it will be recalled that the increase in part-time farming has proceeded apace. Even in those households which remained full-time farmers the man who wants to ensure that his sons stay on the farm is more or less forced to make some concession to their wishes. Hence one can say that a weakening of the household's authority is a general characteristic of the modern Japanese farm family.

As far as inheritance is concerned it is still the general rule that the agricultural property is received as a whole by a single heir, with the other children renouncing their inheritance rights. Holdings are simply too small for division to mean anything but a sharing of poverty. However, although the present situation resembles in form the pre-war custom whereby the eldest son received the entire property, there is in reality a very big difference between younger sons and daughters having no rights and their having rights which they subsequently choose to relinquish. Even before the war, it was not uncommon in the more progressive agricultural districts for an eldest son who showed some ability to be given higher education and sent off to the towns while another son took over the family farm. Nowadays this idea that it does not necessarily have to be the eldest son who inherits the farm has become generally diffused. If there are no obvious differences in scholastic ability between the sons then it is still usual for the eldest son to succeed, but in this case younger sons are no longer treated simply from the point of view of what is in the best interests of the *ie*. One no longer finds, for example, that younger sons are kept at home to provide labour until such time as a bride should be recruited into the family for the eldest son. If the family can afford it, it is the common practice to try to send younger sons to high school, or, if this cannot be managed, to try to make them independent by arranging a job through the mass recruiting system which factories and shops organize among middle-school leavers.[10]

Again there is a change in the nature of the *bunke* branch family. Even before the war, a younger son who had worked on the family holding and was unable to move on to some independent occupation was likely to be given a portion of the family's land during the lifetime of his father, and established in a bunke branch family. But again it was always the interests of the main family which were paramount. Today, by contrast, with the increase in part-time farming, and with a shortage of labour cutting down the size of the manageable holding, the purpose of bunke division is usually to give a younger son who has established himself in some other occupation enough land to grow his own rice. Now, in other words, it is a bunke division in which the interests of individuals are paramount—the aim being to supplement the low income of the bunke itself. Here, too, one can see reflected a tendency for '*ie* consciousness' to disappear.[11]

[10] The tendency not to insist on primogeniture in the more progressive agricultural districts may be seen in the results of a survey conducted in 1953. See Fukutake Tadashi and Tsukamoto Tetsundo, *Nihon nōmin no shakaiteki seikaku*, 1954 (Yūhikaku), p. 102 ff. On inheritance practices in post-war farm families see Nōrinshō, Nōchikyoku, *Nōka sōzoku no jittai*, 1952. Partial results of this survey are also to be found in Watanabe Yōzō and Bai Kōichi, 'Nōson no sōzoku-keitai', *Hōritsu Jihō*, Vol. 26, No. 9, and Vol. 27, No. 2.

[11] For the transition from *bunke* governed by the interests of the *ie* to bunke

As far as marriage is concerned, too, the situation has greatly changed. The aspect of the rural family which has excited the greatest comment since the war, as the prime example of its feudal characteristics, is the position of the young bride and her relation with her mother-in-law. The result has been that farmers' daughters of the post-war generation have developed a marked reluctance to marry into farm families. Instead of the double burden of hard labour both in the fields and in the home, they would prefer, even if it means a sacrifice of income security, to live alone with their husbands, free from the restraining presence of parents-in-law. What is more, they tended to find oppressive the stifling atmosphere of village society in which the size of a bride's dowry was a staple topic of conversation.

With these changes the old type of marriage—the importation into the *ie* of a 'hornless work- and milch-cow'—has ceased to be viable. Even in the villages love affairs have sometimes developed in youth clubs and in agricultural study groups, though this is still by no means a general phenomenon. In fact it is rather rare; most farmers' children are still married through the good offices of a go-between and a similarity in the 'standing' of the family remains a condition for arranging a match. But the mere decision by parents and househeads that a match would constitute a suitable alliance between their houses is no longer a *sufficient* condition for a marriage. The wishes of the young couple themselves have come to be respected, and it is now becoming normal even in the villages for the young couple to see a good deal of each other before marriage to give an opportunity for affection to develop.

As a consequence the status of the bride after marriage has also risen. Today's mothers-in-law may have suffered the scoldings of their own mothers-in-law when they were young, but it is no longer possible for them to mete out the same treatment to their daughters-in-law. They now have to treat their sons' wives with some consideration. Whereas formerly the young bride often depended for a long time on her own parents

governed by the interests of individuals and for the tendency for bunke to become less a matter of 'paternal benevolence', and more a matter of rights, see Ushiomi Toshitaka *et al.*, *Nihon no nōson*, 1957 (Iwanami Shoten), the section entitled 'Ie to sōzoku' by Nakao Hidetoshi and Ishimura Zensuke.

for supplements to her pocket money and for her personal clothing, nowadays it is generally expected that the young bride should be given her own pocket money by her husband's family. And it has become necessary for the nuclear family of the young couple to be respected as a semi-independent entity within the household.

One may assume that these changes have been accelerated in the last few years. In those households which are still full-time farmers it is the general practice for the agricultural income to go into the househead's personal savings account in the Agricultural Co-operative, and its expenditure is still under the househead's control. In some districts, however, the Agricultural Co-operatives have promoted the idea of monthly salaries and in this way the regular expenditure of the family has been freed from the househead's monopolistic control. There are even examples of farms which have turned themselves into legal companies, so that the wife too receives her own separate wage packet. And there are a good many families in which the heir and his wife receive a fixed monthly amount to cover their own personal expenses. Recently, since so many eldest sons are themselves tempted to take jobs elsewhere, there have been serious discussions of 'father-son contracts'—arrangements whereby the son receives a fixed wage for his work on the farm and also receives full control over a part of the family farm which is separated from the estate which has to be shared among his brothers and sisters.

Again, we have already seen that the tendency for more farm househeads to take other jobs has increased the number of house-wife-farmers, and this has led to a tendency for wives to assume something like the househead's role. It has long been common in urban areas for the husband to hand over his wage-packet to his wife. Now this may also happen in those farm families where the husband goes to work away from the farm; the househead has to take second place to the wife who bears the brunt of the farm work. In heavily industrialized districts it is by no means rare for the househead of a farm family, his eldest son and his younger sons, all to commute daily to some other work, and one begins to hear talk of dormitory farms and of farm lodgers. Again, when the eldest son leaves his parents in the village, goes off to work in the town, and finally marries in the town, the family is reduced to nuclear size, with only the old couple remaining—by no means a rarity today. All of these changes signify, to a greater or lesser degree, the dissolution of the traditional *ie* in the villages.

Nevertheless elements of the *ie* still survive. In present-day Japanese circumstances which do not encourage development of the notion that agriculture is a business enterprise, and where, moreover, migration to the city still does not always promise a better or a secure standard of living, the property of the family farm does at least guarantee that one will get enough to eat. Hence the concept of the *ie* does not disappear. Even if the househead's dictatorial authority has crumbled, in the houses of full-time farmers it is still he who holds the purse-strings. Even if, here and there, one encounters the idea of 'father-son contracts', the number of farm families which are in a position for such contracts to be successful is extremely small. The draft laws for special inheritance provisions for farm families have usually envisaged some scheme whereby all land, buildings, large machines and farm animals would be inherited intact by a single heir, while the other children would receive their share in some form of annual payments, but the number of farm families which could keep the farm going and carry the burden of such debts is small indeed. In the present condition of full-time farmers equal inheritance is an impossibility. Even among the part-time farmers, where '*ie* consciousness' has been weakened and where property is divided in the light of individual needs, *equal* division is still not practised because of the need for one child to take over responsibility for the parents or because of the special social responsibilities which will devolve on the son who is considered as the main heir. Even among those farm families which have so little land that they are hardly to be considered farm families at all, the fact that what land they do have supplements their otherwise low income and provides some kind of security for old age acts to preserve the remnants of a '*ie* consciousness'. Where all the children have left home and the old parents continue their painstaking cultivation of the soil alone, although sometimes the eventual solution will be for them to be absorbed in a son's home in the town, it will probably also happen frequently that the son, not having achieved a sufficiently secure livelihood in the town, decides to return to the village and take over the farm. Here too the concept of the *ie* can survive.

Moreover, even though the position of the young bride has improved, given the present circumstances in which farmers live, there is little hope of taking the further step of setting up a new household for a young couple separate from their parents. Recently one notes attempts within the farmhouse to arrange relatively separated living space for the young couple, but given the open structure of the traditional farmhouse it is difficult in the nature of things for the young couple to create a citadel of their own to which they can escape from the frustrating complications of personal relationships within the family. Moreover, even today's brides, once married, are by no means in a strong position and in part-time farming households they may have very heavy farm work to perform. Economic growth has brought a labour shortage and this in turn has raised farm wage rates, so that they are forced willy-nilly to bear the brunt of the work themselves. The example may be extreme, but one hears instances of farmers' wives having an abortion chiefly in order to avoid being pregnant during the agricultural busy season.

Until the farm as a business enterprise becomes fully disentangled from the farm family as a consuming social unit, and until agriculture becomes a profession freely chosen, rather than a 'family occupation' inevitably inherited, the *ie* will not disappear. Until there is an assurance of a decent livelihood in some other occupation, and a guarantee of security in old age, the 'family property', however small it may be, represents the staff of life. Here too is a factor preserving the *ie*. Hence, despite the tendencies for the *ie* system to disappear in the post-war period, Japanese farm families have still not reached the point at which the final dissolution of the *ie* is in sight.

FURTHER READING

Descriptions of the farm family will be found in:

Beardsley, Hall and Ward, *Village Japan*.

Cornell, *Matsunagi*.

Embree, *Suyemura*.

Norbeck, *Takashima*.

Raper, *Japanese Village*.

Smith, *Kurusu*.

Tokyo, International Christian University, Rural Welfare Institute, *A study of rural economy, family life and the new inheritance law*, Mitaka, Tokyo, 1958.

K. Ariga, 'The family in Japan', *Marriage and Family Living*, 16, 1954.

R. K. Beardsley, 'The household in the status system of Japanese villages', University of Michigan, Center for Japanese Studies, *Occasional Papers*, 1, 1951.

H. Befu, 'Corporate emphasis and patterns of descent in the Japanese family', in Smith and Beardsley, *Japanese culture*.

J. W. Bennett and M. Nagai, 'A summary and analysis of "The Familial Structure of Japanese Society" by Takeyoshi Kawashima', *South-Western Journal of Anthropology*, 9, ii, 1953.

G. DeVos and H. Wagatsuma, 'Value attitudes towards role behavior of women in two Japanese villages', *American Anthropologist*, 63, iv, December 1961.

N. Hozumi, *Ancestor worship and the Japanese law*, Tokyo, 1941.

T. Koyama, 'The changing family structure in Japan', in Smith and Beardsley, *Japanese culture*.

Y. S. Matsumoto, 'Contemporary Japan, the individual and the group', *Transactions of the American Philosophical Society*, new series, 50, pt. 1, 1960.

Y. S. Matsumoto, 'Notes on primogeniture', in Smith and Beardsley, *Japanese culture*.

K. Steiner, 'The revision of the Civil Code of Japan: provisions affecting the family', *Far Eastern Quarterly* 9, ii, February 1950.

E. Vogel, 'Nakodo', *Human Organisation*, 20, ii, Summer 1961.

H. Wagatsuma and G. De Vos, 'Attitudes towards arranged marriage in rural Japan', *Human Organisation*, 21, iii, Fall 1962.

CHAPTER V

THE *DŌZOKUDAN* AND KINSHIP RELATIONS

The Dōzokudan *and Patron-client Relations*

As one generation succeeds another a family divides. As marriages take place it develops affinal relations with other families. In both these ways kinship relations are created between one Japanese family and another. When these related families live close by each other and are closely connected in the daily business of making a living, then kinship groups are formed. Among peasant smallholders of low productivity the difficulty of earning a livelihood in complete independence creates the necessity for mutual assistance, and it is first of all from the kinship group that help is expected. Equally, where there are clear differences in wealth and economic power it is usual for the weaker to depend on the stronger, and again it is first of all within the kinship group that an object of dependence is sought.

Such kinship groups in Japanese villages are normally formed on the basis of patrilineal descent. Since Japan lacked the rules of exogamy found in India and in China, marriage was permitted within such patrilineal kinship groups, also—and the two facts are not unconnected—until recently marriages within the same hamlet were fairly frequent. But although these kinship groups thus had bilineal elements, it was generally the case, as we shall see later, that affinal relations, however close, were very much kept in the background in the patrilineal descent group. This patrilineal kinship group is called the *dōzoku* or *dōzokudan*.[1]

[1] The names for these *dōzokudan* vary from district to district. Fairly commonly used are *maki* (Eastern Japan), *jirui* (Eastern Japan and the

A *dōzokudan* may be defined as a 'stem family' and group of 'branch families' which mutually recognize the genealogical relationships by which the branches have divided from the stem. Thus the splitting up of the family is a necessary condition for the creation of a *dōzokudan*, but it is not a sufficient one. For a *dōzokudan* to be created, one *ie* must divide and create another *ie* as its branch family. The branch family is brought into being by the grant of a piece of house-land, a house, and agricultural land and it thereby becomes independent. But at the same time it recognizes the stem family's ritual functions in the worship of ancestors or of special *kami* of the *dōzoku*, and agrees to abide by the customs which normally bind those of inferior and superior lineage. If a branch does not receive this division of the family property and does not conform to this prescribed pattern of social relations then despite the actual fact of fission no *dōzokudan* is created. Again since it is not simply a matter of genealogical relation, it is possible for servants who by the simulation of kinship relations have become household members to be set up as independent branches and so become members of the *dōzokudan*. Similarly, if a younger son of a branch family belonging to such a *dōzokudan* should go to live in the stem family as a servant and later receive a grant from the stem family to establish himself independently, his new household joins the *dōzokudan* not as a branch family of the house in which he was born but as an immediate branch of the stem family, with a similar standing to that of his original household.[2]

Thus in order to understand the nature of the dōzokudan we must examine the forms of family fission by which they are

---

Nagoya area), *kabu* or *kabuichi* (the Kyōto area and western Japan), *ikke*, *ittō, yauchi*, etc. For the distribution of these names see Gamō Masao, *Nihonjin no seikatsu-kōzō josetsu*, 1960 (Seishin Shobō).

[2] For the *dōzokudan* see the following: Ariga Kizaemon, *Nihon kazoku-seido to kosaku-seido*, 1943 (Kawade Shobō), and 'Dōzoku to shinzoku' in Minkan-denshō no kai, *Nihon minzokugaku no tame ni*, Vol. 2, 1947; Kitano Seiichi, 'Dōzoku soshiki to hōken-isei', in Nihon Jimbun Gakkai, *Hōken isei*, 1951 (Yūhikaku); Oikawa Hiroshi, 'Dōzoku soshiki to kon'in oyobi sōsō no girei', *Minzokugaku Nempō*, No. 2, 1940 (Sanseidō). For a discussion of the development of studies of the dōzoku, see Nakano Takashi, 'Dōzoku kenkyū no kiten to kadai' in *Nihon shakaigaku no kadai: Hayashi-kyōju kanreki kinen rombunshū*, 1956 (Yūhikaku).

originally created. We have already mentioned how the feudal authorities of the Tokugawa period, in order to make certain of an adequate supply of tax rice, imposed restrictions to prevent the excessive sub-division of holdings. Hence branch families could not freely be created. However, since new land was still being reclaimed and since there were always families which died out, the establishment of branches, although difficult, was in practice possible. After 1870 there were no restrictions at all on the creation of branch families, but except in those special circumstances where by land reclamation or an improvement in irrigation there was an enlargement of the cultivated area, it was by no means easy for a family to set up a new branch. For to give a part of the family property to a new branch and at the same time not to lower the family's status, was possible only for those upper class families which through the generations had acquired a considerable accumulation of land. And if the setting up of a branch family would have implied a drastic lowering of the status of the stem family it would normally be scrupulously avoided. Consequently the families which managed to create a relatively large number of branch families and to keep them together in a cohesive dōzokudan, were nearly always large land-owning families.

Since such emphasis was placed on the stem family of direct eldest son descent, and on maintaining its standing in the village, the property set aside for the new branch family was always far smaller than that retained by the stem family. In north-eastern Japan, the least developed area, it was common in the more remote villages for younger sons to work for their parental family for some ten or more years after marriage and then eventually to receive an apportionment barely enough to keep them alive. We have already mentioned that this period of working after marriage was spoken of as their 'service' to the stem family. The apportionment of property was looked on as a reward for this period of service and the branch family considered it an *on*—a benevolent favour— vouchsafed by the stem family. This is the source and *raison d'être* of the master-servant relationship which develops between the stem and the branch family. And it was because of this master-servant relationship that the 'servant branch family' could so naturally be created.

Except for the branches of wealthy landlord families, it was rare for such branches to receive enough property to make them fully independent, and even if the stem family was a wealthy landlord family, servant branch families usually received a smaller apportionment than the branches founded by real kin so that after the branch was established it was necessary for it to continue to depend on the stem family. These branch families therefore, even after independence, continued to receive the protection of the stem family; they were tenants on the stem family's land, they were thoroughly integrated into the stem family's production system and they continued to provide personal services for the stem family's household.[3]

As in this way new families gradually branch off from the parent-stem, the dōzokudan takes on a pyramidical structure, typically with an 'original stem family' (sōhonke) at the top, then stem families (from the original stem family's point of view branch families) and finally branch families (from the original family's point of view 'grandchild-branch-families'). Ranking within the dōzokudan depends on the antiquity of a family's branching and on the directness of its descent relationship to the original stem family. When this ranking is supported by differences in real economic power, and paralleled by landlord-tenant relationships, the 'original stem family' can exercise very strong control over all the other members of the group. Whereas in the Chinese clan it is the clan property held in common which serves to unite the group, in Japan it is the 'family property' of the stem family which provides the material basis for solidarity. In a typical dōzokudan the 'original stem family' has central control over the group's farming activities; the celebration of weddings and funerals, the building of houses or their re-thatching, and other activities of daily life, are carried out by mutual assistance within the group; the worship of the kami of the dōzoku and of its ancestors is carried on under the

---

[3] There is also local variation in the name given to stem families and branch families; for example, honke, hontaku, oya, motoya, bunke, bekke, shintaku, shinya, kamado, etc. It was common for servant branch families to be described by a special term, such as yashinai-bekke to distinguish them from the true kin branches called miwakare-bekke, but this did not imply that they were treated as less important than branch families linked by true descent.

auspices of the stem family, and at every New Year and Mid-summer festival the branch families make formal calls to pay their respects to the stem family. In hamlets where the dōzoku-dan occupied an overwhelming position in the hamlet and the original stem family held large land holdings, even households which originally had no relationship with the dōzokudan would become 'commended' branch families and thus be absorbed into the dōzokudan.[4]

Admittedly such typical dōzokudan were not to be found generally in Japanese villages. They were typical only of the least developed areas. And even where they were typically found it was in fact fairly rare for there to be an orderly pyramid of an original stem family, stem families and branch families left intact. For with the passage of time the ranking based on descent and ranking based on economic standing normally ceased to coincide. Very often the original stem family would go into decline and one of its branches would become powerful. When this happened the latter would create a separate dōzoku-dan with its own immediate branch families, and the original stem family, retaining the loyalty of only a few direct branches of its own, would gradually lose its social standing. Sometimes when the original stem family declined and left the village the whole dōzokudan would split up into two or more separate groups.

Again, in the first decades of this century even in the least developed areas most of the stem families with very large land holdings much reduced the area they cultivated directly, so that there was less use for the labour organization of the dōzoku-dan as a whole, and this frequently hastened the break-up of the dōzokudan. In these cases the dōzokudan retained its solidarity chiefly in ritual matters, and the original stem family retained its authority by virtue of the fact that the branches could turn to it for assistance when they struck hard times. Again the reduction in the size of the area cultivated directly meant that there were fewer living-in servants eventually to be

---

[4] For studies of the detailed structure of the dōzokudan see, in addition to the works already quoted, Tamaki Hajime, *Kindai Nihon ni okeru kazoku-kōzō*, 1956 (Sakai-shoten), and my own *Nihon nōson no shakaiteki seikaku*, 1949 (Tōkyō-daigaku Shuppankai).

set up in servant branch families. Hence the dōzokudan became more purely a true patrilineal descent group, and consequently the master-servant aspects of relationships within the typical dōzokudan were gradually weakened.

In the more advanced areas, in fact, the absence of such master-servant relationships was the normal pattern. Here, too, it was usual for the heir to the househead—since it was he who would have to keep up the necessary expenditures in order to maintain the family's status, continue the worship of the ancestors and also provide security for the parents in their old age—to receive more of the family property than was given to branch families. However, it was normal for younger sons to be set up in branch families very soon after they were married and they were not necessarily in a subordinate position to the stem family after they were established. If they did not have enough land to become independent farmers then they usually took on a side job as well. In such districts the landlords had long since become parasitic non-cultivators and a good many of them were absentee. Consequently, there were no servant branch families and one did not find the typical dōzokudan described above.[5]

However, even in these more advanced areas, the superiority of the stem family was to some extent recognized in the relationship between stem family and branch family and in this sense the character of the dōzokudan described above as typical persisted even if in a somewhat attenuated form. In agricultural co-operation and in formalized social relationships the bonds of the dōzokudan were maintained and in emergencies it was around the stem family that the group rallied. The typical case

[5] In my *Nihon nōson no shakaiteki seikaku*, 1949 (Tōkyō-daigaku Shuppankai) I contrasted the dōzokudan principle of organization with the *kōgumi* (purposeful association) principle of organization and discussed the group structure of Japanese village society in terms of this dichotomy, an approach which has since received considerable criticism. See, especially, Kawamura Nozomu and Hasumi Otohiko, 'Kindai Nihon ni okeru sonraku-kōzō no tenkai-katei', *Shisō*, May and June 1958. The dōzokudan centred around a cultivating landlord could hardly be said to be typical of the modern period when Japanese agriculture was characterized by the parasitic landlord system. The dōzokudan is, however, undeniably important as a basic pattern for the social structure of Japanese villages.

described above was at least a basic pattern in modern Japan and if it was not universal, it was at least normal whenever the ranking implied in the stem-branch descent structure coincided with the ranking of economic power. Even if there was no direct relationship of protection and service between individual stem and branch families, generally speaking there was a marked inequality of status between the stratum of branch families and the stratum of stem families. The former, as the Japanese phrase has it, could not 'hold up their heads' in the presence of the latter. There might not be continuing dependency in matters of everyday life, but whenever a branch family ran into trouble it was usually to a better-off stem family that it was forced to turn.

Another topic which deserves treatment in connexion with the dōzokudan is the patron-client relation between what were known as *oyakata* and *kokata*, or alternatively *oyabun* and *kobun*. In Japan the words *oya-ko* have a much wider significance than their common meaning of 'parent and child'. It is sometimes said that the original meaning of *oya* was the stem family as the lineage ancestor. At any rate the farmers of tiny holdings, living constantly on the verge of starvation, frequently sought security by turning to an *oya* who was not in kinship terms a 'parent'. Other families often sought an *oya* in order that, by becoming the dependents of a powerful house, they could raise their status. Thus we find in Japanese villages formal ceremonies for creating fictional parent-child relationships—ceremonies by which even though there was no descent relationship (or, if there was, in order to strengthen that relationship)—a family would 'take an *oyakata*' or 'take an *oyabun*'. There were a variety of types of such *oyakonari*, or 'taking an *oya*'. There was a 'godfather *oya*' asked by one's parents to choose one's name, and there were *oya* who were asked to preside over ceremonies marking one's coming of age or one's engagement—variously called *eboshi-oya*, *o-haguro-oya*, or *nakōdo-oya*. The man who became the *oya* thereafter acted as protector of his *kobun* and the latter rendered service as a 'child' to the former. It was usually the head of a powerful stem family who became an oya and the ko might be a member of a branch family, either linked or not linked by descent, or even a member of a quite different descent group. In the former case the oya-ko relationship strengthened the stem-branch relationship; in the latter the ko, while remaining within his own dōzokudan, came to depend on a household belonging to another.

The oya-ko relationship, by its very nature, is established in the first place as a relationship between two individuals. However, individuals cannot be divorced from their families, and the oya-ko relationship in actual effect became a relationship between *ie*. It was usual to take one's oyakata from the house from which one's father had taken his. This did not always happen of course, but when it did not the reason was generally not a deliberate decision to change the family's oya, but because the oya family advised the ko to turn elsewhere, either because it had fallen on hard times and was no longer economically capable of playing its oya role, or because the head of the oya family was not, at that stage of the family cycle, of a suitable age to become an oya.

Oya-ko customs of this type can be found in their clearest form in the mountain districts of Yamanashi Prefecture. There the protection afforded by the oya was very considerable, and in consequence the kokata was in a position of complete subordination to the oyakata. A similar relationship, however, if not in such a marked master-servant form, was found fairly generally throughout Japan. The relationship between stem family and branch family itself was essentially of the same patron-client kind and whether or not the words oyabun, oyakata, etc. were used, in actual practice relationships of this type may be considered a characteristic feature of Japanese village society. They were, in the briefest terms, a means by which poor families sought powerful protectors in the village and offered them loyalty and service. Economic dependence was always in the background.[6]

It is obvious that the chief of these relationships of dependency

[6] On oyakata-kokata relationships see Kitano Seiichi, 'Kōshū sanson no dōzoku-soshiki to oyakata-kokata kankō', *Minzokugaku Nempō*, No. 2, 1940 (Sanseidō); Isoda Susumu, 'Nōson ni okeru giseiteki oyako-kankei ni tsuite —toku ni sonraku-kōzō to no kanren ni oite', *Shakai-kagaku Kenkyū*, 5, pp.iii-iv, 6, i, 1954–5 (Yūhikaku), etc. There are also a number of research reports by Hattori Harunori to be found in the *Yamanashi daigaku Gakugei-gakubu Kenkyū Hōkoku*.

was that of tenancy. As already mentioned, the ko of the Japanese word for tenant, *kosaku,* is etymologically related to the 'child' ko of the patron-client relationship, thus indicating the framework of familial subordination from which the concept derives. Very commonly some such tenancy relationship lies behind an oya-ko relationship. One consequently finds that owner-cultivators who have enough land of their own, or even small landlords, will deliberately add to their holding a piece of land leased from another landlord in order to enter an oya-ko relationship with him or to strengthen an existing one. Landlords who are at the same time oyakata are sometimes known as *jioya.*

Such tenancy relationships were not simply contracts for the leasing of land in consideration of a rental payment. The landlord oyakata helped the tenant kokata when the latter was in economic difficulties, and if the tenant's stock of rice was running low by the summer the landlord would provide rice from his granaries so that there would be enough to eat during the heavy work of planting. The landlord would stand as guarantor if the tenant joined a credit club and he might occasionally send down a bottle of rice wine. At the gift exchanges of New Year and Midsummer he might do even better than that. The tenant would be often in and out of the oyakata's house, helping in this and that. And it was not uncommon for the rent he paid to be a little less than the standard amount. For the kokata tenant it was a 'favour' to be allowed to till the oyakata's land and his protection and help was responded to with gratitude.

As one would expect, such oyakata-kokata relationships gradually lost their force, and this even in those districts where one found the custom in its clearest form with a single oyakata having many kokata and the more powerful among the kokata themselves having their own kokata. As the rationality of a capitalist money economy came to penetrate the villages and the oyakata landlords began to invest their money outside of the villages and correspondingly reduced the size of their directly cultivated holdings, it was increasingly difficult for the oyakata to show the same family-like paternalism towards their kokata tenants as they had in the past. Again, from the kokata's point of view, the spread of education meant that he no longer had to get the oyakata to read and write letters, and with slightly more secure family finances there was less need to depend economically on the oyakata. Despite a general weakening of these relationships, however, within a circumscribed sphere they did in reality remain. As already mentioned, although in form bonds between individuals these relationships were in fact usually maintained between families on a hereditary basis, not simply for a single generation, and as such were not likely rapidly to disappear.

Again, even in districts where there was no custom of 'taking an oya' it was fairly common for tenants to be 'in and out' of the landlord's house—delivering their rent rice, transporting it, helping on the landlord's land and about his house. The special word *deiri*, literally 'in and out', describes such a relationship which very often coincided with stem-branch or with oya-ko relations. By their very nature, except in the case of large landlords, they were usually restricted to a small number of families, but they were without any question of the patron-client, oya-ko type. These *deiri* relationships also became more restricted in scope and came to imply less overt subordination as the landlords ceased to cultivate their holdings. They did not, however, disappear until the disappearance of the landlord system itself.

The relationships described above—between stem and branch families, between oyakata and kokata, and the looser *deiri* relationship—have all begun to break up as a result of the post-war land reform, but they all formed core elements of the familial social structure of Japanese villages. As the landlord system evolved so these various social relationships too changed in character, but, entangled as they were with the tenancy system, they remained an essential element of the pattern of social relationships in Japanese villages until the landlord system itself disappeared.

The Dissolution of the Dōzokudan *and Kinship Relations*

We have already shown that even in those districts where the dōzokudan showed typical solidarity, as landlords tended to cultivate less land directly themselves, so they had less need for servants. And as the rationality of the money economy penetrated the villages, even if they did employ servants their relations with them were less of a traditional oya-ko kind. It became rare for a man to serve long years in his master's house, to be married off while still living there and to continue to work there afterwards. Consequently, from the beginning of this century even in the least developed districts, it became uncommon for servant branch families to be created. Dōzokudan tended to be exclusively kinship groups.

In the more advanced districts this process had already progressed much further by the beginning of the Meiji period. Dōzokudan were purely kinship groups, and although the branch families were poorer than the stem families they were by no means as subordinate. The more developed districts had, in fact, set the pattern towards which the least developed were progressing.

Moreover, after 1870 the number of branch families newly created in the villages declined. As we have already indicated the number of farm families did not move far from the 5½ million level throughout the whole of the modern period. Immediately after the Meiji Restoration, when the ban on the division of holdings was lifted, there was probably a sharp increase in the number of branch families, but thereafter it would be almost true to say that the creation of a branch family was possible only as a replacement for a family which died out or left the village. And since the Japanese capitalist economy, despite its rapid advance, did not absorb labour fast enough for complete families to migrate from the villages very often, the possibilities of creating branch families were limited. The information comes only from four villages, but according to the results of a survey carried out in 1950, whereas in the previous generation one family in five produced a branch family, in the generation of the present househead the ratio had fallen to one in ten. If one counts thirty years as the length of one generation this means one new branch family annually for every 300 households. The number of households did of course somewhat increase even in the villages, but among the new ones were a good number which, although in legal terms branch families of existing farm households, had in fact received very little of their stem family's property and were not engaged in

farming. As such they lacked the essential conditions for becoming part of a dōzokudan.[7]

Consequently, the expansion and development of the dōzokudan was restricted after 1870 in a quantitative sense, too. Since
there were also the changes in form mentioned above, one can
speak of a dissolution of the classical form of the dōzokudan as
taking place from the end of the nineteenth century when the
typical landlord became a non-cultivator. Much the same
applies to the patron-client oya-ko relationships.

The event which made this dissolution decisive was, of
course, the land reform. The reform destroyed the material
basis for the dōzokudan and for the patron-client relationships
associated with it, since the tenancy relationships which tied the
branches or ko to the stem or oyakata landlord family were,
generally speaking, dissolved. The landlord stem family which
lost its leased-out land no longer had the economic potential to
protect branch families or keep them in a subordinate position,
and the branch families themselves, having become owner-
cultivators, were liberated from dependence and subordination
to the stem family and no longer had any reason for rendering
it service. In districts where the oya-ko pattern had retained its
vigour the oyakata no longer had the wealth to take care of
kokata and even if asked to accept the position would often decline.

Mountain villages were sometimes an exception, since landlords who owned large areas of forest land were still able to
exercise a stem-family type authority by virtue of their forests,
even after they had lost their arable land. Also, of course,
ritual expressions of stem-branch relationships do not immediately disappear as social customs even though their material
basis is lost. Where it was customary for an oyakata to play the
part of go-between at weddings the custom of 'taking an oya'
continued simply out of ceremonial necessity. Even when the
stem family loses its wealth the traditional custom of giving the
head of the stem family the seat of honour at weddings and
funerals is not immediately abandoned. Nevertheless the land
reform marked a great change. In the more advanced areas

[7] See Fukutake Tadashi, *Nihon no nōson-shakai*, 1953 (Tōkyō-daigaku
Shuppankai), pp. 148–9.

branch families came to be created with the interests of individuals rather than those of the *ie* in mind, and in the least developed districts the internal structure of the dōzokudan came to approximate that found in the most developed districts in the pre-war period.[8]

As the importance of the dōzokudan declines greater stress is laid on true kinship relations, irrespective of whether they are relations within the patrilineal descent group or whether they are matrilineal or affinal relations. If relations within the dōzokudan can be looked on as vertical relationships based on the stem-branch pattern, true kinship relations can be looked on, by contrast, as horizontal relationships.

Affinal relationships created by a marriage, unlike the relationships within the patrilineal descent group, gradually weaken with the passage of generations. A stem family and a branch family remain stem and branch family through the generations, but an affinal relation between families is likely to dissolve itself as soon as the individuals who made the marriage die. This process of dissolution is much faster when matches are made across village boundaries so that there is very little everyday contact. We have already seen that in Japanese villages marriages within the patrilineal descent group were fairly common, and the further one goes back into the past the greater the prevalence of village endogamy. The landlord stem families of the very top rank very frequently took their brides from outside since there was no family of equivalent standing within their own village, but it was also not uncommon for them to send a daughter as a bride to one of their branch families. There was also a tendency to look with favour on marriages between branch families within the same dōzokudan in order to strengthen the weakening bonds of kinship. Consequently, a farm family of middling rank was likely to have a good number of families within the same village to which it was related by marriage. In these cases of village endogamy, affinal relations tended to be intimate as a result of constant daily contact, and the connexion between the two families was long remembered

[8] For the dissolution of the dōzokudan and of oya-ko relationships see, for instance, Fukutake Tadashi, *Nihon sonraku no shakai-kōzō*, 1959 (Tōkyō-daigaku Shuppankai).

even after the death of the original partners to the marriage. Even so, the tie certainly did weaken with the passage of time.

Affinal relationships, by their very nature, necessarily have these limits, but in terms of actual intimacy, when a woman graduates to the position of housewife within her husband's family then the link between it and her own family becomes very close. In a good many cases, if there is some sudden serious emergency it is these affinally linked families who are most likely to be turned to for help and advice. The relationship becomes especially close if the two families are in the same or immediately neighbouring villages.

Nevertheless, in places where the solidarity of the dōzokudan is great these affinal relationships are forced into the background. For though the informal link may be a strong one, in formal terms an affinal relationship is looked on simply as a 'private relation'. The relationship between stem and branch families is a permanent one and is a relationship between *ie;* the stem family is the stem family equally for every member of the *ie.* By contrast it is in the nature of affinal relationships that the head of the household will be most closely linked to a different family from his eldest son and heir. This is why affinal relationships, although they are relationships between families for the exchange of individuals by marriage, are looked upon as having a more personal individual element than dōzokudan relationships. This is clear in the case of marriage relationships between member families of the dōzokudan. The descent relationship always formally takes precedence over the affinal relationship. At weddings and funeral ceremonies and on other public ceremonial occasions which concern a family's relationship with its village neighbours, the affinal relatives will normally be diffident about putting themselves forward. Even in family matters with no public reverberations, as long as they concern the *ie* itself, then again the descent ranking within the dōzokudan is the first thing to be considered.

However, as the descent ranking within the dōzokudan loses its importance and the dōzokudan itself becomes little more than a group of relatives so that one ceases to think of the 'stem family' and thinks rather of one's brother's family or uncle so-and-so's family, these actual personal kinship relationships count for much more. As the solidarity of the dōzokudan begins to weaken, and the branch families cease to accept the patriarchal authority of the stem family, and cease to look on the establishment of a branch family as a 'favour' for which they should be grateful, the actual relations between stem and branch family are often not at all close. As long as people considered the mere establishing of a branch family as a grace and favour, there was no room for resentment over the small portion of property allowed it, but as ideas change there is liable to be dissatisfaction and ill-feeling between stem and branch family over the division of property. It often happens as a result that brothers do not get along at all well together. In such cases links with affinal relatives can become far more important than the stem-branch relationships between the families of brothers.

The declining significance of the dōzokudan since the land reform has brought a correspondingly great increase in the importance of affinal relations. This was something already apparent in the more advanced districts, and there are some places where there has long been a special word—*shinrui*, for instance—for the whole group of relatives including the dōzoku-dan and affinal relations equally. Since the war this tendency has been apparent to a greater or less degree in villages throughout the whole of Japan.

This does not of course mean that affinal relations have fully taken priority over dōzoku relations. Nor does it mean that the latter have ceased to have any importance. It has already been mentioned that since the Meiji period the 'marriage range' of Japanese farm families has considerably expanded. As it became standard practice to arrange marriage through go-betweens, and as transport developed and the self-sufficiency of the village economy broke down, the proportion of matches made within the village community decreased and the 'marriage range' tended to extend beyond adjacent villages. Consequently, affinal relatives, however intimately close, are not likely to be within range of daily contact. Such daily contact is more likely between stem and branch families living in the same village and linked by close kinship ties. The misunderstandings and dissatisfactions likely to be generated when the branch is divided from the stem are softened as time passes and the stem family and the branch family do have occasion to turn to each other for assistance. However, their relationship becomes less like that traditional to stem and branch families and more and more simply a relationship between close kin—closer, probably, by sheer reason of propinquity than relations can be with a wife or mother's family.

Dōzokudan do of course remain despite this shift in emphasis. But the hierarchical element has almost disappeared and they are no longer groups welded together by the central authority of a stem family. Even before the war, dōzokudan with an integrated labour organization covering the whole group were a rarity even in the least advanced districts, but now the independence of each household is even more marked and even if there is small scale labour exchange under the traditional *yui* system of co-operation, it takes place not as between stem and branch family but simply as between relatives helping each other out. These tendencies—to stress relatedness outside of the framework of the dōzoku structure and to give equal importance to matrilineal as to patrilineal ties—may be looked on as modernizing tendencies, and in this sense one may say that kinship relations in Japanese villages are approaching a modern western form.

However, kinship grouping still functions through what remains of the dōzokudan structure. As long as the *ie* remains, the dōzokudan, even though becoming more and more just a group of relatives, will continue to be structured in stem-branch terms. It is also true that all kinship relations, including matrilineal and affinal ties, restrict the freedom of the families involved in them. At present, while the *ie* system retains some force and the individual is not released from its constraints, the farm household cannot ignore related families in its action. Although marriage, for instance, is increasingly looked on as an individual matter, it is still something which concerns the *ie* and consequently the opinions of various related families concerning a prospective match always have to be taken into consideration. Since in present circumstances the element of mutual assistance in kinship relations remains important they are of great moment to individual farm families, and the social pressures which they exercise should never be forgotten when seeking an understanding of Japanese village society. For they are also a factor in the crystallization of the political forces which control Japanese villages.

FURTHER READING

On kinship organization see:

Beardsley, Hall and Ward, *Village Japan.*

Cornell, *Matsunagi.*

Smith, *Kurusu.*

H. Befu, 'Patrilineal descent and personal kindred in Japan', *American Anthropologist*, 65, vi, December 1963.

J. B. Cornell, 'Local group stability in the Japanese community', *Human Organisation*, 22, ii, Summer 1963.

S. Kitano, 'Dōzoku and *ie* in Japan: the meaning of family genealogical relationships', in Smith and Beardsley, *Japanese culture.*

M. Nagai and J. W. Bennett, *Dōzoku: a preliminary study of the Japanese extended family group and its social and economic functions*, Ohio State University, Research Foundation, Columbus, Ohio, 1953, (mimeo).

C. Nakane, *Kinship and economic organisation in rural Japan* (*L.S.E. Monographs on Social Anthropology*, 32), London, 1966.

T. Yoshida, 'Social conflict and cohesion in a Japanese rural community', *Ethnology*, 3, iii, July 1964.

PART THREE

THE STRUCTURE OF
HAMLET SOCIETY

CHAPTER VI

THE HAMLET AS AN AGRICULTURAL SETTLEMENT

General Characteristics of the Hamlet

JAPANESE farmers generally live in concentrated settlements, not on scattered farmsteads. These settlements are generally spoken of as *mura,* and although the wider administrative village is also officially known as a *mura,* even now for most farmers it is the small settlement that the word immediately suggests. Here we shall use the word 'hamlet' for the small settlement and keep 'village' for the administrative unit.

The form of such hamlets varies, but generally speaking tightly nucleated patterns are common and the number of scattered hamlets is a very small proportion indeed of the total. The scattered settlements are found in mountainous districts where concentrations of population are ecologically impossible and in a few special valley areas. About a half of Japanese agricultural settlements can be classified as plain villages, a little over 30 per cent. as foothill villages and a little under 20 per cent. as mountain villages. In the plains there are a number of ribbon settlements stretched along a road, but in both plain and mountain areas the most common form is the so-called 'lump settlement'.

According to the 1960 World Agricultural Census, the average size of Japanese farm settlements was 39 farming households and 25 non-farming households making a total of 64.

TABLE XIV

Distribution of Settlements by Number of Households, Total and Number of Farm Households

Criterion of Settlement	Percentage in Size-group				
Size	−19	20–49	50–99	100–149	150+
Number of farm households	23	56	17	3	1
Total number of households	14	47	25	7	7

As Table XIV shows, the number of settlements with more than 100 farming households is a mere 4 per cent. of the total, while no more than 7 per cent. of settlements have more than 150 households altogether. Hence, even if we leave aside the small settlements in mountain areas, the average Japanese hamlet settlement is by no means large. We may look on the typical Japanese hamlet as containing around 50 farm families and certainly no more than a 100 if non-farming families are included.[1]

As already mentioned, these settlements are made up of farmers with holdings incredibly small by international standards. Their main emphasis is on rice production, so much so that even now more than a half of the planted area is given over to irrigated rice. Apart from a very few areas of rain-fed fields, this rice depends on irrigation and on intensive input of labour. It also requires that the farmers within each settlement co-operate with each other. And this co-operation in agricultural production provides a basis on which is built a variety of co-operative forms extending into other areas of life, providing further occasions for farming households to co-operate on a hamlet-wide basis. For Japanese farmers the hamlet ranks next to the *ie* as the most important social unit for group activity.

Irrigated rice agriculture is not something which can be carried on by individual households each exclusively relying on its own labour. When rice fields are levelled and constructed, irrigation channels must be built to carry water to them. In so far as rice fields tend to be small in area and clearly marked off by built-up banks, they are in a sense conducive to a system of

[1] For a summary report of this survey, see Nōrinshō, Tōkei-chōsa-bu, *Sekai nōringyō sensasu: Nōgyō-shūraku-chōsa hōkokusho*, 1961 (Nōrin-tōkei Kyōkai).

private ownership. But the maintenance of an irrigation system by individual operations is impossible. Inevitably the whole community must do this work by collective labour.

Again, when green fertilizer for the rice fields is cut from the slopes and open spaces around the hamlet, some regulation of the use of these lands is necessary in order to maintain production on every farm within the community. These hills and woods are also essential for farmers as a source of firewood and wood for charcoal. Here again some form of management and use control by the community as a whole becomes necessary.

In Japanese villages land was already individually owned, and the individual farming of individual holdings was already the predominant form, even in the Tokugawa period. However, it was extremely rare for an individual family's holding to be in the form of a consolidated block of land. It was generally split up into many parcels scattered over a wide area. Moreover, the irrigation system was not sufficiently developed to provide separate channels to each parcel of land and it was common for many fields to be irrigated by water which flowed off the field of another owner. Consequently, an individual farmer was in no position to flood his own fields freely whenever he wanted to. And irrigation control by the community consequently had to be strict. Similarly the uncultivated areas around the village which supplied fertilizer and firewood were generally the property of the hamlet as a whole and their use was usually rationed, either by fixing a limited period when they could be freely exploited or by fixing a limit to the number of horse - or man-loads each family could take off them each year.

There were some changes in this situation after the Meiji Restoration. The system of private ownership of arable land was given full legal sanction, and it was not uncommon for the collective ownership of common land by the whole village to be broken up in favour of a system of individual property. The fragmentation of holdings, however, remained substantially unchanged despite the land re-planning schemes which began at the end of the nineteenth century. Even where irrigation systems were re-planned, the need for communal irrigation control continued. And in the bulk of the foothill and mountain villages the common lands remained, legally registered either as the property of the hamlet as an entity or of the villagers severally enumerated as joint owners.

Consequently, Japanese villages have been interpreted until recently as being 'village communities' in the technical sense of *Dorfgemeinde*. This concept belongs to a theoretical scheme in which the 'village community' is one stage beyond a 'primitive communal society'. In the latter the communal system is continued and maintained because the level of productivity is too low for an individualistic system of independent production. A 'village community', by contrast, is typically found where, even though individualistic production becomes predominant, a certain amount of co-operation based on communal ownership is an essential supplementary element of productive activity. Thus the constraint of the whole community limits the individual's private activity and these restrictions are reinforced by the fact that the village community is usually isolated and exclusive, a microcosm of its own.[2]

These structural features certainly continued to characterize Japanese villages even after the Meiji Restoration. They are not such as can be simply interpreted as remnants of feudalism. However, since Japanese capitalism, though using agriculture as a spring-board of development, failed to destroy the old system of production in Japanese agriculture, these 'village community' aspects have continued consistently to colour the character of Japanese villages.

If in agricultural production these community-like aspects remained important, it is only natural that the village social life which was built on these economic foundations should also have

---

[2] There have been considerable discussions among a wide variety of social scientists concerning the interpretation of the 'village community' in Japanese villages, particularly since the dissolution of the landlord system after the war. The following works may be consulted: Sonraku shakai Kenkyūkai, *Sonraku kyōdōtai no kōzō bunseki (Kenkyūkai nempō*, 3), 1954 (Jichōsha); ibid., *Sonraku kyōdōtai-ron no tenkai (Kenkyūkai nempō, 6*), 1959 (Jichōsha). Especially useful is the article by Shimazaki Minoru in the latter, 'Sonraku kyōdōtai-ron no keifu to bunken-kaidai'. See also Saeki Naomi, 'Nōson kyōdōtai-ron', in Chūō-kōronsha, ed., *Nihon nōgyō nempō, 6: Sengo nōgyō riron no dōkō*, and Sumiya Kazuhiko, *Kyōdōtai no shiteki kōzō-ron*, particularly the last chapter on the concept of the community in Japanese rural sociology.

a strong communal character. The farmers who made up village society, though far more closely involved in the money economy than in Tokugawa times, were still generally concerned with the production of staple foods, and provided their own family's food. In this sense the hamlet was still not far removed from self-sufficiency; it was still to some extent isolated. For its inhabitants it was still to a certain degree a small microcosm, a microcosm which provided the framework in which farmers produced and consumed. Consequently, the preservation of community forms applied not only to agriculture, but also to other areas of life. The communal unity of the hamlet community continued to be revealed in the various patterns of exchanging help at weddings and funerals, in co-operation for the building and repair of houses and so on.

Hamlets symbolized this unity in their protecting deity—the *ujigami*—and a shrine was a feature of every hamlet. Their relative isolation from outside society, together with frequent conflicts of interest with neighbouring hamlets over water rights and the boundaries of common land, gave members of the hamlet a strong 'village consciousness'. And since every villager, in every aspect of his daily life, was in constant contact with his fellow villagers, interacting with them over a vast range of social activities, it was impossible to live in a village without being aware of one's neighbours. The hamlet, as we have already indicated, was small in size. As long as the life spheres of the villagers were largely restricted to the narrow confines of the hamlet they tended for the most part to come into daily contact with people whom they knew intimately. Again, since mobility was low, practically every household bore a history stretching well back into the past. Thus the hamlet was made up of people who bore a heavy load of historical social relationships, people who knew not only about each other's present, but also about each other's past. And inasmuch as farming could not be carried on freely and individualistically apart from the communal restraints of the hamlet, the weight of these complex and pervasive personal relationships became all the greater.

This is not the end of the story. Japanese village communities are said to be less egalitarian and more hierarchical than those in the West; at any rate the character of the hamlet as a community was closely inter-related with the stratification implied by the landlord system. Farmers who could not survive without communal labour and mutual assistance were involved in a system of landlord-tenant relations and each severally occupied a certain status in the system of social stratification which was based on those relations. More concretely, farm households which were linked in the life of the hamlet as a whole by neighbourhood ties, by kinship ties, by gift exchanges and by the exchange of labour were also linked by tenancy and employment relations. Consequently, the strength of community restraints was greater the lower one moved down the social scale. The independent individuality of those at the bottom of the hierarchy was wholly submerged in the community-like hamlet.

However, it would be a mistake to assume that the features outlined above still continued to characterize the village in the modern post-war world. The situation in which the constraints of hamlet society operated as overwhelming community pressure by virtue of their entanglement with the landlord system, was radically changed by the land reform. Even before that the landlord system had changed; as the big landlords ceased to cultivate or reduced the size of their own farming operations, and as the small farming landlord became the typical landlord type, the kind of dictatorial powers of control which were formerly exercised by the local magnate type of landlord ceased to be at all common. Even when describing the pre-war villages it would be wrong to stress too much their 'village community' character.

The character of hamlets as communities has been changing since the beginning of the Meiji period and the change has accelerated in recent years. Although we said above that the hamlet remained to a certain extent a self-sufficient unit, an exaggeration of this point can lead to a mistaken interpretation. Production for the market developed increasingly after the Meiji Restoration and the villagers' lives ceased to be confined within the boundaries of the hamlet; the sphere of their activities was widened. In the field of agricultural production the range of operations requiring communal work by the whole hamlet was narrowed. More people found part-time work outside the hamlet. Again, the development of the wider village local government units meant that the hamlet ceased to be a self-sufficient, self-governing unit. The hamlet as a 'village community' was gradually being forced along the road to disintegration.

The degree of disintegration, of course, varied from region to region. The closer to industrially developed districts, the closer to towns, the faster this process advanced. By contrast, in mountainous districts and in areas far from the towns, and where there had been little evolution of the industrial structure, these community-like characteristics still remained strong.

And generally in the post-war situation of the present, there has been a considerable dilution of the communitarian flavour of hamlet life. The community framework which once caused villagers to act in concert has now become generally slack and flexible. Despite this, however, hamlets have not wholly lost the characteristics outlined above. To assert this would be as much of a mistake as to assert the contrary view that nothing has changed. The hamlet is still the hamlet. Just as that other important social unit, the *ie*, has not disappeared, so the hamlet too, though headed for disintegration, has still not arrived at that point. We have not reached that happy state in which free individual farmers can cheerfully co-operate with each other, spontaneously and voluntarily, not as a result of the pressures of the 'village community'. This is the problem on which it is the business of this chapter to throw light, but first it is necessary to survey a little more closely the present condition of the villages. An over-all grasp of the present situation is a necessary preliminary to an analysis of the structure of village society, and this will be the purpose of the next section.

The Agricultural Settlement Today

During the Tokugawa period the hamlet settlements which have been the subject of our discussions so far were for the most part independent village units. Sometimes a small settlement would be grouped for administrative purposes with a neighbouring one, but as a generalization it would not be far wrong to say that each settlement was an independent self-governing unit, and at the same time was a taxation unit bearing collective responsibility for the payment of taxes.

By a process which will be considered in more detail in the next chapter such hamlets, after several minor amalgamation measures in the period immediately after 1870, were finally, in 1888, combined into larger administrative units known as *mura* or—when they had town centres of a reasonable size—as *machi*. As the local government unit was thus enlarged, the individual hamlet of the Tokugawa period became a sub-district of the new administrative villages, and as such were generally referred to as *buraku*. By the villagers themselves, however, hamlets continued to be called 'villages'—*mura*. Owing to the low level of political activity in the new local government units and to the poverty of their revenues the hamlets did not become mere administrative sub-districts, but continued certain self-governing functions in their own right. In this way the hamlet settlements directly maintained the character they inherited from the Tokugawa period despite the establishment of the new local government system, and this is one of the factors which explains the continued importance of the hamlet in modern village society.[3]

Just as the Tokugawa division of administrative units did not completely coincide with the settlement pattern, so not every hamlet settlement is at the same time an independent *buraku* sub-unit of the village administration. However, according to the 1960 Census, 76 per cent. of settlements are at the same time *buraku*. The number of settlements which make up an administrative *buraku* together with a neighbouring settlement is no more than 13 per cent. The other 10 per cent. are very large

[3] As will be mentioned later, Suzuki Eitarō, in his *Nihon nōson shakaigaku genri*, 1940 (Jichōsha), used the term 'natural village' to distinguish the hamlet from the *mura*, the administrative village. The word has been widely used, but it is hardly suitable, and in Japanese it is better, if a little cumbersome, to stick to the terms *sonraku* or *buraku*. For a general theory of the hamlet, see the article by Matsubara Haruo, 'Nōson shakai no kōzō', in Fukutake Tadashi, Hidaka Rokuro and Takahashi Akira, eds., *Kōza shakaigaku*, Vol. 4, 1957 (Tōkyō-daigaku Shuppankai), and for a general overview of Japanese hamlets utilizing the results of the 1955 Census, see Sonoda Kyōichi, 'Sonraku-shakai no kōzō', in Fukutake Tadashi, ed., *Nihon no shakai*, 1961 (Yūhikaku).

settlements which are divided into two or more *buraku* in order to avoid the administrative imbalance which would result if one *buraku* in a village were excessively large.

When two or more hamlet settlements make up a single administrative buraku, it sometimes happens that they also have the sociological characteristics of a single hamlet—the same protecting *ujigami*, or commonly owned hamlet property in land or facilities. But this is not always the case; sometimes, however small, each hamlet settlement is entirely independent as far as self-governing functions are concerned, and joins with the other only in a limited range of matters connected with village administration. Again, when a single large settlement is divided into two or more buraku, they may, for instance, share the same *ujigami*, while in matters of internal self-government and property ownership each buraku unit retains a separate identity, or it may be that the separation applies solely to matters of administration connected with the village government, and that in all other matters they are in effect a single hamlet. There is an infinite variety of complications where the buraku and the actual settlement do not coincide.

However, in most cases they do. When a single hamlet settlement is split into two, this is most commonly in order not to make too large the number of households served by a single administrative circular from the village office. And where two or more settlements are combined into a single buraku it is usually the case that in the Tokugawa period one of them was the 'main' or original hamlet and the other is a 'branch' colony. Consequently, we shall not go very far wrong if in what follows we assume that the hamlet as a physical settlement and the buraku as an administrative sub-unit of the *mura* or *machi* governments are by and large identical.

In the previous section we suggested that these hamlets formed relatively independent units of agricultural production. However, even in the Tokugawa period they were not completely independent and self-sufficient. Very often they combined with neighbouring hamlets for irrigation purposes, building and maintaining dams together, and it was not unusual for use-rights over areas of forest land to be shared among a number of villages. However, for most agricultural activities the hamlet was the unit, and it was the hamlet which possessed communal property and communal facilities. It goes without saying that it was these characteristics which made the hamlet a community-like self-sufficient society.[4]

How then does the present situation compare with this? In the first place, with the improvement in irrigation techniques it is to be expected that the area of co-operation would have expanded well beyond hamlet boundaries, but even so the hamlet remains an important irrigation unit.

TABLE XV

(A) Size of Hamlets' Irrigation Systems (1955 Census)

Extent of System	Percentage of total Hamlets
1. Extends to other administrative towns or villages or to non-adjacent hamlets	28.9
2. Extends only to adjacent hamlets	40.8
3. Does not extend beyond the hamlet	20.8
4. Hamlets which only, or also, have irrigation systems confined to a single or several holdings	28.2

(B) Owners of Water Rights

Type of Owner	Percentage of total Owners
1. Land improvement corporation, or administrative unit of at least machi or mura size	38.8
2. Hamlet or ad hoc irrigation union	25.9
3. Joint ownership by group of individuals	30.1
4. Not reported	5.2

As Table xv shows there are still a large number of hamlets which use an irrigation source exclusively their own. When water is drawn from a large river, the system necessarily extends

[4] In saying this I do not ignore the fact that 'it is extremely dangerous in interpreting the nature of the hamlet to look on any collection of physically segregated houses as a single community-like settlement—a village or a hamlet—and to think one has solved the problem by calling it a natural village'. While admitting that very often co-operation in irrigation or in other joint works may be based on a different unit, I look on the hamlet as the unit on which most forms of co-operation are superimposed. See Naka-mura Kichiji, ed., *Sonraku-kōzō no shiteki bunseki*, 1956 (*Nihon Hyōron Shinsha*), p. 7.

over a number of hamlets, but one should not overlook the continuing importance of small water sources. If one looks at the statistics of owners of water rights, nearly 60 per cent. belong to bodies which may be considered as equivalent to hamlets, or at least not very much larger units. It is of course true that in terms of acreage the overwhelming proportion is fed from schemes administered by large land re-planning bodies or by village administrations or by councils drawn from several villages covering areas which include many hamlets, but even in these cases the hamlet often acts as the ultimate unit for the distribution of water at the local level. Regulation of the use of water allocated to the hamlet is generally a matter for purely internal arrangement.[5]

Secondly, as far as concerns hamlet common lands—the remaining traces of communal patterns of ownership—here there have been very great changes. When, at the beginning of the Meiji period, a division was made between state and private property, many hamlets relinquished their rights to forest land which thus became state property, and with the gradual diffusion of commercial fertilizers and the consequent declining importance of such land as a source of green fertilizer a good many hamlets divided their commons among the constituent families. At present the number of hamlets with some kind of common lands is no more than about a third of the total. According to the 1960 Census, about a quarter have land which is used for cutting grass either as fodder or as fertilizer, but the average area per hamlet is only 8.6 hectares. Only 4 per cent. of the total number of hamlets has communal grazing land, averaging 36 hectares in area. Consequently, at present, except in mountain villages where common forest land can be important, the significance of hamlet common lands has generally declined. Where they do remain, however, they have an important bearing on hamlet self-government which will make it impossible to ignore them in the analysis which follows.[6]

---

[5] On the question of water rights, see Watanabe Yōzō, *Nōgyō-suiriken no kenkyū*, 1954 (Tōkyō-daigaku Shuppankai).

[6] Quite apart from those written primarily from the standpoint of legal history, there have been a number of studies of hamlet common lands, beginning with Kaino Michitaka, *Iriaichi no kenkyū*, 1943 (Nihon Hyōrōnsha).

Nevertheless, if we consider developments since the Meiji period there can be no doubt that the water and common land which provided the material basis for the solidarity of the hamlet community no longer have quite the same importance for the hamlet. We have already seen that the modernization of irrigation facilities has expanded the area of operations at the expense of the hamlet. The common lands have largely lost their significance as a source of fertilizer and sometimes been divided up as a result, and even where the common lands provide valuable timber resources their management has generally been somewhat modernized.

In partial compensation hamlets are still required to act in agricultural matters in some senses as a unit. Nearly every hamlet has a *nōji-jikkō-kumiai*—an Agricultural Practice Union. According to the 1960 Census only 5 per cent. do not. In the vast majority of cases (to be precise, in 71 per cent. of cases) a single hamlet has a single Union. In 20 per cent. of cases a large hamlet is divided between two Unions, and in an insignificant 3 per cent. of cases the Union also covers another hamlet. The correspondence with hamlet boundaries of these units dealing with agricultural matters is closer than in the case of the administrative buraku. The actual activities of these Unions varies from hamlet to hamlet and a good many of them are little more than organizations for passing round circulars received from the village Agricultural Co-operative. The range of communal activities that they organize is often very restricted and it would be true to say that there has been a decline in the extent to which hamlet members co-operate for farming purposes, though on the other hand post-war developments in the use of pesticides have created a new need for communal spraying. Some 84 per cent. of hamlets spray their lands together collectively, and in 80 per cent. of these cases the Agricultural Practice Union is the body which organizes it. In other cases hamlets own machinery in common or jointly use pieces of agricultural equipment. Forty-eight per cent. of hamlets make communal use of machinery and in 80 per cent. of these cases

We may mention Furushima Toshio, ed., *Nihon rinya-seido no kenkyū*, 1955 (Tōkyō-daigaku Shuppankai) and Ushiomi Toshitaka, ed., *Nihon ringyō to sanson-shakai*, 1962 (Tōkyō-daigaku Shuppankai).

the machinery is owned either by the hamlet or by the Union, rather than by the Agricultural Co-operative which covers the whole village area. Then there are some 40 per cent. of hamlets which have some communal facility such as a workshop, a silk-worm hatchery, a fruit grading station, a milk collecting shed or a marketing collection point. And 70 per cent. of these were built by the hamlet or by the Union itself.

Quite apart from these forms of agricultural co-operation there is collective effort in other fields too, the communal facilities involved being in this case nearly always owned by the hamlet. Nearly half the hamlets have some kind of citizens' hall or meeting place and 20 per cent. even have loudspeaker broadcasting facilities. Some 31 per cent. have the use of a nursery school for young children during the agricultural busy season, and in the majority of these cases it is a hamlet nursery owned by the hamlet. The wire broadcasting and telephone systems linking every farm-house which have been diffused at such a rapid rate in recent years are normally operated on a village-wide basis or by the village Agricultural Co-operatives, but very often in the establishment of these facilities the hamlet participates as a hamlet unit. Twenty-three per cent. of hamlets have such facilities.

In addition to these facilities hamlets very frequently own traditional buildings which they have inherited from the past such as the shrines of the hamlet protecting deity or of other Shinto and Buddhist gods. (Buddhist temples, as we shall see later, rarely become hamlet property, though it is difficult to consider them apart from the hamlets in which they are found.) Again, the roads which run through and around the hamlet, whether officially they are village roads or unadopted roads, are generally looked on as the hamlet's roads—including agricultural and forest tracks—and their maintenance and repair is generally looked on as a matter for the hamlet as a whole.

This common property, these communal activities and communally owned facilities, provide the basis for an integrated hamlet social life. They are looked on as property or facilities which belong to the *whole* hamlet, and communal activities are looked on as activities in which the *whole* population of the hamlet should participate. Consequently, despite distinctions between farming and non-farming households, or among farming households between the bigger and the lesser farmers, between the full-time and the part-time, the hamlet is nevertheless a united body. The Agricultural Practice Unions, by their very nature exclude the non-agricultural households, but they are nevertheless inextricably bound up with the hamlet. The hamlet exercises strong restraining social pressures on every inhabitant.

However, these pressures have been weakened as the material basis of solidarity symbolized in common lands and common water has gradually lost importance. Especially in the post-war period, with the dissolution of the landlord system which formerly reinforced these community-like pressures, the social pressures of the hamlet have become far looser than before the war. With the growth of part-time farming in recent years, with the consequent division of interests between the full-time farmers bent on developing commercial production and the part-time farmers concerned with not much more than producing their own rice, and with the further growth in the number of non-agricultural households, it has inevitably become more difficult to maintain the unity of the hamlet. As we shall see later there has had to be a separation between the Agricultural Practice Union concerned with agricultural production and the hamlet itself; the system by which the hamlet as an all-embracing unit contained every activity within itself was subject to too much strain.

These strains produced a tendency for all kinds of special functional associations to split off from the hamlet. The traditional groups in the hamlet were all to a greater or lesser degree identical with the hamlet as a social unit, and the functional associations formed in the modern period have also followed the same pattern of being identical in membership with the hamlet as a whole. Now they are achieving a separate identity, though this is as yet nothing more than a tendency which has recently begun to show itself. Associations which though formally devised for special purposes in fact automatically include every member or every household of the hamlet are still widespread, and even if the hamlet does show a tendency towards differentiation, it still provides a tight social framework constricting the lives of Japanese villages. The hamlet imposed on its members an ideal of hamlet unity and hamlet harmony as the highest possible good, and although that ideal is losing its power to suppress individuality, it has still by no means disappeared.

CHAPTER VII

THE HAMLET AND SOCIAL GROUPS

The Internal Organization of the Hamlet

In the social life of the hamlet, as one would expect, each household has the closest relations with its nearest neighbours. It very often happens, of course, that neighbours are at the same time linked by stem-branch family relations, but even without such reinforcing links, it is with neighbours that one has the most intimate ties, second in importance only to those with kin when it comes to celebrating marriages and funerals, while in more everyday matters contacts are even more close and continuous.

Nevertheless, these relationships with two or three houses—traditionally spoken of as the 'three houses opposite and the one on either side'—do not necessarily create coherent social groups. A is intimate with B and C; B with A and D; C with A and E; and so on. Coherent local groups are, however, created in most hamlets, groups based on the neighbourhood but bigger than the range of any one family's close neighbourhood ties. Very small settlements may not have such *kumi*, as these groups are called, but in anything slightly bigger it is almost universal for the hamlet to be divided up into a number of *kumi* which provide convenient units for various social activities.

This kind of neighbourhood group system of the *kumi* has a very ancient history, and in the Tokugawa period the so-called five-man group system—a system of shared legal responsibility, whereby each person was responsible for the crimes of others—became practically universal throughout the country, especially, in the first instance, as a part of the drive against Christianity. Later on in the period, their function broadened beyond that of mere policing and they were used for moral instruction as a means of encouraging habits of thrift and diligence in order to maintain the farmer's tax-paying ability. The registers of the five-man *kumi* were given homiletic prefaces which, whenever the occasion offered, were read aloud to the assembled villagers who then had to sign a declaration of their intention to obey.[1]

This five-man kumi system was not institutionalized by the Meiji Government. It found no place in the official scheme of things when the local government system was created. Consequently, in those hamlets which were too small really to need kumi, and in those in which dōzokudan groups effectively performed the functions of kumi, the old system declined and was gradually forgotten. The kumi are, that is to say, entirely non-compulsory groups which have remained in the hamlets—where they have remained—because of the necessary functions they served.

In the thirties, after the great depression, at the time of the so-called 'economic rehabilitation movement' in the villages, a good deal of attention was again paid to these neighbourhood groups and attempts were made to reinforce systems of co-operation within the hamlet on a kumi basis. Later, as soon as the war started, these neighbourhood groups were created throughout the country, in towns and cities as well as in villages, as a means—as the official phrase had it—of 'transmitting the will of those above to those below'. Thus the kumi were revived in all villages.

This neighbourhood group system, together with its super-structure of hamlet meetings and town ward meetings, was denounced after the war as a system designed for prosecuting warlike purposes, and ordered to be disbanded. But just as the kumi continued to exist after the Meiji Restoration, although they received no institutional support from the central government, so they have continued to perform since the war those functions for which the social life of the hamlet creates a

[1] See Hozumi Nobushige, *Gonin-gumi seido ron*, 1921 (Yūhikaku); Tamura Hiroshi, *Gonin-gumi seido no jisshōteki kenkyū*, 1936 (Ganshōdō Shoten); Nishimura Seiichi, *Gonin-gumi seido shinron*, 1938 (Iwanami Shoten).

necessity. At present only some 27 per cent. of Japanese agricultural settlements do not have any kumi system, and one can
assume that the great majority of these are hamlets too small to
need division. (More than 20 per cent. of hamlets have less than
20 households.) Consequently, it is not much exaggeration to
say that nearly every hamlet has a kumi system.

Although the modern kumi system derives from the tradition
of the old five-man groups, it is by no means usual for groups to
consist only of five households. This was true even in the
Tokugawa period, and today generally speaking the average
size is about ten households. And in some of the bigger hamlets
there is a second-order system of larger units—ō-gumi—which
combine a number of kumi. For instance, a hamlet might be
divided into the upper and lower, or the eastern and western
section, and each of these contain a number of kumi. Again,
when a number of geographically distinct settlements form one
social hamlet, each of the settlements acts as an ō-gumi, as a
constituent unit of the buraku, while possibly containing kumi
within itself. In such circumstances, these ō-gumi perform
important functions and the small neighbourhood kumi tend
to be very small—of from five to ten households—and to confine
themselves very much to traditional activities. By contrast,
when there is no system of ō-gumi, the neighbourhood kumi
have both the traditional functions of the small kumi and also
the functions of the ō-gumi in the large settlements, and they
tend to contain a larger number of households.

These kumi in exceptional circumstances may be formed on
a genealogical basis, irrespective of physical proximity, but
normally they are based on strictly territorial criteria. Occasionally, that is to say, a new branch family would remain a
member of the kumi of the stem family from which it sprang,
even though its house was built at some distance. As time
passed, however, the inconveniences of this geographical
dispersal would cause a reshuffling on a straightforward area
basis. This kind of dispersal and reshuffling of the kumi was
common only for the small neighbourhood kumi and it was
extremely rare for a larger ō-gumi ever in this way to be split up.

The names for these kumi divisions vary from region to
region: examples are kōchi or tsubo, and there are some of very

ancient origin like *kaito* (literally, inside the fence) or *kōji* (literally, the little road). Where there is a double banked system with small kumi inside an ō-gumi, the small kumi may be known as *jikko-gumi*, *gochō-gumi*, or *han*. The ō-gumi are often given proper names—geographical names, a point of the compass, or perhaps the house-name of a former kumi chief—while the small kumi are generally known by numbers.

Hence kumi, strictly speaking, can be divided into the small kumi as neighbourhood groups, and ō-gumi as sub-units of the hamlet. However, it is impossible here to go into all the details necessary to explain the differences between the larger settlements and the smaller, so we shall in principle ignore the neighbourhood group which exists simply as a means for the dissemination of information from a superior group level and confine the discussion to kumi in general, by which will be meant the ō-gumi, or those smaller kumi which (in the absence of an ō-gumi level) combine the functions of the small neighbourhood group unit with those of the ō-gumi. And since, as we shall see in the next section, a wide variety of traditional groupings go by the name of kumi we shall distinguish kumi in the sense referred to above by the name 'hamlet kumi'.[2]

These hamlet kumi perform a good many functions as constituent units of the hamlet. For instance, in agricultural matters, such as the maintenance and repair of field tracks or the cleaning of irrigation ditches, each kumi is likely to have a certain area allotted to it for which it is responsible. Again, Agricultural Practice Unions are generally divided into a number of *han*, these *han* and the kumi being identical in composition. It was not uncommon, either, for kumi of this sort to act as rice-planting groups, working together on each member's fields in turn. If we except those areas where the dōzokudan formed the unit of work organization, these hamlet kumi provided an important frame-work for farming co-operation, the more important the further one goes back into the past when productivity was low.

The hamlet kumi acted in other matters too besides agriculture, providing a system of mutual assistance for all the

[2] See Takeuchi Toshimi, 'Kumi to kō', *Sonraku-kyōdo kenkyū kōza*, Vol. 2, 1957 (Kadokawa Shoten).

emergencies and celebrations of human life. Very often they were identical in membership with the funeral kumi which will be described later. Sometimes a kumi would own collectively the dishes and bowls and trays necessary for the celebration of weddings and funerals at any member's house. Very frequently they acted as the unit of co-operation for re-thatching, for most Japanese farmhouses were thatched and the periodic business of re-thatching was a necessary task rather laborious for a single family. In some hamlets each kumi had its own little area of waste land which grew the *kaya* reed used for thatching and this would be cut annually, the houses of the kumi being thatched in rotation.

Further, the hamlet kumi acted as constituent units of the *ujiko* organization attached to the shrine. As we shall see later, *ujiko* organizations were often of considerable complexity but generally all the inhabitants of a single hamlet were *ujiko* ('children') of the hamlet's god, and in large hamlets each kumi took turns in looking after the various jobs that had to be done in preparation for the shrine festivals. In other matters of religious ritual too, for example for celebrations connected with the *kōshin-kō* or the *himachi-kō*, although the whole hamlet might celebrate simultaneously, if the whole hamlet was too big to act in unison the hamlet kumi usually acted as independent units.

Thus, as far as the situation in the recent past is concerned, it would be no exaggeration to say that the functions of the hamlet kumi extended to every aspect of life in the hamlet. However, as time passed, and agriculture became sufficiently productive for individualistic farm operation to be possible, the range of the kumi's functions was correspondingly contracted. In agricultural matters they did not go beyond acting as a work group for the maintenance of hamlet facilities; in rice transplanting, for instance, the unit of co-operation tended to get smaller and to include simply a few households of kin or neighbours—not necessarily belonging to the same kumi. And as living levels rose there was less necessity for collective ownership of the equipment for celebrating weddings and funerals and fewer places where the custom persisted. As more and more farmhouses had tiled roofs, it became less and less common to arrange re-thatching on a collective basis as a kumi activity.

Furthermore, many of the special traditional groupings which will be described in the next section, although at first organized in units which coincided with the hamlet kumi, have under some circumstances got out of line so that they might now bestraddle two or more kumi. As a consequence the functions of these groups have ceased to be looked on as functions of the hamlet kumi. What is more the very significance of these traditional groupings has decreased with the passage of time; they are taken less seriously. Even when special purpose associations created in the modern period have coincided in their boundaries with the hamlet kumi this coincidence may not, depending on the nature of the association, necessarily cause the two to be identified, and so may not have the effect of strengthening the hamlet kumi. For instance, although the *han* into which the Agricultural Practice Union is divided coincide with the hamlet kumi, non-farming households do not belong to these associations, and hence the kumi and the Union han are not thought of as identical.

Thus, in just the same way as the hamlet inevitably comes to be disentangled as a social unit from various functional associations of the hamlet members, so the hamlet kumi, from being traditional groups which coincided with the sub-units of various associations, have gradually transferred their functions to these special associations and become little more than a unit of convenience within the hamlet. Like the small neighbourhood groups within ō-gumi mentioned earlier, they tend to become mere units for spreading information through the hamlet in those matters for which the hamlet itself functions as little more than the smallest unit of the local government system.

Just as the hamlet itself has not entirely thrown off its character as a holistic group with undifferentiated functions, so the hamlet kumi have not been completely transformed into mere units of geographical convenience or organizations for the dissemination of information. Although they may have lost many of their former functions and seen many others demoted in importance, the hamlet kumi remain essential elements of the internal structure of the hamlet.

Traditional Groupings in the Hamlet

The traditional hamlet of the past carried on a unified hamlet social life, in which the hamlet kumi played a part as subordinate organs. The hamlet had, however, a variety of social groups apart from the hamlet kumi. A good many of them were identical in membership with the hamlet itself; one can, in other words, look on them either as separate groups or simply as aspects of the hamlet community. The hamlet kumi can similarly be looked on as a grouping with a variety of functions, or as the framework for organization of a variety of special groups. It was, however, by no means rare for other groupings to be formed which did not include everyone within a hamlet or hamlet kumi but only those who fulfilled certain qualifications or were concerned with pursuing certain particular objectives. Even these groups were, of course, founded on quite different principles from the modern functional association voluntarily created by its members. They were, characteristically, groups which everyone with certain qualifications or placed in certain circumstances was expected to join irrespective of any personal interests he might have.

In what follows we shall describe under the general heading of traditional social groups those which coincide in membership with the hamlet or with hamlet kumi and also those in which membership was in effect compulsory under certain conditions.

One kind of grouping differs radically from the hamlet kumi in that it did not, like the latter, divide the hamlet as it were horizontally on a geographical basis. These were the age groups. They were not necessarily found in every hamlet in Japan. Nor were they always all-inclusive where they did exist. In some villages they did not admit members from families of certain statuses. For instance, there are a good number of examples in which the eldest son of a house of *oyakata* rank did not normally belong to the young men's kumi, and in other cases those who came into the hamlet from outside were not allowed to become members. There were also hamlets with two parallel sets of age groups, one for the upper stratum of families and the other for the remainder. The actual age grades also varied from region to region and more often than not there would be only a kumi for adolescents and young men, and nothing for younger or older ages.[3]

With these reservations one might generalize as follows. The chief age grades were: children's kumi, young men's kumi, a 'middle-old' kumi and an old men's kumi. Of these the children's kumi, usually under the name of *kowaka-ren* or *tenjin-kō*, came into its own at village ceremonies and festivals. However, it was, if anything, rare for them to take on a clear and continuing organizational form; particularly in recent times. By contrast, the young men's groups, the *wakamono-gumi*, or as they are also sometimes called *wakashū-gumi* or *wakaze*, were the most common of the age grades, found fairly generally throughout Japan. It was not uncommon, too, for these young men's groups to be subdivided according to age or according to the order of entering the group. And it was usual for them, under the direction of their chief, to perform protective police duties, and to play an important role in communal work tasks and the celebration of hamlet festivals. They usually had a monopoly of such functions until youth organizations and fire brigades were formed in the modern period. The 'middle-old' kumi was extremely rare, for those who moved out of the young men's group formed in effect the dominant body of members of the hamlet itself, though the name 'middle-old' was very commonly used to describe those who acted as patrons and leaders of the young men's group. Organizations for men between the ages of 25 and about 40—known usually in Japan as *sōnen*, 'men in their prime'—were primarily a product of the war period when formal *sōnen* organizations were created. Consequently, in the absence of other organizations, in some districts the young men's organizations despite their name in fact included a good number of men in their late twenties. Finally, the 'old men's kumi' was also very rarely fully institutionalized, though it was very common for those who had passed their sixtieth birthday *kanreki* celebration and retired from the headship of their house-

[3] See Seki Keigo, 'Nenrei shūdan' (*Nihon minzokugaku taikei*, Vol. 3, *Shakai to minzoku*, Part I), 1958 (Heibonsha). See also the examples cited in Suzuki Jirō, *Toshi to sonraku no shakaigakuteki kenkyū*, 1956 (Sekai Shoin).

holds to form a variety of religious *kō*, and in these cases, as we shall see later, there was usually no sexual division; men and women joined the same groups.

The second type of kumi to be considered are the funeral kumi which are often coextensive with the hamlet kumi. Both weddings and funerals require expensive celebration, but whereas the former are to a certain extent foreseeable the latter come unawares, and as a consequence villagers have that much greater need for mutual assistance. In districts where dōzokudan are tightly organized it is possible for a group of stem and branch families to carry out funerals with only minor assistance from neighbours, and in such districts special funeral kumi may not be formed. Again in those areas where villages have a special caste of families whose job it is to dispose of the dead, the ordinary hamlet kumi can do all the rest that is necessary without forming special funeral kumi. Also in small settlements, since the hamlet as a whole takes part in funerals, here again there is no need for special funeral kumi. However, even if there is no special association, the functions of a funeral kumi are catered for in practically every settlement. According to the 1955 Census of agricultural settlements some institutionalized system for funerals was found in 94 per cent. of settlements. Sometimes the hamlet kumi is at the same time a funeral kumi; sometimes two or three small kumi will join together to make one funeral kumi; sometimes quite separate funeral kumi will be established. But whatever the form it is generally true that some kind of kumi provides the framework for co-operation in carrying out funerals. When a death occurs in one household the other members of the kumi provide prescribed amounts of money or rice and take care of all the details for the funeral. They divide among themselves the various jobs of notifying relatives and the family's temple, getting together the necessary ritual implements and the coffin, digging the grave, bearing the coffin in the funeral procession, greeting and entertaining guests at the funeral, and so on. Usually a funeral feast will be served, and the women of the kumi will take care of all the catering. It is the general custom for the kumi to keep a register to record who does the most troublesome jobs such as going to inform distant relatives, or bearing the coffin and digging the grave, so that

COMMUNAL LABOUR ON ROAD RECONSTRUCTION

HAMLET CITIZENS' HALL AND A FIRE-BRIGADE
STOREHOUSE

A HAMLET SHINTO SHRINE

BUDDHIST TEMPLE AND GRAVESTONES

these duties can be distributed according to a strict roster.[4] Next there are a number of groups which are concerned with religious belief and ritual. Of these the most important is the group of *ujiko*. A special characteristic of the Japanese shrine system is the fact that the *ujigami*, literally the 'clan-god', is at the same time the *hamlet* protecting deity. In ancient times members of a dōzokudan worshipped their own ancestral god so that the *ujigami* really was the god of a clan. Later, as the dependent serfs of the true clan members became established in separate independent households within the hamlet, they too came to take part in the religious rituals as *ujiko*. Thus the *ujigami* came to be the protecting deities of hamlets defined by territorial rather than by kinship criteria. There were also a good number of instances where, depending on local traditions or the social structure of the hamlet, not all the ujiko were on a footing of equality as members of the ritual group, and there was no exact equation between the ujiko group and the hamlet. It might be that an 'original stem family' which had founded the settlement retained a special position as 'keeper of the shrine key' (*kagimoto*) by virtue of its traditional claim to be the family that had originally established the shrine. In other cases the so-called *miyaza* system persisted until quite recent times, a system whereby a small group of households inherited special functions in ritual matters which marked them off from the rank and file ujiko.[5] These houses would, for instance, take turns in acting as 'head house', performing the main ritual functions at annual festivals. However, these systems of stratification within the ujiko group have tended to disappear with the passing of time. The ujiko group has, except in rare instances where, for instance, new-comers are denied immediate admission, become homogeneous and identical in composition with the hamlet. The festivals of the shrine were the festivals of the ujiko as a whole, carried out under the direction of the ujiko representatives (*ujiko-sōdai*), and, depending on the form which the festival

---

[4] See Takeuchi Toshimi, 'Sonraku-shakai ni okeru sōgi no gōryoku-soshiki', in *Kazoku to sonraku*, Vol. II, 1942 (Nikkō Shoin). For the 1955 Census, see Norinshō, Tōkei-chōsabu, ed., *Shōwa 30-nen rinji nōgyō kihon chōsa kekka hōkoku*, Vols. I-VI, 1955-9 (Nōrin-tōkei Kyōkai).

[5] See Higo Kazuo, *Miyaza no kenkyū*, 1941 (Kōbundō).

took, it was fairly common for the various hamlet kumi to take turns in performing the major tasks of preparing and organizing the festival.

There is another type of religious grouping which must not be forgotten, namely the *kō*. The word *kō* derives from *kōgi*, meaning to expound the Buddhist *sutras*, from which it gradually came to mean the group of people who gathered together to listen to such expositions. There is such a variety of types and forms of religious *kō* in the various districts of rural Japan that it is extremely difficult to generalize about them. They can, however, be roughly divided into *kō* which are identical in membership with a whole hamlet or with an ō-gumi, *kō* which collect contributions from their members at every meeting in order annually to send one or more representatives to the temple or shrine of the Shinto god or Buddha in whose honour they are formed, and *kō* in some way based on an age or sex group—*kō* for the old people or for women, for instance.

Examples of the first kind are the *yama no kami kō, ta no kami kō, kōjin kō, daishi kō,* named after their patron gods, of the forest, of the rice field or of the kitchen, and *himachi kō*—night-vigil *kō*. It is usual for their members to bring either rice or money to meetings so that food and drink can be served. The *hōon kō* found in hamlets belonging to the Shin sect (the feast of 'returning thanks' to the sect's founder, Shinran) are basically of the same type, though the celebrations are on a grander scale. Examples of the second kind are the *Ise kō*, the *Kompira kō*, the *Akiba kō*, etc., which usually not only send representatives to worship at these famous shrines or temples, but also hold regular meetings at the houses of each of their members in turn—food and drink again being served at such meetings to strengthen the bonds of friendship. This second kind of *kō* differs from the first in that only certain houses, not whole hamlets, take part; for one thing it is a necessary qualification for membership to be able to afford contributions for the representative's journey. As for the third type, there are children's *kō*, and for women the *koyasu kō* (easy childbirth *kō*) or the *Kannon kō* in honour of the Buddhist Goddess of Mercy. Formerly, for women who had graduated from the status of *yome* in their household, these represented practically their sole opportunity for enjoyable recreation.

There were also old people's *kō*, commonly called *nembutsu kō*—
nembutsu being the 'Hail Buddha' invocation. Old people used
to gather regularly for a feast at the hamlet temple or at one of
the small unattended wayside shrines—the *dō*—which housed
Buddhist images.[6]

With the passage of time the recreational aspects of these
religious *kō* groups have become more important than their
strictly religious functions. Consequently, as the opportunities
for other forms of entertainment have increased, they have
declined in importance. Especially during the war *kō* meetings
were often suspended because shortage of food ruled out feasting, and many were not revived. Nevertheless, according to the
1955 survey of settlements, there were no more than 35 per cent.
of settlements which had no religious *kō*, while 43 per cent. had
two or more, 17 per cent. had three or four, and 5 per cent. had
more than five.

Another type of *kō* which should be mentioned in connexion
with the religious *kō* are the *tanomoshi kō* or *mujin*. These mutual
credit and saving societies began as subsidiary functions of
religious *kō*, hence their name, though they gradually became
separated and no different from the secular *mujin*. Such credit
and saving societies, however, are now very much a rarity. In
some villages there used to be special *mujin* for special kinds of
savings, a 'thatch *mujin*' for buying the material to re-thatch the
house, a 'horse *mujin*' to save up for buying draft animals, a
'bedding *mujin*' for purchasing household furniture and so on,
but these are of insignificant importance today.

A final form of traditional grouping in the hamlet is the
'parishioners' group'. As part of its measures for the suppression
of Christianity the Tokugawa Government insisted that every
household should be a registered *danka*—a 'parishioner household'—of some Buddhist temple or other. Since many hamlets
had no temple, households individually attached themselves to
a temple outside the hamlet, preferably one with which it had
some past connexion. Even if a temple had been built within
the hamlet it quite often happened that as a result of the family's
history it had become established as the *danka* of a temple in

[6] See Wakamori Tarō, 'Shinkō shūdan', in *Shakai to minzoku*, Part I
(*Nihon minzokugaku taikei*, Vol. 3), 1958 (Heibonsha).

some other village. Hence it was by no means regularly the case that the hamlet and the parishioner group coincided, with one temple per hamlet and all the hamlet members belonging to the same sect. This is in contrast with the Shinto worship of the *ujigami*. Everyone who lived in the hamlet was automatically an ujiko of the Shinto god by virtue of his hamlet membership, but this did not prevent each household from having its own individual and separate connexions with different Buddhist temples. However, this was not always the case and it was by no means rare for a hamlet to have its own temple and for the majority of the households to be parishioners of that temple. In such cases even the households which were not parishioners proper might become involved in the rituals carried on at the hamlet temple; they would take part as *shinto*, i.e. 'believers' who do not, like the *danka*, call on the services of the hamlet temple and its priest to bury their dead or perform family memorial services.

With certain special exceptions most of these traditional groupings were coextensive in membership with either the hamlet or with hamlet kumi. Very few of them, as already mentioned, were groups which one could choose voluntarily to join or not to join. The *kō* which sent pilgrim representatives to shrines and had something of the character of a holiday savings society might seem on the face of it to be relatively voluntary organizations, but as soon as they are established their membership tends to become fixed and traditional; sons take over from fathers and it is not easy, once one belongs, to withdraw. In principle one could freely choose one's temple, but given the emphasis on respect for the ancestors built into the *ie* system that was in practice not possible. Hence the justification for including them in the category of traditional groupings. As indicated about each one of these groups severally, there has been a general decline in their importance in recent years. The young men's *wakamono-gumi*, the most universal type of group, was gradually absorbed into the Youth Groups organized at the behest of the central government. The majority of the *wakamono-gumi* simply disappeared, the only exceptions being in those hamlets where they retained special functions in looking after hamlet common land or in the shrine festival celebrations. The funeral kumi still function but the scope and content of co-operation has tended to narrow and they are of lesser significance than they used to be. The ujiko groups have become increasingly egalitarian; it is now very rare for particular families to retain particular privileged functions. The families which monopolized special ritual roles have for the most part suffered from the land reform and are no longer able to bear the expense involved, and people are in any case no longer willing to tolerate the persistence of this kind of status distinction in ritual matters. The religious kō are also a shadow of their former selves. A decline in religious belief is one reason for this, but even more important, since the holiday excursion aspect was such a prominent aspect of the kō's function, is the fact that villagers nowadays have so many other opportunities for recreation. Again, the special women's kō have been replaced by the new Housewives' Associations.

To sum up, apart from those which still perform necessary functions, traditional groupings in the hamlet have generally declined in importance and been replaced by other groups. Those which remain and continue to provide a framework for traditional customs no longer have the importance for hamlet society that they once had. This is not to say that these groups can be ignored in any analysis of the modern hamlet. The fact, for instance, that co-operative funeral groups still exist, even though less important than they were, is not without its influence on villagers' behaviour, and in the jokes and conversation of a traditional kō feast, the hamlet still preserves significant channels of communication.

Special Functional Associations and the Hamlet

We have had several occasions to mention the establishment of the modern local government system in 1889 when the new towns and villages were created, amalgamating a number of what had formerly been autonomous hamlet settlements and making them what were called buraku sub-units of local government areas. Since that date a number of new groups have been formed on the basis of these new local government units, most of them having branches or sections in each buraku—which, as we have seen, can for practical purposes be equated with the hamlet settlement.

The chief of these were the Youth Group, the Housewives' Association, the Girls' Youth Group (sometimes known as the Maidens' Association, *Shojokai*), the Fire Brigade or Watch Brigade, and the Reservists' Association. We have already mentioned that these special functional associations often superseded traditional groups.

However, none of them were formed by the voluntary and spontaneous adhesion of the villagers. They were, rather, created first in the village local government units on instructions and models provided by the central government and, utilizing the hamlet's traditional capacity for unified action, branches of these organizations were then created in every buraku. But these were not the kind of organizations that villagers had freedom to enter or leave voluntarily as they desired. Formally one could refuse to join, but in practice if one fulfilled the requisite qualifications one was automatically made a member. The Youth Group, for instance, included everyone in the hamlet who had left school and had not reached a certain age. At least one woman from every household was expected to be a member of the Housewives' Association. And the same applied to the Fire Brigade. In this sense these were organizations of the whole community.

The nature of these organizations shows both how strong was the social unity of the hamlet and also how deep was the penetration of the political power of the central government into the remotest corners of the country. Administrative guidance has been a preponderant influence in the formation of associations in Japanese villages. Because there was little exercise of voluntary initiative from below, it was not difficult for political authorities to create and use official associations.

From the point of view of the hamlet, since these new associations were associations of the whole hamlet they were in fact little more than aspects of the hamlet community. In this sense they were no different from the traditional groups. Consequently it was looked on as quite natural that the hamlets should be expected, out of meagre hamlet funds, to subsidize the Youth Group and the Housewives' Association and to provide the expenses for the Fire Brigade. Since these were not independent organizations, they in fact had the effect of strengthening the unity of the hamlet. This was especially the case with the Fire Brigade which with the Youth Group took over the functions of the former *wakamono-gumi*. It not only went into action against fires and floods, but also exercised some continuous policing functions.

Very similar in form were most of the Local Farm Unions (*nōka kogumiai*) created throughout the country in the period after the depression of the thirties. Beginning with the Producers' Co-operatives Law of 1900, co-operatives were created throughout the country until by the late twenties they were found in every district. These too were usually formed on a one-per-administrative-village basis. The Local Farm Unions—the predecessors of the present Agricultural Practice Unions—were then formed on a hamlet basis, in part as sub-units of the village co-operatives, there usually being one, or perhaps two, such unions in each hamlet. Sometimes these were further subdivided into *han* which, as we have already seen, corresponded to the hamlet kumi. Once more it was a case of every farm family in the village having to join these unions whether they wanted to or not. Here again the principle of hamlet holism was applied. It was in fact the intention of the political authorities to utilize the social pressures of the hamlet to mobilize the farmers. The unions were expected to play a major role in the economic rehabilitation movement, the drive to pull the countryside out of the depression by forcefully inculcating habits of diligence and thrift.[7]

These unions were, of course, only for the farming members of the hamlet. Nevertheless, in most cases they were looked on as identical with the hamlet itself. It was common, for instance, for contributions to the Local Farm Unions to be collected through the general purpose organization of the hamlet. The

[7] Tanahashi Hatsutarō, *Nōka kogumiai no kenkyū*, 1955 (Sangyō-tosho Kabushiki-kaisha). According to a Ministry of Agriculture survey (Nōrinshō, Nōmukyoku, *Nōka kogumiai ni kansuru chōsa*, 1936) a half of these local unions covered an area of less than one hamlet, but the majority of them were formed for the purpose of communal farming operations and for this reason in large settlements two or more might be necessary. In general, however, they may be considered to correspond with the hamlet.

same applied to irrigation unions. The latter were increasingly formed as the modernization of irrigation systems proceeded. It was usual for their membership to be confined to landowners so that irrigation fees were paid only by landlords and owner cultivators and not by tenants, but even in these cases, it was not uncommon for irrigation fees to be collected through the general-purpose organization of the hamlet.

If most of the pre-war functional associations were in this way indistinguishable from the hamlet itself, there was one major exception—the Farmers' Unions which developed from around 1920. These were organizations of tenants and part-tenants formed in order to demand reductions in rents from landlords. Consequently by their very nature they could not become organizations of the hamlet as a whole. In many cases the poorest strata of tenants were prevented by their very dependence on landlords from joining such unions, so that they never succeeded even in recruiting all the tenants in the hamlet: in the pre-war village it was no easy matter to create an association which was *not* an association of all the hamlet members. On the other hand, in districts where there were landlords with very large holdings so that some hamlets might consist almost exclusively of tenant-farmers, it was not uncommon for everybody to be forced into joining the union and for the landlord's manager or the tenant foreman to be practically ostracized. Under certain conditions, therefore, the principle of hamlet holism operated in the formation even of class interest groups.[8]

However, Farmers' Union branches never numbered more than 5,000 even at their strongest, and their peak membership was around 300,000. They succeeded in drawing into the movement farmers from all over Japan, as is evidenced by the fact that in some years nearly as many as 7,000 disputes were recorded, but not every village had an organized union by any

[8] There are very few analyses of the Farmers' Union movement which consider them in relationship to the structure of the hamlet. The reader may consult my own description of the famous dispute in Kizaki Village of Niigata Prefecture, an important landmark in the history of the movement, included in my *Nihon sonraku no shakai-kōzō*, 1959 (Tōkyō-daigaku Shuppan-kai), and also Kawamura Nozomu, 'Kosaku-sōgiki ni okeru sonraku-taisei' in the 7th Annual Volume of the Sonraku-shakai Kenkyūkai, *Seiji-taisei to sonraku*, 1960 (Jichōsha).

means. And as the country moved on to a war footing they were faced with stern repressive measures and either forced to dissolve or reduced to functionless inactivity. Simultaneously the principle of hamlet holism was even further reinforced from above under the slogan 'construction of villages worthy of an empire'. The shortage of labour resulting from the war effort required a good deal of co-operative labour on the part of hamlets and kumi, while the social pressures of the hamlet were also used by the Government to ensure food deliveries, and correspondingly strengthened in the process.

TABLE XVI

Farmers' Unions and Tenancy Disputes: 1925–35

		Number of		
Year	Farmers' Unions	Union Members (thousands)	Disputes	Participants in Disputes (thousands)
1925	3,496	307	2,208	135
1930	4,208	301	2,478	59
1935	4,011	242	6,824	113

These circumstances changed considerably in the post-war period. At the time of the land reform the landlords did their utmost to repossess tenanted land, so that as owner-cultivators they could save their land from expropriation, and Farmers' Unions were formed on a wide scale to combat these efforts. The class dividing line on which these unions were formed naturally conflicted with the principle of hamlet holism, and the resulting tension caused extremely interesting results in the villages. However, the work of dismantling the landlord system was forced through by political authority backed by the orders of an occupying army, and the social tension in the villages was dissipated before it led to any serious conflicts. Consequently, the Farmers' Unions too either disbanded or became merely formal organizations after the end of land reform. Nevertheless, the social cohesiveness of the hamlet had been weakened and its holistic character had been largely destroyed.

Thus, for instance, in the post-reform villages agricultural study groups were often formed as voluntary organizations, usually by young farmers—househeads or eldest sons in full-time farming households—who were keen to study new techniques and so raise their productivity and their incomes. Some enthusiasm, not just hamlet residence, was a necessary qualification for joining. Such study groups were not organized in every village in Japan, but they are of considerable interest as marking a new pattern of group formation. Before the war any attempt to form such groups would doubtless have had to make them agricultural study sections of the hamlet organization, and every farming househead would have had to become formally a member whether he was interested or not.

Again, with the further development of commercial production since the war, co-operatives and joint marketing associations for fruit, dairy, poultry, pigs or silk cocoons have been formed on a scale far greater than in the pre-war period. These by their very nature include only farm households concerned with these crops and very often, to be big enough to be worthwhile, they are formed on the basis not of a single hamlet but of an administrative village as a whole. Consequently, except when the majority of houses in a hamlet grow the same special crop, very few of them have any connexion with the hamlet as such. Organizations such as these—silkworm co-operatives and fruit co-operatives—were also formed on a scale bigger than a hamlet basis before the war, but then it would have been usual to create a hamlet sub-unit which was identified with the hamlet itself.

Since about 1955 new types of group have been formed for co-operation in actual agricultural production—again small groups of households which have come together without reference to the hamlet as such. There is a great variety of these co-operative groups, ranging from those which simply perform a few operations jointly, to those which have completely merged their farms into a single unit, but they all, to a greater or lesser degree, are different from the traditional forms of co-operation. This is, indeed, one reason why these groups have often run into difficulties. For farmers who are only accustomed to forms of co-operation which resolve conflicts of interests by simply requiring 'selfishness' to be suppressed 'in the interest of the hamlet' as a whole, these new forms of co-operation represent an entirely new experience. In short, farmers today are still accustomed to groups formed on the basis of hamlet holism, and the principle of 'everyone without exception' is still very much alive.[9] The same observations might be made of other groups. For instance, the Youth Groups which were re-formed after the war started off as a new type of club for both sexes, without the principle of compulsory membership which operated before the war. The same applied to the Housewives' Associations and to groups like the 'young bride's schools'. Nevertheless the members of these groups have not lost the sense of belonging as a matter of compulsory obligation. And since there is no real spontaneous interest to support them they frequently lapse into inactivity. (The Youth Groups have suffered particularly from another factor, the recent large outflow of young people from the villages either as permanent migrants or as daily workers.) The Housewives' Associations too are rarely very active. The Agricultural Co-operatives have tried to fill the gap by starting women's sections and youth sections within the co-operatives. These have the same catchment area as the co-operatives themselves, an area larger than a single hamlet, but even so they usually create sub-sections in each hamlet. It is still thought advantageous to use the principle of hamlet unity as a method of group formation.

This characteristic is even more marked in the Agricultural Practice Union which has a tradition stretching back to the pre-war period. The compulsory forms of co-operative labour which developed as a response to the wartime labour shortage (one of their original *raisons d'être*) rapidly disappeared after the war, but the unions continued in existence as subordinate organs of the Agricultural Co-operatives. The development of agricultural techniques since then has created a need for new kinds of co-operation through the Agricultural Practice Union. We have already mentioned one of the most important, com-

[9] On co-operative farming see Wataya's analysis in Sakamoto Kusuhiko and Wataya Takeo, *Nōgyō kyōdōka no jittai*, 1960 (Toshi to Nōson o musubu Henshūbu), and for many individual examples there are the two volumes, of Nōrinshō, Nōrin-keizaikyoku, *Nōgyō kyōdōka: jittai to tembō*, 1960–1 (Nōrin-tōkei Kyōkai). See also an analysis of three examples, respectively by Matsubara Haruo, Hasumi Otohiko and Takahashi Akiyoshi in the Survey Report edited by the author, *Nōgyō kyōdōka to sonraku-kōzō*, 1961 (Yūhikaku).

munal spraying against pests and diseases. In the present state of technology, if only from the exigencies of these pesticide measures, every household in the hamlet has to belong to the union.

For all that, even the Agricultural Practice Unions show a tendency to be detached from the hamlet as such. Although in a good many villages the two are still looked on as identical, as the members of the hamlet become more and more differentiated into full-time farmers, part-time farmers and non-farmers and as the diversity of their interests and orientations increases, the possibilities of united action on the part of the whole hamlet correspondingly diminish. In other words, the interest-association character of the organizations becomes much more overt. This tendency is still not very accentuated, but the trend towards a dissociation between the hamlet as a small society and special functional groups within it may be seen to a greater or lesser degree in every kind of grouping. And it is from a further development of these processes of dissociation that the possibilities lie for the creation of new village communities.

CHAPTER VIII

THE STRUCTURE AND FUNCTIONING OF HAMLET SELF-GOVERNMENT

Self-Governing Organizations in the Hamlet

IN the Tokugawa period each village had its own set of rules or village by-laws which might or might not be written but which were sanctioned by the village assembly. Village life was controlled by the village headman (*nanushi, shōya* or *kimoiri*), by the heads of kumi (*kumi-gashira*) and by the 'farmers' representatives' (*hyakushō-dai*). (These various leadership positions were conventionally known as the 'three village offices'—*jikata-sanyaku*.) And sanctions were applied against anyone who offended against the rules. Despite the limitations imposed by their subordination to the control of the feudal lord, the villages themselves may be said to have had their own legislative, executive and judicial powers. The creation of the Meiji local government system meant that these villages ceased to be self-sufficient and self-governing units as groups of them were amalgamated to form the new administrative towns and villages. Hence, as far as the national law was concerned the former village units were denied recognition as independent legal entities.

These changes did not, however, mean the real end of hamlet government, as has already been mentioned and as will be explained in detail later. The new administrative units were not strong enough to absorb all the self-government functions of the former villages and these still had to be carried on. Moreover, the new local government law said specifically in Article 68 that 'for purposes of administrative convenience sub-divisions of towns and villages may be created and a division chief and one deputy may be appointed'. In most cases the sub-divisions which were formed and usually called buraku corresponded with the former village units. There were obvious administrative advantages to be gained from using the former villages with their established system of self-government for this purpose.

In this way the former villages—what we have called 'hamlets'—took on a dual character, combining with their role as self-governing units their new function as sub-divisions of the village administration. In addition, where hamlets had formerly possessed fairly extensive holdings of common land, they were permitted to form what were called 'property corporations' (*zaisanku*) to manage them, thus further complicating the situation by adding another corporate role to the community. All the same, as we have already seen, the correspondence between the hamlet, the Tokugawa village, and the settlement was not exact and the buraku as an administrative sub-unit was not always exactly the same as the hamlet as a functioning social unit. But even if it over-simplifies the situation to equate the hamlet with the administrative sub-unit, with the property corporation and with the Tokugawa village this was in fact the case in the majority of instances and it is this typical situation which will be assumed in the discussion of hamlet self-government which follows.[1]

It must be noted that there was no necessary correspondence between the membership criteria for the two main aspects of the hamlet's identity. As a sub-unit of the village administration it included every individual living in the defined geographical area. Sometimes, however, as a self-governing social unit it did not admit to equal membership everyone who lived within that area. Generally speaking only those who had been resident for a minimum period of time, had paid their hamlet contributions, performed their share of hamlet labour tasks, and conformed

---

[1] It is said that the word buraku was the word used to translate *Gemeinde* in the draft plan for local government drawn up by Albert Mosse, a German adviser employed by the Cabinet. In this draft plan the new city town and government units were all called *Gemeinde* which was translated as 'self-governing buraku'. It is thought that the present usage of the word buraku evolved from this translation. See Kikegawa Hiroshi, *Meiji chihō jichi seido no seiritsu-katei*, 1955 (Tōkyō-shisei Chōsakai), p. 132.

to the normal conventions of exchanging gifts and help at weddings and funerals were recognized as members of the hamlet. A household which moved in from outside could only be recognized as a constituent household of the hamlet after these conditions had been fulfilled; until then the newcomers were thought of as resident strangers. It was not uncommon, in hamlets where rights in communal hamlet property had considerable importance, for the entrance qualifications to be quite strict, including for instance the payment of membership money. In consequence it often happened that there was differentiation among residents within the hamlet with respect to their rights and obligations.[2]

However, in the majority of the villages it was not so very difficult to become a member of the hamlet, and the number of villages in which the process of *kabuiri* ('gaining a share') is of any great importance is today relatively small. Changes in this respect correspond, of course, to changes in the structure of hamlet society in modern times, and in turn they also affect the process of change in hamlet self-government. This is an important matter which will be considered later. Here we shall begin our discussion of hamlet government by a brief review of its organizational structure.

First, then, to begin with the appointed officials; every hamlet, of course, had its head. In the early Meiji period he was usually called *sōdai*, but after the establishment of the local government system and the subdivision of the new administrative villages into the sub-districts (originally *ku*) which generally coincided with hamlets, the most common title became *kuchō* head of the *ku*. Officially the *kuchō* and his deputy were to be appointed by the members of the village Council, on the recommendation of the Mayor, but in actual practice he was normally appointed within the hamlet. His duties included both traditional hamlet self-government functions and also tasks delegated to him in connexion with village administration, and since self-government extended over a wide range of diverse activities, these duties were quite onerous. Consequently,

[2] For an example, see the analysis of a village in Nagano Prefecture described in Furushima Toshio, ed., *Warichi-seido to nōchi-kaikaku*, 1953 (Tō-kyōdaigaku Shuppankai), p. 82 ff.

the position generally carried considerable weight. It was usually the case, however, as we shall see later, that the members of the *village* Council were more powerful than the *kuchō*, so that the latter was not always drawn from the very first rank of men of influence. Again, in some hamlets the *kuchō* was little more than the executive errand-boy of the hamlet Council which will be discussed later. It might also be the case, where commonly owned hamlet land was of considerable value, that the real men of influence were concerned to monopolize the special positions (as officials of the 'property corporation') which gave control over this property, so that the post of *kuchō* consequently was of lesser importance. Generally in the pre-war period, however, the authority of the *kuchō* as the head of the hamlet was considerable, and his powers were quite extensive.

The majority of hamlets also had a small Council with the function of assisting the *kuchō*, variously called *hyōgiin, kyōgiin,* or *kukai-giin*. In practice one may assume that hamlet affairs were effectively controlled by the member or members of the village Council who were elected from the hamlet, by the kuchō, and by the hamlet Council. In hamlets which did not have such a Council, it was common for the heads of the various hamlet kumi to perform this function collectively. Like the kuchō, these chiefs of hamlet kumi were also, under the kuchō's direction, given the task of conveying information to, and acting as intermediaries for, their members in matters concerned with village administration. Posts on this hamlet Council were naturally usually occupied by members of fairly powerful families within the hamlet. As we shall see in the next chapter, in some hamlets this group of influential families made up a relatively stable hereditary group. Where formal hamlet Councils existed, the position of kumi chief was generally of rather slight importance, involving little more than messenger functions and filled on a rotating basis by all the househeads in the kumi. Where, however, there was no such special Council, the kumi chiefs fulfilled a role rather similar to that of the heads of kumi in the Tokugawa period, and consequently the post was filled by men from relatively powerful families within the kumi.

Other offices found in the hamlet include the hamlet Treasurer, the Lands Officer (*sanya-iin*, sometimes also called the *yama-sōdai*), the Irrigation Officer (*suiri-iin*), and the Public Works Officer (*doboku-iin*). Treasurers were not found in every hamlet; in small hamlets or in those with only a small budget, accounts would be handled either by the kuchō himself or by his deputy. Similarly, it depended on the circumstances of the hamlet whether or not a separate lands officer to deal with hamlet common land, irrigation officers, or public works officers would be appointed. However, as in other cases, when these matters had considerable importance for the hamlet's economy, these offices were usually filled by men of influence who thereby carried considerable weight in the hamlet structure of self-government.[3]

There are many other offices which, while not strictly offices of the hamlet itself, were thought of as such because of the undifferentiated nature of the hamlet as a community. Among the traditional ones were, for instance, the positions of *ujiko-sōdai* concerned with upkeep of the hamlet shrine, or the position of Chief of the young men's group. Similarly, since the Agricultural Practice Union was in practice identical with the hamlet, the position of Chief counted as an important hamlet office, and so did the positions of hamlet Branch Chief of the organizations which were incorporated at the administrative village level—the Fire Brigade, the Youth Association, and the Housewives' Association. Where committees at the village level were made up of members drawn one from each hamlet and in practice appointed by the hamlet, membership of these committees too came to be considered as hamlet offices. Examples were the tax committee, the school committee, the health committee, or in the post-war period, the welfare committee or the citizens' hall committee. (The committee member in the latter case generally acted as Director of a hamlet Branch Citizens' Hall.) The same applied to the village Agricultural Co-operative, seats on whose executive committee were generally allocated to particular hamlets. Properly speaking these organizations were distinct from the hamlet, but some-

---

[3] For a general description summarizing a number of studies of hamlet government structure, see Ushiomi Toshitaka, ed., *Nihon ringyō to sanson-shakai*, 1962 (Tōkyō-daigaku Shuppankai). This work also summarizes the results of surveys in a good number of other fields.

times there would be a parallel structure, the hamlet Council itself having, for instance, a Youth Section Chief who was at the same time Chief of the hamlet branch of the village Youth Group, a Culture Section Chief who was at the same time Director of the hamlet Branch Citizens' Hall, a Production Section Chief who was at the same time the Chief of the Agricultural Practice Union—and so on. A good many of these offices might be concentrated in a few hands, with one man filling a number of offices at once.

These offices make up, as it were, the hamlet's administrative structure. Appointments to them are made by the hamlet general meeting. Under the traditional name of *mura-yoriai*, these gatherings have an old history. Formally at least they represent the hamlet's highest decision-making body and its legislative body. General meetings are regularly held around New Year during the agricultural slack season or else twice a year, though emergency general meetings might be held when important issues arise. The meetings are usually attended by one person from each household, in principle the househead. This remains the general practice in most hamlets even today, since the constituent units of the hamlet continue to be not the residents as individuals but households.

At the regular general meetings, elections are held for those offices whose incumbents' terms have expired, each household having a single vote. In the past actual voting did not always take place. The men of influence who made up the hamlet Council would previously agree on a list of nominees which was then recommended to the general meeting, the recommendations generally being approved unanimously. The regular general meeting would also receive a report on the hamlet's finances, though as we shall see later it was rare for a budget for the following year to be presented and discussed. Also, since the general meeting is formally the legislative organ, it might be the occasion for establishing new hamlet rules, and if any changes were necessary in the annual round of hamlet activities this is when they would be decided. Decisions might also be taken about the use or management of hamlet property and buildings and, if necessary, on the formal admission of new members to the hamlet or on the sanctions to be taken against hamlet residents who had offended against hamlet regulations.

It was the general rule that unanimity was required for these decisions. Just as it was thought preferable to select hamlet officers by recommendation rather than by competitive voting, so for other matters every effort was made to avoid decisions by majority vote, for it was considered that voting would damage the solidarity and harmony of the hamlet. What this meant in effect was that, although the general meeting was in form the highest decision-making organ, in actual practice decisions were left to the influential members who made up the hamlet Council, and there was no effective division between legislative and executive functions. What had been previously agreed by the kuchō and the other men of influence was simply accepted at the general meeting as a unanimous decision.[4]

Hamlet self-government has, of course, changed with the times. One must not assume that the *mura-yoriai* of the Tokugawa period still lives on in the hamlet general meeting. The hamlet offices, too, have changed not only in name; the range and nature of their functions is now very different, nor are the personalities of the men who filled them the same as they once were. These changes we shall discuss in a later section after a brief discussion of the way the system worked.

The Functioning of Hamlet Self-Government

The hamlet did not normally have any special building as an office for its self-governing activities. Most hamlets had a meeting hall, nowadays commonly the Branch Citizens' Hall, and this would be used for hamlet general meetings. But it was rare for such a building to be used as the kuchō's office, and except in very large hamlets where a great deal of business had to be transacted the kuchō usually carried on his work from his own home. During his term of office the documents chest which contained all the necessary records would be taken to his house

[4] Some hamlets have preserved detailed minutes of hamlet general meetings and of the meetings of the hamlet Council. See for an example, Yoden Hiromichi, *Nōgyō-sonraku-shakai no ronri-kōzo*, 1961 (Kōbundō). Pages 97–174 contain the records of one hamlet for a whole decade of the pre-war period.

and left in his charge, and it would be up to him to discuss necessary business with the other officers of the hamlet.

The workings of this system of self-government followed practices handed down from the past. If the hamlet general meeting took new decisions about procedures, etc., it would of course be necessary to follow them but the greater part of the business to be transacted followed well-worn lines laid down in the quite distant past. These well-worn lines—the hamlet customary law as it might be called—in some hamlets was committed to writing. Sometimes the rules—ranging from prescriptions of the rights and duties of residents to regulations covering every aspect of hamlet life—were set out with great precision in several score, or sometimes even a hundred or more, articles. Alternatively, instead of one consolidated body of hamlet regulations there might be several sets, each covering one particular area of activity. Whatever the form it is possible to consider this process of formalization as a response to the tendency for the traditional customary order to lose its binding power—an attempt to reassert and strengthen the traditional unwritten law by putting it clearly into writing. This, however, would be an over-simplification, for the process was also influenced by the special circumstances of particular hamlets and by simple diffusion. Villagers might be brought into contact with the national laws when some conflict over water rights or rights to common land was taken to the courts. This might lead them to put their own customary practices into writing, even though there was no particular need to reaffirm them, and their example might then be followed by neighbouring hamlets. However, taking a general over-all view, hamlets with clearly formulated written regulations have remained a minority. Systems of hamlet self-government have not, after all, disintegrated to the point where it has become difficult to run the hamlet on the basis of unwritten custom.[5]

[5] I have given an example of one extremely detailed set of hamlet regulations in my *Nihon sonraku no shakai-kōzō*, 1959 (Tōkyō-daigaku Shuppankai). Another set is printed as an appendix to Yoden Hiromichi, *Nōgyō sonraku-shakai no ronri-kōzō*, 1961 (Kōbundō). For examples of village regulations dating from the Tokugawa period see Ono Takeo, *Nihon sonraku-shi-kō*, 1941 (Tōkō Shoin) and Maeda Masaharu, *Kinsei sompō no kenkyū*, 1950 (Yūhikaku).

Nevertheless, the process of written formalization has been facilitated in recent decades, as villagers have generally become literate and as there had been some weakening of the cohesive solidarity of the hamlet. It has at least become common for newly agreed regulations—modifications in customary practices required by changes in circumstances—to be put in writing. For example, as village poverty became a more pressing problem around the turn of the century, and as it consequently became more necessary to intensify efforts to economize, there were frequently hamlet agreements to reduce expenditures on the mutual feasting and display attendant on weddings and funerals, and these were normally put in writing. So too were the moral codes sometimes drawn up in similar circumstances—sets of moral precepts embodying the traditional rural philosophy of diligence and thrift. Alternatively, with a loosening of hamlet cohesion and with a growing tendency for individual families to display a more overt 'family egotism' in their behaviour, the arbitrary exercise of authority by the hamlet ruling stratum being no longer acceptable it became necessary to formalize the rules, especially their penal provisions, making quite clear the sanctions attendant on infringements. Examples of written rules prescribing sanctions of this type are not uncommon in mountain hamlets.[6]

All the same, exceptional circumstances and districts apart, for the most part hamlet affairs could be run on the basis of unwritten custom. Even when custom was modified, villagers would remember the change without it being put formally in writing; at least it usually sufficed if the new modification was recorded in the minutes of the hamlet general meeting.

As to the precise nature of these customary forms of hamlet self-government, it is difficult to give a general summary description for the very reason that it was a matter which national legislation left unprescribed. As far as the national law was concerned, it did no more than give legal recognition to the

---

[6] In north-eastern Japan it was not uncommon for hamlets to be considered as 'contractual associations' (contractual *kō*), and in these cases the hamlet regulations were always in written form. For examples of fragmentary special-purpose regulations, see the notes in my *Nihon nōson no shakaiteki seikaku*, 1949 (Tōkyō-daigaku Shuppankai).

hamlet as a sub-unit of village and town administration, and formalize the nomenclature of the head of such a unit and his deputy. Beyond that, depending on the circumstances and traditions of each hamlet, there was great variety, not only, as we have seen above, in their internal structure and systems of titles, but also in the way such structures operated.

One safe generalization that one can make about these infinitely varying practices is that the great majority of hamlets used regular levies on their members as a source of hamlet funds. The names given to these levies vary (*buraku-kyōgihi, kuhi, ōaza-hi*, etc.), but under some such rubric they were collected in at least 77 per cent. of the hamlets covered in the 1955 settlement survey. An indication of the uses to which these funds are put may be gained from Table XVII which shows that the most common items of expenditure were for roads, for festivals and for expense allowances to officials.

TABLE XVII

Items of Hamlet Budget Expenses

	Percentage of Hamlets budgeting for this Item	
Item	For direct Expenditure	On behalf of a separate Organization in the Hamlet for which it acts as Collecting Agent
Road repairs	54.4	—
Irrigation	24.4	16.7
Production facilities	28.0	8.4
Sanitation and medical	35.3	6.1
Road lighting	29.4	—
Festivals	48.2	25.2
Expense allowances for officials	57.2	—

And if one includes not just hamlet levies proper, but also those contributions collected (along with the hamlet levy) by the main hamlet organization on behalf of other organizations within the hamlet, a large number of hamlets are also involved in the financing of irrigation works and agricultural production facilities. In these latter cases, of course, the bodies on behalf of which the main hamlet organization collects are respectively Irrigation Unions and Agricultural Practice Unions. One may see in this, therefore, a symptom of the tendency (to be discussed in the next section) for separate functional organizations to become differentiated from the hamlet organization as such, but the fact that the hamlet still does the collection shows the limits to this tendency.

In addition to these levies on residents, some foothill and mountain hamlets are able to supplement hamlet funds by income from hamlet common lands, and in some cases that income is sufficient to make the collection of hamlet levies unnecessary. However, according to the survey, in 90 per cent. of the hamlets which had a hamlet budget some levy was collected. The method of assessment varies, but usually involves a combination of an equal per-household levy, a levy proportionate to the area of land farmed or owned, and a levy proportionate to assessed wealth or income. In principle, festival funds would be levied on a per-household basis, irrigation expenses on a land area basis, and other expenditures on an income or wealth basis, with each household being graded for the latter purpose in one of a determinate number of categories. Some hamlets would collect each levy separately on these different bases, maintaining separate accounts for each; others would make a consolidated levy for a single budget but collect, say, 40 per cent. of the total on an area basis, 40 per cent. on an income basis and 20 per cent. on a per-household basis. There has been a considerable rationalization of methods of collection since the war. Table xviii summarizes the information yielded by the 1955 survey concerning the methods then used. It will be seen that a still high proportion of hamlets use a combination of two or more methods of assessment.

TABLE XVIII

Methods of Collecting Revenue for Hamlet Expenditure

Method	Percentage of Hamlets Studied
Equal contributions of more than 500 yen from each house	7.5
Ditto, less than 500 yen	23.5
According to 'family standing'	8.7
According to size of holding, municipal tax or income tax	20.8
A combination of more than one of these methods	39.4

Of the various combinations, those which use as a basis the size of holding, the local citizen's tax or the national income tax may be considered relatively highly rationalized, though not necessarily fair in their incidence. And it will be noted that the equal per-household tax or the tax based on a wealth assessment determined by the traditional 'standing' of the family are still by no means uncommon. These aspects will be touched on again later, but meanwhile it is worth noting that the burden of hamlet levies tends to weigh more heavily on the lower income groups in the hamlet, even to a greater extent than the local citizens' taxes which are themselves much more regressive in their incidence than national taxes.[7]

As for the procedure for collecting the hamlet levies, in smaller hamlets with not very large budgets it was not uncommon for special collections to be made as the need arose, or for the hamlet head to pay out on behalf of the community from his own pocket and recover the money later. In larger hamlets where greater sums of money were involved it was usual to make regular collections fixed on the basis of expenditure in previous years; it was rather rare for a detailed forward budget to be prepared. Even in 1955 the survey found that only in 53 per cent. of hamlets could the procedure be categorized under the loose heading 'hamlet residents approve expenditure in advance', which may be taken as an indication that some kind of budget target was fixed, if only in global terms.

The other sources of hamlet funds, besides levies on residents, are income from hamlet property and subsidies from the village or town administrations. However, the survey showed that only 23 per cent. of hamlets had access to the former and only 48 per cent. to the latter. Moreover, it should be noted that the concealed effect of using income from hamlet property for hamlet purposes is in reality to increase the proportion of the hamlet

[7] If, for example, one uses the figures of the Farm Household Economy Survey to compare the incidence of taxation respectively on farmers farming less than 30 ares and those farming more than 2 hectares one finds that while, for national taxes, the latter pays 35 times as much as the former, for local taxes the ratio is one to five, and for the item 'other public charges and levies' (which includes hamlet levies) the ratio is one to less than three. On the relation of hamlet finances to the structure of the hamlet see Takahashi Akiyoshi, 'Buraku-zaisei to buraku-ketsugō', *Shakai-kagaku Kiyō*, No. 9, 1959 (Tōkyō-daigaku Shuppankai).

budget deriving from equal per-household contributions. As for subsidies from the village administration, these are usually for special purposes and granted on the condition that the hamlet devotes funds of its own to those purposes—generally for an amount larger than the subsidy. These are in other words often devices whereby activities which it is properly the duty of the village administration to support are pushed on to the hamlet in exchange for a tiny subsidy—a matter which will concern us again later in a discussion of the double incidence of taxation.

The operation of hamlet self-government has another important aspect besides the levying of hamlet monetary taxes, namely the mobilization of labour from hamlet members. In the days when the villages were still not deeply involved in the monetary economy, the amount of actual cash required to run the hamlet was small; it was enough if there was money to buy paper and ink and brushes. Most jobs could be done by going to the hamlet's forest land and cutting down a little timber, work accomplished by the unpaid labour of hamlet residents. With the development of a commercial economy the size of cash budgets increased and monetary levies became general, but the system of labour *corvées* for communal hamlet works persisted—at the very least for the repair of roads or for cleaning irrigation ditches. The most universal form was road-mending, usually carried out twice a year in spring and autumn. Ninety-four percent. of hamlets covered in the 1955 survey had such a system and in nearly all of these (96 per cent. to be precise) each household was expected to send one person to join the work gang. This is still usually unpaid labour; only 11 per cent. of hamlets paid a work allowance—and that usually a token amount.

It is estimated that the average hamlet requires some six days a year of such unpaid labour from each household. Its effect is to exaggerate the tendency of equal per-household money contributions to weigh disproportionately on the poorer members of the community, for the benefits derived from the labour thus equally contributed often accrue in greater measure to the more wealthy farmers. When ditch-cleaning or road repair or the repair of field paths or forest tracks are carried out on a one-person-per-household basis, it is much easier for the farmers with a bigger holding to release labour in the agricultural slack season than it is for the smaller farmers who have to use this period to supplement their earnings through some kind of non-agricultural work. Not only that, the farmers with the bigger holdings also use more of the water that flows through the cleaned ditches and get more use out of the roads that have been repaired. Very often, also, this kind of 'hamlet works' labour is mobilized for other purposes besides the regular repair of hamlet roads because of a shortage of funds in village administration. Works which should properly be carried out as the official activities of the village administration are at least partly accomplished by requisitioning labour on the principle that 'the burden should fall on the local beneficiaries'.

What this in effect means is that the patterns of hamlet self-government which have been handed down from the period when the hamlet was a unified whole, producing as a community on the basis of mutual aid, begin to run into serious difficulties as the individual family farm economy becomes increasingly differentiated from the community-based sub-sistence economy. But since in most cases the individual farm family cannot dispense with certain community services, the traditional patterns of hamlet government are maintained, preserving methods of collecting hamlet funds and requisitioning hamlet labour which derive from the past. They are at once conditioned by the system of stratification in the hamlet and contain the seeds of conflict between the strata. Such conflict was not absent even in the old 'village community' forms, but then the tenants and poor farmers did get, in exchange for an excessive burden of unpaid labour, the assurance of protection from the landlords and richer farmers. The latent conflict of interest was not felt as such. The structural changes of the modern period, however, have not permitted the preservation of these traditional ties between strata in their original form. It has become increasingly difficult to compensate for the tendency towards conflict between the classes. Again, although the hamlet has retained a certain judicial autonomy and continued to have the power to impose sanctions for the infringement or neglect of hamlet rules, these sanctions have gradually grown weaker. The suspension of the rights attaching to hamlet residence, or even the full ostracization known as *mura-hachibu* have ceased to be quite the awesome punishments that they once were. Consequently the traditional patterns of hamlet self-government, with their implications of potential conflict between social strata, could not remain unaffected. There was bound to be a change in the direction of rationalizing these contradictions and adapting the patterns of hamlet organization to the needs of new circumstances.

Changes in Hamlet Self-Government

The difficulties of hamlet self-government, we have said, increase with the growing independence of each individual farm household, and with the increasingly heterogeneous differentiation of the composition of the hamlet. In a commercial economy each individual family becomes more aware of its own discrete interests and more independent in its own farm operations, while the community becomes more stratified; there is an increase in the number of part-time farmers and of non-farming hamlet residents. The hamlet ceases to be a homogeneous settlement of farming families. Even in mountain villages which contain few non-farming families, because forest products come to acquire greater monetary value, villagers become much more exclusive and protective about their rights to forest land; such rights are restricted to old residents, and thus a division is created between the endowed and the non-endowed members. Hence in such villages too some adjustment may be required in the patterns of hamlet self-government.

At the same time, as contradictions arose from internal differentiation and stratification, hamlets have also faced the difficulty of reconciling their traditional self-governing functions with their functions as sub-units of the village administration. This was especially the case after the late war when there were great changes not only in hamlet structures, but also in the ideas and attitudes of farmers. The result was an acceleration of the rate of change in both the structure and the functioning of hamlet self-government.

Considering first the offices and office-holders of the hamlet, there has generally been a lowering of the prestige attached to the post of hamlet chief. This used to be an honorary office filled, for relatively long periods at a time, by a 'powerful man' of the first rank, an office second only in importance to that of member of the village Council. As overseers of all the affairs of the hamlet they usually had the services of an underling to act as a messenger and runner of errands. The latter was usually given a small annual salary in rice or cash and chosen from a poor low-status family. More recently however—and partly because the job was a mark of low status there has been no one available and willing to be recruited for such a menial task—the hamlet chief has had to run his own errands. What was formerly an honorary post now has to carry some kind of expense allowance. Again, as a variety of differentiated associations have been formed (including those coextensive in membership with the hamlet), there being a limit to the extent to which offices can decently be combined, they have often had separate individual chiefs, so that the hamlet chief has ceased to be the director of all the hamlet's affairs. What is more, his duties (as indeed the common title for the position, *kuchō*, indicates) have come to include an increasing proportion of tasks delegated by the village administration. The wartime period was the climax of this particular trend, when hamlet chiefs were kept perpetually busy with the tasks of 'transmitting the will of those above to those below'. Then, in the post-war period, when the neighbourhood group system was banned and the title 'hamlet chief' was replaced by some such term as 'local officer' or 'liaison officer', the tendency for his job to consist of administrative message-carrying was further enhanced. With more work to be done and less prestige to be earned by doing it, in a good many hamlets the job of hamlet chief became something to be avoided.

A rather similar process of declining prestige has affected the post of hamlet councillor—a process aided, as we shall see later, by the virtual disappearance of a 'councillor stratum' as a hereditary status group. They have become of no greater importance than kumi chiefs, and much the same may be said of the variety of other types of hamlet offices. Occasionally, where for instance a hamlet shares valuable rights in forest land with other hamlets and needs a 'forest representative' with some forcefulness and negotiating skill, the post may carry with it a certain amount of authority, but the majority of hamlet offices have come to be burdensome without earning one, to a commensurate degree, the respect of one's fellow hamlet residents. The majority of these offices, including that of hamlet chief, are now filled, not by the recommendation of the 'powerful men' of the hamlet, but by election. This has come about, not only because they carry lesser prestige, but also because of a change in farmers' attitudes and ideas—a change which has become even more decisive after the end of the land reform.

Secondly, the pattern of hamlet general meetings has also changed. They are no longer simply a means of rubber-stamping the decisions of the inner group; no longer the old kind of 'hamlet gathering' at which seating positions were determined by the family's traditional status in the hamlet, with the poorest families sitting at the back of the room and not daring to say a word. Occasions may arise when the old method of reaching unanimous decisions no longer works, and differences of opinion make it necessary to decide by majority vote—and this is especially the case since the land reform. We have already mentioned that the voting is still usually on the principle of one-household-one-vote, but there are some hamlets which have adopted the one-vote-per-person principle. Then again, as a result of such changes, general meetings are often unwilling to be satisfied simply with a financial report for the previous year and have demanded the right to approve the budget for the next year. Similarly, all those matters which used to be dealt with as hamlet business, irrespective of how small the proportion of hamlet members who stood to gain or lose anything from them, can no longer be treated in the same undiscriminating way. Different conflicting interests are brought out into the open; hence the tendency for specialized associations to become differentiated from the hamlet as such. And one result of this is that when the hamlet general meeting has no very important business to conduct the attendance is often small and it is difficult to hold an effective meeting, for it has become impossible to compel attendance or to enforce sanctions on those who fail to attend.[8]

[8] It was not uncommon for some fine to be imposed for non-attendance at hamlet meetings. See for instance the example of hamlet regulations in my

There has also been a tendency to rationalize the methods of collecting hamlet dues. The statistics quoted earlier showed that a good number of hamlets used the method of equal per-household levies which in effect leads only to a false equality. As such it can hardly be called a rational method, but even so it is an improvement on traditional practices which involved arbitrary, subjective assessments by hamlet leaders. It seems certain that the number of hamlets which collect the total amount of the budget by equal contributions has increased since the war, which in some ways may seem a retrogressive step, but there is another aspect to the matter. Even if the older methods did in effect weigh more heavily on the poorer and less on the richer members of the hamlet, nevertheless in absolute amounts the richer paid bigger contributions. Consequently, they were looked on as granting charitable favours to the poorer strata which meant in effect that the latter were felt to have less right to a say in hamlet affairs. In some cases, therefore, the adoption of equal contributions has been part of a claim to an equal voice in the making of decisions. The statistics quoted earlier also showed that the dues for various separate organizations within the hamlet were sometimes collected by the hamlet along with the hamlet levy, but at least the fact that these various dues are conceptually separate shows the tendency for the differentiation of functional associations and represents a more rational method than the former practice of covering all expenses from a single hamlet fund. There is, moreover, an increasing tendency for these various associations to collect their own dues individually, without reference to the main hamlet organization.

There have been changes, too, in the performance of hamlet works. People no longer simply take them for granted as proper and natural duties. Whereas they would formerly work at them with a will because they believed they were working for the good of the hamlet, now the more usual attitude is that they are unavoidable chores, and hamlet work has become a synonym for slack and inefficient work. Whereas it was practically un-

---

Nihon sonraku no shakai kōzō, 1959 (Tōkyō-daigaku Shuppankai). The regulations were several times amended over the course of the years, and in the latest version the penal provisions had disappeared.

heard of not to turn out for hamlet tasks, hamlets have now had to give a chance to work later to those who found the appointed day inconvenient, or have had to levy fines for non-appearance. In some hamlets where the breakdown in solidarity has gone furthest there has been no alternative but to turn a blind eye to failure to appear.

TABLE XIX

Treatment of those who fail to turn out for Communal Hamlet Tasks

Treatment	Percentage of Hamlets Studied
Offence passed over in silence	32.6
Work required later	15.7
Fine collected	37.0
Other measures	1.3
Question never arises	13.5

Table XIX shows the findings of the 1955 settlement survey concerning the way hamlets deal with the problem. With the increase in non-farming households, it becomes ever more difficult to enforce their participation, in spite of all the arguments that they use the hamlet paths as much as the farmers. The survey showed that 75 per cent. of hamlets impose the same obligations in this regard on non-farming as on farming households, but there is little doubt that this will become more difficult in future, and it will be increasingly necessary to resort to paid labour instead of voluntary labour. Although the rates paid are generally well below the ruling rates for unskilled labour, the number of hamlets which do make some payment is increasing.

It is unnecessary to repeat that behind these changes in hamlet self-government lie changes in the structure of the hamlet. One aspect of these—changes in the stratification system—will be discussed in the next section. The other is the increasing occupational differentiation which makes it necessary to hive off the Agricultural Practice Union and the Irrigation Union as dealing with activities which can no longer be considered the concerns of the hamlet as a whole. Formerly, expenses for maintaining the irrigation system and commonly-used agricultural facilities were paid out of general hamlet funds together with expenditure for stationery, for festivals, for roads and bridges, for fire equipment, for sanitation, for lighting on hamlet roads and in the hamlet hall, for taxes on hamlet property and so on, and as far as possible cash expenditure would be saved by using the unpaid labour of all the hamlet members. But when there are large numbers of non-farmers in the hamlet it becomes difficult to cover such expenditures from hamlet funds which they help to contribute. Hence the need for Irrigation Unions and Agricultural Practice Unions to collect their own funds, though as a transitional phase, as already mentioned, the hamlet might collect these separate levies on these Unions' behalf.

A similar process can take place with respect to hamlet property. Those who have rights in the property may, if they do not comprise all the residents of the hamlet, form a separate group, distinct from the hamlet itself. They may not go so far as to take on a legally incorporated form, but they become recognized as a separate group able to prevent the income from their property being simply absorbed into hamlet funds. Similarly, agricultural facilities do not become common hamlet property, but property of the Agricultural Practice Union. As part of the process of rationalizing the structure of the hamlet, this tendency will inevitably grow.

As these functional organizations hive off from the hamlet organization itself, the latter is more and more purely confined to administrative work delegated from the village administration. Even now the latter has generally become the more important part of its work. If the system of town and village administration were to change in such a way as to make these functions of the hamlet unnecessary there would be little left for the hamlet organizations to do, beyond the minimum tasks required for a group of neighbouring householders to coexist in close proximity. Hamlet funds as such would all but disappear, on the one hand into contributions to specialized associations in the hamlet, on the other into the public finances of the local administrations.

At present the situation is far from tending in that direction. Despite the tendency for functional groups to acquire separate identities, the hamlet organization is still a fairly comprehensive organ of hamlet self-government. What keeps it so is not simply the fact that the structural differentiation of the hamlet is still incomplete and the attitudes of the villagers on these questions still undeveloped, but also the fact that the town and village administrations still rely on the hamlet a great deal. Since the post-war reforms hamlets are no longer legally designated as official administrative sub-units, but they have nevertheless continued to be used as such. In agricultural districts they have still been the units for the allocation of subsidies, and they have continued to be used as channels for the dissemination of information. Nor has this been changed by the wholesale amalgamations of local government units which have taken place since 1953. On the contrary, the larger the area centrally administered, the greater has been the need to enlist the services of hamlet organizations. Thus the dual nature of the hamlet organization is preserved. And since the associations which have become functionally differentiated are also organized on a village basis with hamlet sub-units, these sub-units can continue to be integrated with the hamlet organization. At present it is only in the suburban agricultural areas close to the big towns where the population is already highly heterogeneous that there has been a clear separation between the hamlet organization as such and the Agricultural Practice Union. In most hamlets, there may be strains set up, but the differentiation process seems to be marking time.[9]

However, questions of the relation between local government and hamlet self-government go beyond the scope of this chapter and will be taken up at a later stage. First, though, it is necessary to get a general perspective on the authority patterns in the hamlet which have supported these forms of hamlet self-government.

[9] For examples of the separation of the hamlet and the Practice Union see the relevant chapter in my *Nihon sonraku no shakai-kōzō*, 1959 (Tōkyō-daigaku Shuppankai).

CHAPTER IX

THE POWER STRUCTURE OF
THE HAMLET

The Stratification System of the Hamlet

ONE may picture the traditional hamlet as typically consisting of one or two landlords, about one-third owner-farmers, about one-third who owned a part of their land and rented the rest, and about one-third who owned none of their land and were wholly tenants.

These divisions according to land-owning status were in the typical case overlaid by relations between stem and branch family or between *oyakata* and *kokata*. Thus we may draw up an ideal-typical picture of hamlet structure as follows: at the top came a landlord family which was also a stem family and an oyakata family; next, the upper middle consisted of owner farmers—the immediate branches of the top family, the stem families of lesser *dōzoku*, and families which, themselves kokata of the top family, were also oyakata to small groups of lesser families. Finally, the lower middle and the lower strata were made up of tenants and part-tenants who were the 'grandchild-branch-families' at two stages removed from the top family, or the branches of lesser dōzoku groups, or kokata clients of families of higher ranks, or several of these things at once. In some hamlets, indeed, these status distinctions were apparent even in the terms of address used within families; children of the top rank would, for instance call their father *otōsan*, those of the next rank *oto*, of the next *tete*, and of the lowest *dede*.[1] These were, in

---

[1] Many examples of graded kinship terms have been found in villages in the north east and on the northern Japan Sea coast. On the general question of stratified status groups see Kawashima Takeyoshi, 'Nōson no mibun kaiso-sei', in Iwanami-shoten, ed., *Nihon shihon-shugi kōza*, 1954, vol. 8.

other words, distinctions of no mean significance, marking off groups whose personal prestige status was sharply differentiated.

As we have seen, when landlord-tenant relations are overlaid by stem-family–branch-family relations or oyakata-kokata relations they become something more than a contract for the lease of land at a fixed rent. If the tenant was in difficulties, he could expect the landlord —the stem family, the oyakata—to hold out a helping hand. If rice ran out before the harvest, he could expect a loan from the landlord's granary. If he needed a guarantor to take part in a *kō* type of loan club, the landlord would stand in for him. From time to time he could count on the odd present from the landlord of a bottle of rice wine. In return the tenant—the kokata, the member of a branch family—would be 'in and out' of the landlord's house, always ready to be of service. When summoned to appear, he would be ready to drop everything and go at a moment's notice. Landlord and tenant were, in effect, master and servant in the most familistic sense; the exploitative tenancy relation was concealed under a layer of paternalism appropriate to the bonds which joined them as stem family and branch, oyakata and kokata. Their status differences, while ensuring that each kept his proper position, united them, too, in a familistic whole.[2]

One must quickly point out, of course, that such a 'typical' stratification system was found only in a very small number of villages. Where it did exist it was usually as a survival of early medieval forms where an original local magnate type of landlord had preserved his power. Even in the Tokugawa period it was far from being the general form and in more recent times it has been, if anything, a rarity.

But some of the outline features of such a system have been common. Even in villages which formed part of the large estates of merchant-money-lender landlords, there were generally small farming landlords within the hamlet who at the same time acted

---

[2] For the structure of such hamlets see my *Nihon nōson no shakaiteki seikaku*, 1949 (Tōkyō-daigaku Shuppankai), for the section on the 'north-eastern type' of hamlet. Also, for instance, see the analysis of two villages in northern Akita prefecture by Tsukamoto Tetsundo and Matsubara Haruo included in Fukutake Tadashi, ed., *Nihon nōson shakai no kōzō-bunseki: sonraku no shakai-kōzō to nōsei-shintō*, 1954 (Tōkyō-daigaku Shuppankai).

as local managers for the big landlords and formed a distinct upper stratum. Again, even where the landlords were of the 'thrifty-peasant' type whose estates were acquired gradually piece by piece, there would still be a system of status ranking— landlords, owner-farmers, part-owners, tenants—which had something of the nature of hereditary caste-group distinctions. It was a complex social order in which descent and economic dependence, tenancy relations an'd the bonds of communal work groups and common membership in a holistic community, were subtly intertwined.[3]

This social order began to disintegrate as the villages came into increasing contact with the capitalist economy and as the productivity of agriculture itself began to increase. The tenancy system which supported it changed *pari passu* and the landlords became increasingly parasitic. The change did not take place at a uniform rate throughout the country, however. To oversimplify the situation a good deal, one can make a distinction between those areas where agricultural productivity was already fairly high in late Tokugawa times and where the subsequent progress of industrialization was rapid, and those areas where productivity had always been lower and industrialization was slower. It was in the latter areas that one was most likely to find hamlets closely corresponding to the polar type outlined above and these were also the areas in which change occurred most slowly. There was, therefore, a widening of the gap.

The two types have often been distinguished as the 'north-eastern' and the 'south-western' hamlet type, but since one could find 'north-eastern' type villages also in the south-west, it will be best here to use the terms 'developed' and 'underdeveloped'.[4]

[3] For villagers' own perceptions of status distinctions in their hamlets see the analyses by Ushiomi Toshitaka in two books edited by Furushima Toshio: *Sanson no kōzō*, 1949 (Nihon Hyōronsha, later Ochanomizu Shobō), and *Warichi-seido to nōchi-kaikaku*, 1953 (Tōkyō-daigaku Shuppankai). These are also summarized in the third chapter of Ushiomi Toshitaka, *et al.*, ed., *Nihon no nōson*, 1957 (Iwanami Shoten).

[4] In my own *Nihon nōson no shakaiteki-seikaku*, 1949 (Tōkyō-daigaku Shuppankai), I tried to draw a distinction between the 'dōzoku' type of village and the 'kō and kumi type' of village, identifying these with the north-eastern and south-western types respectively. See also Isoda Susumu's

In the underdeveloped regions the occupational structure was still of a simple kind and communications were primitive so that hamlet residents had fewer opportunities of visiting the outside world or of finding employment there, irrespective of whether they belonged to the upper landlord stratum or to the lower ranks of the tenants. The penetration of the money economy had not gone far, commercial agriculture was little developed; their farming was still of a predominantly subsistence nature. There was little mobility, either geographically or vertically in a social sense, between the economic strata, and so little disturbance of the stratification system. Since the landlords had little opportunity to transfer to other occupations and move into a purely parasitic relation to agriculture, they usually continued to farm even if they did somewhat reduce the size of the holdings under their direct cultivation. They employed members of the lower strata within their hamlets on their own farms, and by virtue of this fact they maintained their interest in agriculture, kept up close relationships with the other members of their hamlets and so preserved intact the hamlet status order.

This status order was reinforced by the village-community-like nature of hamlet society. In such hamlets green fertilizer, and consequently the waste land from which it was cut, played an important role in the farming system, so that the common ownership of waste lands tended to be maintained, thus preserving the solidary bonds of the hamlet community. This tendency was further reinforced by the fact that the modernization of irrigation systems was rarer in such regions so that traditional methods of water control continued to help to hold the community together. Add to this the continuing need for labour co-operation in an agricultural system of low productivity—the need to organize communal roof-thatching and so on—and the fact that in the absence of other opportunities for recreation the traditional festivals and occasions for mutual feasting retained their original significance. In these overlapping patterns of co-operation members of the hamlet were caught up in a tight network of community constraints which helped to

analysis, which hangs on the distinction between the 'family-status type' and the 'non-family-status type' village, in his 'Sonraku kōzō no futatsu no kata', *Hō-shakaigaku*, 1, 1951.

preserve the status system intimately bound up with the traditional patterns of hamlet life.

The typical hamlet of the more developed type was a contrast in all these respects. Industrialization provided greater opportunities for transfer to other occupations outside the village, not only for the upper landlord class who profited from the chances for higher education which their wealth secured, but also, as labourers, for the poorer tenant groups. The landlords thus tended to withdraw completely from farming, and even among the tenants who remained in the villages a number became part-time farmers commuting to other jobs. Nor was it only opportunities for geographic mobility which were notably increased; with the increasing penetration of the monetary economy and greater cash cropping there was also increased social mobility as between the economic strata of the hamlet. There was a further blurring of the divisions between hereditary strata, divisions which had never in these regions been very sharply marked in the first place. The landlords had ceased at an early stage to farm large holdings of their own; now they tended further to become absentee, or if they stayed in the hamlet to travel to salaried employments elsewhere, thus losing all direct connexion with hamlet society. There were, moreover, much quicker fluctuations of fortune within the landlord group than in the less developed districts, so that the traditional authority of established landlord families was more likely to suffer decline. And even if new farming landlords did rise to the top to replace them it was usually beyond their power to claim the same kind of status superiority and re-order the status system in a traditional mould.

The restraints of community solidarity were also more quickly eroded in such districts. As agricultural techniques developed there was greater reliance on commercial fertilizers, and the common hamlet lands which had formerly provided silage—and which were generally of smaller extent than in the less developed regions in any case—tended to be divided into individual lots. The relative increase in the productivity of labour led to the break-down of co-operative labour systems. Irrigation systems, also, to a greater or lesser degree were reorganized by modern engineering methods and traditional patterns of community control became less significant. With increasing contact with the towns there were new opportunities for recreation which overshadowed the old feasts and festivals. And the breakdown in the isolation and exclusiveness of the hamlet, combined with changes in the composition of the strata themselves, contributed to a general weakening of the stratification system.[5]

Despite all these differences between the two types of region, it remains true that the trends were similar in both. Not even the least developed districts were wholly sheltered from the effects of the developing capitalist economy, and there was a general tendency, though differing in degree, for stratification systems to lose their rigidity.

They did not entirely break down, however, as long as the tenure system which underpinned them remained. Even if some of the bigger landlords retained only the loosest ties with their villages, many farming landlords remained and the distinction between owner-farmer and tenant was still a real one. Even if hereditary status distinctions ceased to matter very much in everyday matters, even if generally speaking it was wealth and ability which seemed to count for most, a sense of 'family status' still remained—to be activated, for instance, when marriages were in question.

It was, of course, the land reform which struck the decisive blow. Its effects were not uniform. The completely parasitic landlords of the more developed districts, being generally absentee landlords, lost all their land and their power in the village as well. By contrast, those landlords in the less developed districts who continued to farm large holdings were allowed to retain their farms up to the maximum permitted size. But even the latter, and for that matter the remaining farming landlords of the more developed districts too, though they might still

[5] For an example of such hamlets see the chapter on the 'south-western type' in my *Nihon nōson no shakaiteki seikaku*, 1949 (Tōkyō-daigaku Shuppankai) and also Furushima Toshio, *Kisei-jinushi-sei no seisei to tenkai*, 1952 (Iwanamai Shoten). See also the examples of village structure in Kondō Yasuo, *Mura no kōzō*, 1955 (Tōkyō-daigaku Shuppankai). The latter author remarks that 'the crucial difference between the north-eastern and the south-western village lies in its employment structure—whether it is simple or complex', (ibid. p. 13).

retain some of their wealth had lost their erstwhile authority. They remained in the upper stratum of villagers, but the gap between them and the owner-farmers and part-tenants who emerged from the reform with largish holdings was conspicuously narrowed, and in terms of economic status there was little to choose between them.

Apart, then, from those landlords who retained large areas of forest land (untouched by the land reform) and consequently remained powerful, the former landlords lost their positions at the pinnacle of the hamlet hierarchies and became members of a broader upper stratum defined as 'the farmers with the larger holdings'. In consequence they could no longer maintain their traditional superiority as stem families in stem-branch relations between households, nor could they claim the traditional prestige or continue the traditional roles of oyakata. Though there are still recognizable differences in the degree to which the old order has disappeared as between the more and the less developed regions, the marked differences of the pre-war period have disappeared. Now the vast majority of Japanese villages have much the same kind of loose stratification system as characterized those pre-war hamlets of the more developed regions which lacked any dominant resident landlord family.

The post-war increases in agricultural productivity and the growing impact of urban influences have furthered this trend by hastening the disintegration of communal work patterns and modifying the social customs of the villages. The community solidarity which supported the status system has weakened, thus furthering the pattern of disintegration caused by the collapse of the tenancy system.

The qualification should be added that the land reform did nothing to equalize discrepancies in the size of holdings. The differences between the wealthy farmers with large holdings and the poor farmers with small ones remain. Villages have not become egalitarian unstratified communities. Nevertheless, the differences which remain are no longer differences between distinct status groups. Former landlords and former tenants are now all owner-farmers and in that sense of the same status. Moreover, the tendency towards part-time farming has further altered the system. Farmers with only small holdings can now belong to the upper economic stratum if they have a lucrative side occupation. If the immediate post-reform change was from a status system based on land-ownership to an economic ranking based on size of operated holding, the subsequent increase in the numbers of part-time farmers and non-farming hamlet residents has further complicated the picture. Whereas farmers used to be rated by their 'family status', a compound of genealogy and the form and extent of their 'family property', nowadays what counts is the wealth and income which they currently command. And this represents a big change in the stratification system of the hamlet.

The Power Structure of the Hamlet

We have already described how the Tokugawa village was controlled by the holders of the 'three local offices', those of the headman (nanushi), kumi chiefs (kumigashira) and farmers' representatives (hyakushō-dai). The office of headman was usually hereditary in a wealthy family at the pinnacle of the hamlet hierarchy, or, if there was no outstandingly wealthy family, it might circulate among a number of influential families. The other offices would be filled by members of the next rank of farmers. These were collectively known as the 'senior farmers' of the village (osabyakushō) and, unless there was some drastic decline in their families' fortunes, membership in this group would be inherited. In other words the ruling stratum of the village was more or less fixed in terms of a small number of families. The rest of the village—the komae-byakushō with small holdings, the mizunomi with nothing better than tenancies—submitted to their hereditary rule, while at the same time their lives were circumscribed by the constraining bonds of the solidary community.[6]

The system continued under different names even after the beginning of the Meiji period. The former nanushi often became the new kochō in the system initially established after the Restoration. When, later on, the new local government system was

[6] For the government of the Tokugawa village see, e.g., Ono Takeo, Nihon sonraku-shi gaisetsu, 1936 (Iwanami Shoten), and Kodama Kōta, Kinsei nōmin seikatsu-shi, 1957 (Yoshikawa Kōbunkan).

finally promulgated it was generally a man from a family of the highest rank who became the hamlet's member of the new Village Council, and someone from the next rank of families who became head of the hamlet. The notion of a group of 'senior farmer' families which formed the hamlet council and filled the hamlet and village offices long survived the Tokugawa period. They were known in modern times as the *omodachi*—the 'prominent'—and they were usually oyakata of the other families in the hamlet.

We have seen in the previous section how the authority of this upper stratum was maintained through their positions as landlords, as oyakata and as stem families, through their paternalistic protection of the lower strata of the village, and through their effective control over the common property of the hamlet and the hamlet work organization—a control which was not much affected by the fact that decisions were formally taken at hamlet general meetings, for those who did not belong to the circle customarily observed a compliant silence on these occasions.

Despite considerable changes in this pattern after the creation of the new local government system, it would not have been difficult to find hamlets in the least developed parts of the country which still fitted this description right up to the end of the last war, hamlets where the group of families which made up the hamlet council was fairly rigidly fixed and gaps in their ranks left when families died out or lost their wealth could only be filled by others which had acquired ownership over at least a minimum area of land. Appointments to hamlet and village offices would be decided in such cases by consultation within the group, and the more important offices would be reserved by the group for themselves. The other members of the hamlet put up no resistance to their power, for to resist would be to be cut off from the life of the hamlet. If there was dissension and conflict within such hamlets it was factional conflict arising from a split within the ruling segment itself, for there was no room for conflict between the strata to develop.

However, hamlets in which the traditional patterns showed this degree of stability right up to the recent war made up a minority of the whole. In most hamlets there was a shift in the power structure during the first quarter of this century. This was particularly marked in those villages where the upper landlord families lost their fortune in the sharp economic fluctuations of the first half of the Meiji period. Even where this was not the case the gradual extension of the suffrage removed the formal mark of the hereditary oligarchy's separateness—there was no longer a distinction to be drawn between those who were first-class citizens of the nation and those who were mere residents of the hamlet. The process might begin, for instance, with the demand that the lesser farmers should be represented on the hamlet Council, and a kind of 'people's tribune' might be formally included as their representative. In hamlets where Farmers' Unions were formed and the first stirrings of class tension and conflict were heard, the tenancy disputes over rents and security of tenure might be paralleled by a movement to democratize the government of the hamlet. As a final step the whole system of a Council of hereditary 'prominent men' might be abandoned in favour of an elected body on which the old upper stratum families no longer had a monopoly but were also joined or replaced by members of the middle groups.[7]

The change in the power structure of the hamlet reflected on the one hand the withdrawal from agriculture of the landlords and the growing economic strength of the owner-farmers and part-tenants which resulted from the development of a capitalist economy. On the other, it was also a reflection of the fact that by the turn of the century the upper strata of villagers no longer had a monopoly of literacy. With the spread of school education even a middle-ranking farmer of ability was perfectly equipped to manage the hamlet's affairs. Nor should one overlook the fact that hamlet residents all became citizens with equal rights in a legal sense. After the enactment of universal manhood suffrage in 1925 it ceased to be possible in a good many hamlets for a small privileged group to maintain its hereditary monopoly over official positions.

[7] On the relation between hamlet government, tenancy disputes and the development of Farmers' Unions see the essay on this subject in my *Nihon sonraku no shakai-kōzō*, 1959 (Tōkyō-daigaku Shuppankai). See also Teruoka Shūzō, *Jinushi-sei to kome-sōdō*, 1958 (Tōkyō-daigaku Shuppankai) and Takahashi Iichiro and Shirakawa Kiyoshi, *Nōchi-kaikaku to jinushi-sei*, 1955 (Ochanomizu Shobō).

For all that, the upper stratum still maintained its predominance. Since these offices were usually honorary or at most carried only a small expense allowance, they were beyond the means of the poorer tenants or part-owners. Even though many of the bigger landlords ceased to farm, or left the villages entirely, the smaller farming landlords, the richer owner-farmers and the managing agents of the larger landlords retained their authority—by virtue of their greater wealth, of their positions at the top of the traditional status hierarchies, and through their ability to manipulate the community solidarity of the hamlet. Their position was reinforced by the fact that in absolute terms they contributed larger amounts in hamlet dues—though relative to their incomes their burden in this regard might be lighter than it was for the poorer residents. One might say that a man's voice in hamlet affairs continued to be proportionate to his contribution to hamlet finances, and that it was simply the narrowing of the contribution gap between the upper and the middle strata which brought hamlet offices within the reach of the latter.

The land reform changed this situation, however. As we have already seen, it created a new and broader top stratum which contained not only landlords brought down from their commanding heights by the ending of tenancy relations and the declining importance of all kinds of patron-client ties, but also of owner-farmers and ex-tenants with large holdings. The status hierarchy was weakened, not least by the formation at the time of the land reform of Farmers' Unions which stood in declared opposition to the landlords. In a good many hamlets, it is true, the traditional slogans of hamlet unity and hamlet harmony did succeed in muting the class-conscious activities of the Farmers' Unions. Movements which sought to create a sense of class solidarity stretching beyond the confines of the hamlet were denounced as destructive of hamlet harmony— hence the failure of the Farmers' Union movement to acquire a real class character and hence also its loss of direction and rapid decline after the land reform was completed. However, the very existence of the movement is proof that there was some stirring of resistance against the traditional status order, and the movement itself can share—along with the actual destruction of the landlords' power by the land reform itself—the credit for delivering a powerful blow to the traditional status system.[8]

As a result the hamlet community, once so effective in smothering the development of class divisions, could no longer be so easily mobilized under the leadership of its upper stratum. At hamlet general meetings the poorer villagers too began to make demands and proposals reflecting their own particular interests. The post of hamlet chief became something to be avoided, and there was an increasing tendency for the post of kumi chief to be filled on a turn-and-turn-about regular roster. Even in the least developed districts there was no longer a group of hereditary hamlet councillors. Since the traditional authority no longer attached to those who occupied hamlet offices, they no longer could command the implicit obedience of hamlet residents. Hence it was not unnatural that even those in the upper stratum often came to consider involvement in hamlet affairs primarily as a waste of valuable time.

Nevertheless, it inevitably happens that it is the stratum of richer farmers who have to take these offices; a group of men, all much of a muchness in terms of their wealth and standing, who take these posts in turn. The payment attaching to these posts—usually a small allowance paid partly from hamlet funds and partly from the village office —is usually slight. Even for a job as onerous as that of hamlet chief it is little more than enough to keep him in cigarettes. This is now, in fact, the basis of his authority; the very fact that he has to make considerable personal sacrifices for very small reward restrains the villagers' criticism. The other source of his authority is the fact that he acts as the liaison man with the village authorities and with other organizations which transcend the hamlet. Nowadays, the hamlet chief is less the chief of the hamlet as a community than of the hamlet as a sub-unit of the administrative system. His work in this respect has come to make even greater demands

---

[8] On the Farmers' Union movement and its relation to hamlet structure, see the essay on hamlet 'harmony' in my *Nihon sonraku no shakai-kōzō*, 1959 (Tōkyō-daigaku Shuppankai). And see also Furushima Toshio, Matoba Tokuzō and Teruoka Shūzō, *Nōmin-kumiai to nōchi-kaikaku*, 1956 (Tōkyō-daigaku Shuppankai).

on his time since the amalgamations of local government units. Hence a farmer who is fairly well-to-do and has a good number of supporting workers in his family is preferred for the job. The kind of man who has real power and the ability to dominate the hamlet is much more likely to become the village or town councillor, or a Director of the Agricultural Co-operative. At any rate, the position of hamlet chief has lost its prestige; in some cases it has become a messenger-boy job that everyone has to take his turn at, and in few hamlets does anyone occupy the post for many years running. It has now become a job suitable for an old man who has practically handed his farm on to his son, and needs something to keep him from being bored with his retirement.

By contrast, younger men, who are in full control of their holdings and keenly interested in farming them better, are the ones who take on the job of chief of the Agricultural Practice Union. Other offices, too, reflecting the separation between the hamlet community and functional associations, and reflecting also a general trend to avoid letting any one man have too many jobs, are likely to be widely distributed. Power ceases to be concentrated; there is no centre of authority formed around the office of hamlet chief from which the activities of a united hamlet can be directed. In hamlets now more differentiated into farmers and part-time farmers, the holders of official positions now exercise leadership only within their circumscribed sphere. They may still be drawn predominantly from the upper strata, but they do not exercise anything like the same authoritarian dominance of the pre-war leaders. In this sense the hamlet has become less capable of unified action.

But the upper strata still manage to maintain control over the hamlet for in most hamlets there is still no complete separation between the hamlet community as such and the functional associations it contains. As long as the two remain undifferentiated, these associations will not become the unadulterated special-purpose bodies they are supposed to be. Nor will it be easy to develop democratic patterns of leadership through elections designed to fit the man to his function.

FURTHER READING

On the structure of hamlets and of groupings within them, further information will be found in:

Beardsley, Hall and Ward, *Village Japan.*

Cornell, *Matsunagi.*

Dore, *Land reform.*

Embree, *Suyemura.*

Grad, *Land and peasant.*

Raper, *Japanese village.*

Smith, *Kurusu.*

R. J. B. Braibanti, 'Neighborhood associations in Japan and their democratic potentialities', *Far Eastern Quarterly*, 7, 1948.

R. P. Dore, 'The day the fire brigade went fishing', *Japan Quarterly*, July 1956.

I. Ishino and J. W. Bennett, *Types of Japanese rural community*, Ohio State University, Research Foundation, Columbus, Ohio, 1953 (*mimeo*).

E. Johnson, 'Perseverance through orderly change: the traditional *buraku* in a modern community', *Human Organization*, 22, 1963–4.

E. Norbeck, 'Common interest associations in rural Japan', in Smith and Beardsley, *Japanese culture.*

M. Titiev, 'Changing patterns of kumiai structure in rural Okayama', University of Michigan, Center for Japanese Studies, *Occasional Papers*, 4, 1953.

R. J. Smith, 'Co-operative forms in a Japanese agricultural community', in University of Michigan, Center for Japanese Studies, *Occasional Papers*, 3, 1952.

R. J. Smith, 'Community relations with the outside world: the case of a Japanese agricultural community', *American Anthropologist*, 59, 1957.

R. J. Smith, 'The Japanese rural community: norms, sanctions and ostracism', *American Anthropologist*, 63, ii, pt. 1, 1961.

T. Ushiomi, 'La communité rurale au Japon' (trans. by P. Anouilh), *Bulletin de la Maison Franco-Japonaise*, n.s. 7, ii-iii, 1962.

PART FOUR

THE POLITICAL STRUCTURE OF JAPANESE VILLAGES

CHAPTER X

THE DEVELOPMENT OF LOCAL GOVERNMENT IN THE VILLAGES

The Organization of Village Local Government

WE have many times mentioned the fact that the modern formal system of local government in Japanese villages dates from 1888. Over the two succeeding years the old independent units which had existed since the Tokugawa period were combined to make new local government units called towns or villages.

The beginnings of this system can be traced to the early Meiji period. In 1871 when the Government passed the Family Registration Law it also appointed officials whose main task was to see that the registers were kept up to date. Thus in 1872 the whole country was divided into districts and sub-districts. Each district had a district chief and a vice-chief who were appointed by the government, and each sub-district also had an officially appointed chief known as the *kochō*. Each of the towns and villages within a sub-district had a deputy *kochō* who was to be elected by all property-owners. At this time there were about 80,000 towns and villages.[1]

Then followed the so-called 'Three New Laws' of 1878—the law for the Formation of Towns, Villages and Districts, the Regulations for Prefectural Assemblies and the Regulations concerning Local Government Taxation. Henceforth *kochō*

---

[1] See, for instance, Ono Takeo, *Nihon sonraku-shi gaisetsu*, 1936 (Iwanami Shoten), p. 331 ff., and Kikegawa Hiroshi, *Meiji chihō-jichi-seido no seiritsu katei*, 1955 (Tōkyō Shisei Chōsakai), p. 24. According to the former there were 620 towns and 79,600 villages.

were to be appointed in every town or village and were to take over, not only the traditional local government functions continued from the Tokugawa period, but also certain administrative functions which they were to perform as the local agents of the central government. Henceforth the villages had to bear the cost of an increasing involvement in government administration which for local units then containing on an average only 100 households was no easy matter.

Education in particular did not lend itself to management in units of this scale. As the old reading and writing schools, which in the Tokugawa period had usually taught only the children of the upper strata of the villages, gave way to the new elementary schools designed to provide compulsory education for all, it was beyond the capacity of most hamlets to establish and maintain such schools independently. So it become common practice for a group of hamlets to combine in the building of a school. In many other fields besides education it was impossible for units the size of these old villages to reach the level of administrative efficiency which the central government required. As a consequence the first attempt at amalgamation came in 1884 when village offices were established in a ratio of approximately 1 for every 5 former villages, or every 500 households, and an officially appointed *kochō* was put in charge of each office. However there were often difficulties and misunderstandings between the new offices and the old village units, and it soon became the general view that a new system of local government was required.

Moreover the demand for greater local self-government had not disappeared, even though the People's Rights Movement which developed throughout the country in the early days of the Meiji period had by this time been reduced by government repression to a rather low ebb of activity. The Government's concern was to establish a bureaucratic system of control. Plans were already laid for the enactment of a constitution and the establishment of a parliamentary assembly, but the Government wished first to impose from above an officially designed system of local self-government so that by at least formally granting local autonomy it could choke off the development of a democratic movement from below. It sought also, by putting local government bodies under the direction of the central government, to turn them into instruments for the day-to-day administration of central government business which should be substantially under bureaucratic control. But in order for the central government to be able to hand over even more administrative functions it was necessary to amalgamate the existing towns and villages and thus by strengthening the revenue base of each unit, improve its power to maintain an adequate administrative staff.

Consequently the establishment of the new local government system was accompanied by the amalgamation of village units. A gradual process of *ad hoc* amalgamation up to this point had already reduced the number of local government units to about 71,000, but now this number was further reduced by about 80 per cent. Henceforth Japan was divided into 39 cities and 15,859 towns and villages. These amalgamations, it is unnecessary to add, were carried through by the political authority of the central government not as a result of any local expression of popular desire. Moreover, the Government, in establishing this new system, was not recognizing the right of residents democratically to control their own affairs; it was imposing a system which it was the duty of the people to operate.[2]

Thus the new local government units were formed, but not all their residents had the same rights. Residents were divided into those who were fully-fledged citizens (*kōmin*) and those who were not. *Kōmin* were defined as males over the age of twenty-five who had resided in the area for two years or more and who paid a land tax or some other direct national tax of more than two *yen* per annum. Voting rights were confined to *kōmin* as thus defined, and at the time the electorate amounted only to about 10 per cent. of the population.

Moreover, there were even distinctions between different grades of *kōmin;* for village government purposes there were two classes distinguished according to the amount of tax they paid. The system worked to give the wealthier first class considerably greater voting rights than the second. It meant that in effect a

---

[2] For the history of these amalgamations, see Shima Yasuhiko, Miyamoto Ken'ichi, and Watanabe Keiji, *Chōson-gappei to nōson no hembō*, 1958 (Yūhikaku).

member of the first class could become a councillor with a very small number of votes.

Members of the Council held office for six years, half of them being re-elected every three years. They elected a Mayor and Vice-Mayor for four-year terms from among the *kōmin* of the village and the effective administration of the village was in their hands. The Mayor was also at the same time to be the chairman of the Council. Thus the villages acquired at least the form of a modern system of local self government, with the residents delegating their powers to a Mayor and Council.

The substance, however, was somewhat different. Both the Council and the Mayor were placed firmly under the supervision and control of higher officials. The Council could be dissolved by the Minister of Home Affairs, and the Prefectural Governor (an appointee of the Home Ministry) could employ a variety of sanctions against all village officials from the Mayor downwards, including dismissal from office. In these circumstances it is not surprising that the village office was less an office of the village than an outpost of the central government by which it exercised control through the prefectural government.

The system of local government which thus began in 1888 quite naturally, with its limited suffrage and system of differentiated electoral classes, came under the dominance of the local notables, that is to say the landlords, while remaining effectively under official supervision. And thus it continued for many years; it was not until after the defeat at the end of the Second World War that the system underwent any fundamental change.

There were, certainly, revisions of the system in 1911, and 1921 and 1926, but its essential character was not altered. In 1911 the term of office for village Councils was changed to four years, every member being elected at the same time. There was also a strengthening of the powers of the Mayor and simultaneously of the power of central government control. With the wave of so-called 'Taishō democracy' in the second and third decades of this century, however—a period towards the end of which Farmers' Unions were formed in the villages—the trend was in the other direction. In 1921 the qualifications for the status of *kōmin* were reduced to simple payment of village taxes. Thus the electorate was enlarged and the system of electoral classes was abolished. In the 1926 revision, as a logical consequence of the establishment of universal suffrage in national elections, all tax qualifications for the local government suffrage were removed. These changes may be seen as reflecting a decline in the power of the parasitic landlords in the villages. They may also be seen as an attempt to prevent the development of acute class conflict. In any case, however, these revisions did not imply any fundamental change in the character of the local government system. Particularly in the late thirties, as the country was increasingly mobilized for war, there was a further reinforcement of central government control, and during the last war local *self*-government was reduced to a mere formal framework.[3]

After the war there were great changes in local government and the institutions have taken on a fundamentally different character. The new Constitution contains a chapter on local government (something completely lacking in the old constitution) which guarantees the right of local self-rule. The Local Government Law which was based on this chapter is quite different from the old.

Firstly, all adult residents of more than three months' standing who are aged twenty or more, of either sex, have the right to vote, and all aged twenty-five or more, are eligible for election.

Secondly, the Council elects its own chairman, and the Mayor (who was formerly *ex-officio* chairman) is now to be elected directly by the villagers.

Thirdly, a fixed quorum of electors can at any time demand by signed petition the establishment or revocation of by-laws, the audit of any particular accounts, the dissolution of the Council, or the dismissal of the Mayor or of councillors. There has thus been a remarkable increase in the powers of residents.

Fourthly, as far as the formal institutions go, national control over the Mayor and Council has almost disappeared, and there are no powers comparable to the former ability of the Minister

[3] For an outline of the institutional changes in local government, see Kikegawa Hiroshi, *Chihō-seido shōshi*, 1962 (Keisō Shobō), Fujita Takeo, ed., *Chihō-jichi no rekishi* (*Kōza chihō jichitai*, Vol. I), 1961 (San'ichi Shobō). On the relationships between village structure and the changes in the system see the seventh annual volume of the Sonraku-shakai Kenkyūkai, *Seiji-taisei to sonraku*, 1960 (Jichōsha).

of Home Affairs or the prefectural government to dissolve the Council or dismiss a Mayor. In other respects too the constraining power of the central government is weakened and the right of local government units to *self*-government is given clear legal specification.

However, these institutional reforms were part of the democratization policy of the occupation army, not something achieved by the spontaneous efforts of the people themselves. Consequently, the situation changed somewhat with the subsequent change in occupation policy. Also, as we shall describe in the next section, in the matter of the financial powers which must support local government, the autonomy of local government units has been seriously compromised by their dependence on central government funds, despite the absence of formal institutional central government control.

Thus, for instance, the system of local police forces which was created after the war, and also the decentralized educational system based on elected local education committees, did not last long. Most towns and villages were operating on a deficit and were forced to depend on the central government in order to function. Thus the local government system was forced into a position where revision became necessary, a revision which revealed the weakness of a system which was not created by popular efforts to cater for felt popular needs but, like the original local government system of the nineteenth century, was imposed from above. The revision was carried through less as a means of improving the local government system itself, than as a means of rationalizing the national system of administration.

The main feature of the revision was the amalgamation of local government units which followed the Law for the Promotion of Amalgamations of Towns and Villages of 1953. The purpose of these amalgamations was to strengthen the revenue basis of local governments, and by economizing on overhead expenditure increase their capacity for capital investments. Officials, drawn from a wider area, would be of a higher calibre, while the rationalization of the personnel organization would improve administrative efficiency; amalgamation would contribute to the welfare of the residents and make it possible to provide a more complete range of public facilities: such were the slogans of the amalgamation movement and such was its promise. However, just as the amalgamations in 1888 had their origin in the central government's desire to strengthen the financial foundations of local government units and improve their administrative efficiency, so, in the most recent phase too, the real starting point was the demand of the central government for more efficient execution of national policy while escaping the need to cover deficits in local government finance. It is little exaggeration to say that 'improvement of popular welfare' was little more than a decorative slogan. The amalgamations were, in effect, a way of resolving the difficulties of government finance at the expense of local government units, by creating 'local government on the cheap'.[4]

These amalgamations were, moreover, if not with the same speed as after 1888, carried through quite rapidly under the authoritarian direction of the state and prefectural governments. The fact that this process which should have been carried through democratically and by the spontaneous wishes of the inhabitants and with full regard to the long-term future of local government could be rushed through in this way is an indication of the fact that local self-government is still not *popular* self-government and that the spirit of self-rule is still relatively underdeveloped.

At any rate, as a result of these amalgamations local government is at present carried on in far larger units than hitherto. Although the population size set as a standard for the new units was 8,000, in fact many are even larger. During the period from October 1953 to September 1956, which was that set in principle for the operation of the amalgamation law, the number of local government units fell by more than 6,000. In the process there sometimes arose disputes and conflicts between towns and villages which led to opposition to particular amalgamation proposals of the prefectural authorities, but there was hardly any movement of opposition to the amalgamation policy itself, and in the short space of three years, there emerged a system of

---

[4] See the final chapter, on the amalgamations and local government, in Hoshino Mitsuo, *Nihon no chihō-jichi: Jūmin-jichi to hoshu-kakushin no taiketsu*, 1958 (Tōyō-keizai Shimpōsha).

local government units much larger than the existing ones. Especially notable is the fact that, as shown by Table xx, there has been a marked decrease in the number of villages and a sharp increase in the number of cities. This means that many of the new cities contain large rural areas. Hitherto it has been possible to discuss rural local government almost exclusively in terms of town and village government, but now city administrations are also deeply involved. The political structure of rural areas has also changed since these amalgamations. The significance of these changes will be discussed in the subsequent sections.

TABLE XX

Trends in Numbers of Cities, Towns and Villages: 1930–60

Year	Cities	Towns	Villages	Total
1930	99	1,528	10,292	11,919
1940	125	1,706	9,614	11,445
1950	235	1,862	8,346	10,443
1953	286	1,976	7,606	9,868
1957	501	1,920	1,365	3,786
1960	555	1,930	1,023	3,508

The Present State of Local Government Finance in the Villages

The new towns and villages of the early Meiji period were required by the state to perform more administrative functions than were the villages of the Tokugawa period. Even in the Tokugawa period village headmen had been required by the feudal authorities to maintain a variety of administrative records, but their range was vastly extended by the policy needs of the new government when it set out, after the Meiji Restoration, to acquire at least the essentials of a modern nation state. In addition, as we have already seen, the cost involved in establishing a new educational system also imposed a heavy burden on local governments.[5]

These burdens became even heavier after the establishment of the new local government system. The increased village office expenditure and educational expenditure was, needless to say, necessary for the state authorities as part of their endeavour to build a modern capitalist state, but the local govern-

[5] See Shima, *et al.*, *Chōson-gappei to nōson no hembō*, 1958 (Yūhikaku).

ment units created by the new system were not given sufficient resources to play their part. In principle local government was to be chiefly financed by income from publicly owned property and by fees and charges for registrations and other services, while as an auxiliary income source, towns and villages were allowed to collect a supplementary levy which represented a fixed proportion of national and prefectural direct taxes. They were much discouraged from levying any independent taxes, which were to be used only as an exceptional source of revenue. In effect the 1888 system created new local government units without new sources of revenue, and since in the majority of cases, the property of the hamlets—the old village units—was not transferred to the new towns and villages, what was supposed to be their main revenue source turned out to be of only nominal importance—on an average providing only about 3 per cent. of annual revenue in the early days of the system. Financially the new local governments were very badly off indeed.

What is more, under the new system villages were not permitted to refuse to foot the bill for work required of them by superior echelons of authority. This was known as the 'compulsory budget system'. Hence these delegated administrative duties became the first charge on the impoverished budgets of the new villages and they were necessarily forced to hold down expenditure on the business of local government proper. As Table xxi shows, after they had met their commitments for maintaining the village office and for education they had very little leeway for anything else. Public works also claimed a fair share of expenditure, but the emphasis here was on the need for roads and bridges to accomplish the transition from a subsistence economy of isolated units to a national capitalist market economy. Local governments found it difficult to cover expenditure on agricultural roads and irrigation systems which were directly necessary for agricultural production. Such funds as they could provide were usually insufficient, and it was necessary to rely on the monetary contributions and unpaid labour of those residents directly affected.[6]

[6] See Shibata Tokue and Miyamoto Ken'ichi, *Chihō zaisei*, 1963 (Yūhikaku). Table xxi is derived from the appendix tables of this book.

TABLE XXI

Trends in Financial Structure of Towns and Villages:
Percentage Composition of Income and Expenditure: 1882–1945

Income	Year	1881	1891	1906	1921	1930	1945
Local surtax on national taxes		91.5	63.3	61.4	62.2	20.3	15.5
Independent taxes		—	1.8	1.3	1.1	22.5	5.5
Grants and subsidies from central government		—	11.5	5.3	7.1	18.2	40.9
Local government bonds		—	1.4	6.6	3.4	10.2	1.5
Other sources		8.5	22.0	25.4	26.2	28.8	36.6
Total		100.0	100.0	100.0	100.0	100.0	100.0

Expenditure							
Salaries and administrative expenses		17.1	35.6	29.0	27.9	18.5	32.0
Education		35.3	32.7	40.6	44.4	42.6	13.0
Public works		34.2	26.3	8.7	8.8	8.0	10.9
Industry and commerce		0.6	0.5	1.4	1.6	1.8	10.6
Social security		—	—	—	—	2.6	—
Servicing of debts		—	1.0	5.8	1.8	7.0	5.0
Other expenditures		12.8	3.9	14.5	15.5	19.5	28.5
Total		100.0	100.0	100.0	100.0	100.0	100.0

These financial arrangements were therefore an additional reason why the new local government system did not create units capable of dealing with local affairs and carrying through the local projects which were within its proper sphere. This was one of the factors which left the old village units—the hamlets—with an important role to play. If there were insufficient village funds for public works, the upkeep of farm roads and irrigation systems which was formerly organized by the old villages continued to be in charge of the hamlets. Even further, since the new towns and villages were so poorly endowed, they were forced to use the hamlets—as administrative sub-districts—for the convenient performance of their basic administrative functions.

This system became even further entrenched as Japanese capitalism became established and the framework of a modern state came to require an even more extensive degree of administrative control. In a Japan whose growth depended on her increasing military strength sufficient funds could not be spared for internal administration, and it became the established practice to delegate more and more administrative functions to the towns and villages in exchange for a small subsidy. As an inevitable result of this policy of administration by subsidy, the autonomy of local government units was further reduced and their dependence on the state and the prefectural authorities increased.

This system of state subsidies made advances in all fields after the world depression which began in 1929. The government tried to tackle the problem of rural poverty by starting public works projects and by organizing its rural rehabilitation movement. But these measures were insufficient to rescue the villages from their economic depression and a further increase in the volume of state subsidy became necessary. Later with the development of industry linked to the armament programme the degree of regional economic imbalance was intensified and the government found it necessary to establish a system of local government equalization grants to assist those local governments which were in the financially weakest condition. Inevitably this further increased the degree of centralization of public finance.[7]

This tendency was carried even further during the war. The hamlets which, ever since the rural rehabilitation movement started, had been emphasized as the basic units for 'rural self-help' programmes, were incorporated (along with the city wards) into the formal administrative system. They became means for the prosecution of national policy, and as such were placed under the supervision and control of town and village Mayors. Local *self*-government was repressively restricted and state authority penetrated into the remotest corners of the villages.

Thus until the end of the war there was very little real self-government in the local government system. Subordinated as they were to the central administration and forced to give first priority to their delegated duties, it was as much as the towns and villages could do to keep the schools going. Matters which were really of local concern could only have devoted to them

[7] On the subsidy system, see Ouchi Tsutomu, *Nihon nōgyō no zaiseigaku*, 1950 (Tōkyō-daigaku Shuppankai).

such funds as were left over, and in these matters too a good deal of reliance was placed on the hamlet organizations—another factor which tended to preclude any positive policies, since, apart from anything else, rivalry and clashes of interest between hamlets acted as an inhibiting factor. But more of this later.

We have seen how the whole local government system was given a new look after the war. However, the financial system which provided the basis for operating the new local government structure was not immediately changed to correspond with that structure. The institutions of local government finance were not basically reformed until 1950, three years after the promulgation of the Local Government Law. Thereafter local governments were allowed to collect a resident's tax and a tax on immovable property. Compared with the previous system this change enhanced the financial independence of local governments. In the poorer areas, however, these new taxes were not sufficient to cover local government expenses. Faced with the extension of the compulsory education period and the need to build new middle schools many local governments would have found themselves bankrupt but for equalization grants or treasury subsidies paid from the national budget. Equalization grants were paid to those local governments whose income was less than a national standard, but the amount granted was always much less than the amount requested. The funds available for subsidies were also small so that the local government's counterpart contribution to subsidized projects tended to represent a heavy burden. Nevertheless the fact that they were forced to rely on state financial assistance meant that despite their structural independence, local government units were very much restricted in their freedom by the authority of the central government.

The amalgamation of local government units was promoted by the government as a means of reducing grants and subsidies or at least of utilizing them more efficiently. Despite the effect of these amalgamations in increasing the volume of local government revenues they have not always led to an improvement in their financial health. In some cases over-ambitious development plans which were worked out in the amalgamation negotiations have meant that the financial situation of these local governments, far from improving, has in fact become worse.[8]

The amalgamations began at a time when local government finances were reaching a high level of indebtedess, and in 1954 the Government replaced the system of equalization grants by an equalization tax rebate and set a maximum limit to the total amount. It also sought to reduce the range of local governments' activities and to strengthen their taxing powers as a means of curing their indebtedness. The result was a further limitation of local government independence. At present local governments mobilize about two-thirds of their revenues from their own resources and depend on the national treasury for the remaining third. This does not mean that two-thirds of their budget is under their own independent control, however, since they have to commit a good deal of their own funds as counterpart contributions in order to receive the additional grants from the state. Local governments have still not escaped from their subordination to a large measure of state control.[9]

A further measure of central government limitation over local government finance has resulted in the recent years of rapid economic growth from the emphasis of national financial policies on strengthening the industrial base. Local governments too have responded by adjusting their policies to conform to the government's objective. Measures designed to bring security to the people's livelihood and to increase public welfare have been forced to take second place. As a means of curing indebtedness the attraction of industry to their district seems to be considered a universal panacea, and 'regional development planning' is now the fashionable slogan. The trend affects even towns and villages, but it is even more important for the rural areas which have recently been incorporated into the new city administrations.

In addition to these tendencies towards greater central

[8] For an example of local government finance after amalgamation, see Fukutake Tadashi, ed., *Gappei-chōson no jittai*, 1957 (Tōkyō-daigaku Shuppankai). For examples dating from before the amalgamations, see Uno Kōzō, ed., *Nihon nōson-keizai no jittai*, 1961 (Tōkyō-daigaku Shuppankai).

[9] For these points, see the chapter on central control and local government finance in Fujita Takeo, *Gendai chihō-zaisei nyūmon*, 1962 (Nihon Hyōron-shinasha).

government control, we should not overlook the tendency towards greater centralization of power within the local governments themselves as a result of the amalgamations. With the extension of the area covered by each administration, there has been a renewed tendency for the local government to make greater use of hamlet organizations. There is a tendency also for the urban centres of the new local government units to dominate the whole and for their development to be promoted at the expense of the rural fringes, something which is particularly marked in the case of the largest units, the new cities. In the new bigger units the rural areas have moved even further from self-government—another sense in which one can no longer discuss rural politics in purely rural terms. This is one of the central problems of the political structure of villages today.

CHAPTER XI

THE AUTHORITY STRUCTURE OF THE VILLAGES

Village Government and the Hamlet

WE have seen in the last chapter how the subordination of local governments to the purposes of state policy meant that most of the real business of local government remained the function of the hamlet units, and that, even further, in the prosecution of the tasks imposed on them by state policy, local governments were forced to rely on the hamlets for a good deal of the detailed administrative work.

Nevertheless, after the first creation of the local government system in 1888 the official status of the hamlet was limited to its recognition as a sub-district for administrative convenience, and as far as the intentions of the government were concerned, the policy was to weld the old independent hamlet-sized villages into new and fully-integrated units. The original intention to rely largely on town or village property as the main source of revenue for the new local government units presupposed that the common property of the old villages would be taken over by the new. In practice, however, this rarely happened, in most cases the common lands and forests remained the property of the hamlets. This was one factor contributing to factionalism between hamlets. In 1910 the government again tried to consolidate hamlet property and put it in the hands of local governments, but this policy met with strong resistance and in most cases, even if the property was nominally transferred to the village, in effect the traditional patterns of use and control by members of the hamlet remained substantially intact. In some cases hamlet property was transformed into the joint possession of a group of named individuals—the current residents of the hamlet—the group being given no territorial definition, or the opportunity was taken to divide the common hamlet lands among the villagers for individual ownership. The Government also encouraged the unification of the hamlet shrines which were symbols of the hamlet's identity. All the hamlet gods were to be transferred to a new village shrine—a symbol of the village's unity—and worshipped jointly. This policy did not have very much success either; the hamlet clung tenaciously to its identity.

The Government having thus failed in its attempts to obliterate the hamlet by *force majeure*, policy later swung in quite the opposite direction—towards strengthening and utilizing the hamlet's cohesion. We have already seen how, despite a tendency for the weakening of hamlet solidarity as the power of the landlords declined, after the upheaval of the twenties and especially with the beginning of the rural rehabilitation movement after the Great Depression, the attempt was made to strengthen community activities in the hamlet—a policy which was carried to the point of giving institutional recognition to hamlet associations after the war had started, especially for the purpose of ensuring food deliveries as a part of the programme of total national mobilization.[1]

Thus the relationship of the hamlets to the towns and villages as affected by central government authority underwent several metamorphoses, but the hamlet remained consistently an identifiable unit within local government areas and, because of the weakness of local governments, retained its cohesion. For this reason town and village politics rarely became anything more than a mechanism for adjusting conflicts of interest between different hamlets. In such circumstances it was too much to expect that local government finances could be used for positive policies designed to promote the interest of the village as a whole, over-riding the divisive boundaries between hamlets.

[1] For these institutional developments, see Ari Bakuji, 'Chihō-seido: Burakukai chōnaikai-seido', in Ukai Nobushige, *et al.*, ed., *Kōza Nihon kindai-hō hattatsu-shi*, Vol. VI, 1959 (Keisō Shobō).

Consequently, each hamlet was concerned, in village politics, to promote its own interest. It was difficult to divide the meagre sums available for public works and agricultural development between the hamlets in any rational planned way or to establish priorities between projects to be started in successive years. The tendency was for funds to be divided widely and thinly so that everyone had something, and in the share-out the strength of each hamlet, as represented by its members in the village or town Council, was a strong determining factor. These representatives were also expected to ensure that their own hamlet was let off lightly when quotas were allocated for the household tax which provided an increasingly important source of local government revenue. Until 1911 when the regulations for local government household taxes were promulgated, the criteria for these taxes were ambiguous, and very often they were based on a general estimate of a household's financial standing. Since a variety of factors had to be taken into account—income, property, size of family and so on—the hamlet's representatives in the Council had to be well acquainted with conditions in their hamlet as well as strong promoters of their hamlet's interest.

In consequence, each hamlet sought to elect as many members to represent its interests in the Council as the votes available to it made possible. So a hamlet might divide itself into two sections and allocate all the votes of each section to a single candidate. Alternatively, a small hamlet which did not have enough votes to ensure the election of its own candidate might reach an agreement with a neighbouring hamlet to combine votes and elect a representative drawn alternately from each hamlet. This was considered a normal procedure and hamlets which could not in this way control their own votes but sometimes let votes leak away to the candidates of other hamlets were spoken of scornfully as 'open grassland'. If there was a powerful landlord in the hamlet then, of course, he would be the natural person to be chosen for the hamlet's representative, but if there was no such obvious leader, then a unified candidate would be agreed. As, in more recent decades, the number of men with the ambition to become village councillors increased, it became a common practice to conduct a kind of primary election in order to decide on a single candidate. Every effort was made to ensure that those elected should represent their hamlet. If such agreement could not be reached, rival candidates might try to gain votes in other hamlets, counting on the votes of relatives, of tenants or of their employees or of people with whom they had business connexions, but still the majority of their votes would come from their own hamlet. Even when there were disputes between landlords and tenants which led to the formation of Farmers' Unions, and the appearance of a clear rift within the hamlet, still the votes of the rival candidates came mainly from within their own hamlets. The function of the councillor to represent the interests of his hamlet remained a consistent feature of the system.[2]

This function of representing the interests of their own hamlet was not confined to members of the local government Council. The town or village was also the unit for many other bodies whose officials also took on the character of hamlet representatives. This was so, for instance, in the case of the Producers' Co-operatives which were formed under the Producers' Co-operatives Law of 1900, with the early Farmers' Associations which were largely landlords' associations, and also in the Agricultural Associations which were formed as an amalgamation of the two during the war. Not all these associations were formed like the Co-operatives on a national scale in one single drive, but most of them shared the same characteristic of being officially designed and established in accordance with specifications imposed from above. They consequently never became independent voluntary associations capable of action promoted by movement from below, and their officials were normally elected on a hamlet basis in the same way as members of the village Councils. They also had subordinate organizations at the hamlet level and were similarly, in structure, more or less federations of hamlets.

This situation did not change after the war. Despite the 1947 ban on the official use of hamlet organizations and despite the improvement of local government finances it was still impossible to do without the self-governing functions of the hamlet and it

[2] For an example, see the chapter by Ishida Takeshi in Isoda Susumu, ed., *Sonraku-kōzō no kenkyū*, 1955 (Tōkyō-daigaku Shuppankai).

VILLAGE OFFICE AND A FIRE-BRIGADE STOREHOUSE

THE GENERAL STORE OF AN AGRICULTURAL
CO-OPERATIVE

PRIMARY SCHOOL

MIDDLE (JUNIOR HIGH) SCHOOL

was still necessary for the hamlets to protect their own interests
vis-à-vis the administration of the village. Consequently, the
basis of representation of members of the village Council did not
change. Although it was no longer the landlords who controlled
village politics, councillors continued to be elected by their
hamlets as their hamlets' representatives—and this even in those
districts where during the land reform a strong Farmers' Union
had developed and clearly set itself in opposition to the conservative forces dominated by the landlords. It was true, of course,
that the hamlets were less cohesive than before the war and that
community controls were weaker, so that it became rare for the
system of hamlet sponsorship to work so well that the number
of candidates exactly equalled the number of seats available and
voting became unnecessary. Nor was it any longer true that as
soon as a hamlet's candidate was decided the votes of the hamlet would automatically accrue to him without any further
effort. It became more necessary deliberately to mobilize votes
and prevent them from leaking away to candidates from outside the hamlet.[3]

The recent amalgamations, however, have changed the
situation somewhat. Formerly the relation between the number
of hamlets and the size of the village Council was such that most
hamlets could count on getting at least one candidate elected,
but in the new local government units there is generally only
one seat available for several hamlets. Even under the old
system, as mentioned above, small hamlets sometimes had to
combine to elect a member alternately, but in the new system
it has become infinitely more difficult for several hamlets to
combine in controlling the distribution of their votes. Thus the
conditions have been created for a change in the representative
character of members of local government Councils—from
being representatives of territorially defined local interests to
being representatives of occupational groups. Under the old
system it was very difficult for leaders of village Youth Groups

[3] For an example of a case where even candidates sponsored by a Farmers' Union which tried to organize united opposition to the landlords
still gathered their votes chiefly from their own hamlets, see the chapter on
hamlet harmony and class tension in my *Nihon sonraku no shakai-kōzō*, 1959
(Tōkyō-daigaku Shuppankai).

or Housewives' Associations to get elected to the village Council unless they were sponsored by their own hamlet and could draw on a solid basis of their hamlet's votes. In the new units it is easier for such representatives of generational or professional interests to draw votes over a wide area. It is still true, as we shall see later, that a kind of territorial representation tends still to exist, though the unit is enlarged from the hamlet to a district or perhaps to the pre-amalgamation village unit. The tendency of voters to elect, if no longer their hamlet's representative, at least a 'local' candidate still persists. Local government politics have still not become the arena of class interests or of conflicting occupational interests. Nevertheless it remains true that the hamlets are no longer the main protagonists in local politics and this in itself represents a big change in Japanese rural self-government.

At the same time, for the purposes of village administration the hamlet remains the smallest identifiable administrative unit even after the amalgamations. In a sense the expansion of the area controlled by each local government has made it even more necessary to use the hamlet for the practical work of administration. Generally speaking, after the amalgamations, the offices of the old village units have remained in being as branch offices of the municipality. These, however, deal only with such matters as civil registration, rationing, and tax payments, and are simply a nominal concession to local residents who would object to losing the convenience of having an office close at hand. They were not deliberately established as a means of carrying municipal policies down to the grass-roots level, and the new administrations, like those of the old villages, have continued to use the hamlets for cheapness and convenience of administration. So the practice often continues of sending a single copy of announcements to each hamlet for circulation around the hamlet, of using hamlet chiefs as a cheap means of collecting taxes, of appointing hamlet collectors for community chests and other charitable contributions, and of using the hamlet associations in order to carry out public health activities. Similarly the practice continues of distributing the meagre funds available for road repair and other public works as widely and evenly as possible so that in exchange for a subsidy from the municipal administration hamlets are expected to make their own contributions to works which should properly speaking be wholly financed by the local government.[4]

It is unnecessary to add that these practices serve to preserve and strengthen the identity of hamlets and inhibit their dissolution. As long as hamlets continue to be utilized by local government administration and to define communities which are something more than mere geographical notions local politics will not cease to operate on the principle of 'local interests', a principle the vague neutrality of which will continue to have the irrational effect of concealing conflicts of class interest. This is a matter of some importance which will concern us in the next section.

The Mechanisms of Town and Village Government before the Recent Amalgamations

From the beginning of the local government system it was largely dominated by landlords. The limited suffrage with its division into two classes made it easy for the big landlords to become members of the Council, and when hamlets chose their candidates to represent them it was natural that, given the typical hamlet status structure, a landlord—probably someone who was at the same time an oyakata and head of a powerful main family—would be chosen. The Mayor and Vice-Mayor chosen by such councillors were likely to be either the most powerful landlords or else lesser landlords who could be relied on to work in the latter's interests. It was not uncommon for the sons of such lesser landlord families to start life early as officials in the village office and to work their way up through the position of Treasurer and Vice-Mayor until they finally achieved the mayoralty, having shown that they were men in whom the powerful landlord members on the Council could place complete confidence.

Thus the basis of village politics lay in the landlords' dominance of the hamlets. Its major tasks lay in securing a balance

---

[4] On these points see Shima Yasuhiko, ed., *Chihō-zaisei no riron to jittai*, 1955 (Yūhikaku) and also Seikatsu-kagaku Chōsakai, ed., *Chōnaikai, Burakukai*, 1962 (Ishiyaku Shuppan-kabushiki-kaisha).

between the hamlets which continued in large measure to look after their own needs. How were the small sums available for public works to be divided among the hamlets? How were the various levies and charitable contributions required from the village to be collected from each hamlet? In setting up standards for the household tax, how was a balance between the hamlets to be preserved? These were the matters in which councillors were expected to protect the interest of their hamlets. The strength of each hamlet's influence in these matters depended not simply on its size and its social and economic power, but also on the strength of its landlords and especially on the landed wealth of the particular landlord who represented it in the council. As a consequence the actual policies which resulted from the council's decisions were not only determined by the interests of the various hamlets but also coincided with the class interests of the landlords themselves. We have already seen how funds provided for road or irrigation works in the hamlets had to be supplemented by the hamlet's own contributions in cash or in unpaid labour. These projects were spoken of as being for the good of the hamlet, but the actual profit went in larger measure to the landlords than to anybody else. And of course the benefit was all the greater for those with extensive estates which extended into several hamlets.

This coincidence between hamlet interests and landlord interests was not fundamentally altered even after a good proportion of the landlords had withdrawn from farming and even after, with the abolition of suffrage classes and the enactment of universal suffrage, councillors came to be drawn from the owner-farmers and even from the upper strata of part-tenants. The interests of their very own hamlet was an idea which made an immediate appeal to the farmer's mentality, but in this concept of the hamlet interests the real class interests of the lower strata of poor farmers tended to be obliterated. It was a seemingly class-neutral concept but in effect the interests of the hamlet tended to be equated with the interests of the landlords and richer farmers.

Thus village politics tended to be a matter chiefly of attaining compromise between the interests of different hamlets, in effect between the interests of different landlords. Consequently, if there were in the village a few landlords who were powerful enough to dominate it and enforce such a compromise things tended to go quite smoothly. If there was a single landlord whose property was extensive enough to allow him to dominate the whole village there might even be some positively forward-looking policies adopted. But where such a central pivot of authority was lacking the landlord delegates, backed by their separate hamlets, tended to cling tenaciously to their positions. The maintenance of a mechanical kind of balance was about as much as could be expected. Any new positive departures would threaten to disrupt that balance and consequently a negative attitude of avoiding controversy tended to dominate village politics. There were some villages in which, from the beginning of the local government system, deep-seated rivalries between landlords from different hamlets admitted of no compromise, with the result that factional conflict was continuous and no Mayor could ever be secure in his position. Since local government funds were in any case severely limited, in such villages where every policy proposal led to conflict, the possibilities of positive developmental policies became even more remote.[5]

Consequently, those who were elected to the village Councils were not men qualified by the ability or the breadth of vision necessary to consider the interests of the village as a whole and carry it forward by measures of enlightened reform. They considered themselves to be honorary representatives of their hamlet. And to fulfil their function of ensuring that nothing was done to damage their own hamlet's interests it was necessary only that they should have some social standing in the village backed by sufficient land ownership and a certain amount of experience in hamlet and village affairs. Provided that they maintained their hamlet's relative position, whatever their bargaining activities produced by way of a share-out would be considered by the residents of their hamlet as something to be grateful for. Since the patterns of hamlet self-government were

[5] Factional rivalries in the Council commonly tended to make the position of the Mayor insecure. It was not at all uncommon for Mayors to resign before the end of their term of office. For example, see Fukutake Tadashi, ed., *Nihon nōson-shakai no kōzō-bunseki: sonraku no shakai-kōzō to nōsei-shintō*, 1954 (Tōkyō-daigaku Shuppankai), p. 110 ff.

left more or less intact, they considered it as entirely natural that hamlet works should be done by the hamlet, and hence even a small subsidy from village funds was likely to be much appreciated as the result of their representative's efforts. Likewise if their quotas for village levies and charity contributions were kept at a reasonable level, they would consider this also to be thanks to their representative's efforts in speaking up for his hamlet. In point of fact the business of reaching a reasonable compromise between the interests of various hamlets—or in effect between the interests of different landlords—was generally a matter of fairly simple arithmetical adjustment. Consequently, most business was settled in informal discussions before the Council meetings. The minutes of village Councils are usually a bland and simple record of a series of motions carried by unanimous approval.

In the twenties, it is true, local government ceased to be government by a handful of landlords. The lower strata of tenants and poor farmers did not succeed in getting their interests reflected in village politics, but as the bigger landlords became more purely parasitic and as members of the owner-farmer and part-tenant groups were elected to the Council, it was no longer possible for the interests of the landlords and the interests of their hamlets to be simply equated. And in the local government units which had a small town as a nucleus, the conflict of interest between town and village became more marked. It consequently became more difficult to preserve a satisfactory balance between districts, and the minutes of Council meetings came to record a certain number of decisions carried not unanimously but over the dissent of a minority. This was more especially the case in those towns and villages where Farmers' Unions were organized and succeeded in getting some of their representatives elected to the council.

These nascent tendencies were, however, nipped in the bud as the country moved on to a war footing in the thirties. Local governments became the subordinate units of a central government bent on total mobilization, and all local autonomy was destroyed.

We have already seen how it was revived after the war and institutionally given a wholly new look. The town and village

Mayors who had played the key role in the grass-roots war effort, and occupied *ex officio* the positions of divisional directors of the Imperial Rule Assistance Association, were purged from public office. Under the new system Mayors were to be directly elected—and at a time when the land reform was creating turmoil in the villages. By virtue of their direct election the Mayors occupied a stronger position than before the war. No longer simply the chairmen of the village Councils, chiefly concerned with securing compromise agreements among the members of the Council, they were now able to pursue positive policies of their own.

The Councils, too, as a result of the structural changes brought in the villages by the land reform, were no longer dominated by landlords. Councillors were drawn from a much wider stratum of villagers, and men who had been part-tenants or even wholly tenants could get elected, if they had the ability. The voting age was lowered and women were given the vote. As a result it was possible for relatively young men to secure election, and there were even women councillors, though they were few in number.

These changes did not, however, imply a definitive change in the mechanisms of village politics. As Table xxii shows, a high proportion of mayors and village councillors were still drawn from the landlord stratum. And as we have seen, elections for the village Council were still generally on a hamlet basis and those elected were still expected to act as representatives of the interests of their hamlets. It is unnecessary to add that even after the dissolution of the tenancy system the interests of the hamlet were largely interpreted in terms of the interests of its richer members.

TABLE XXII

Holders of Village Offices by Pre-land Reform Ownership Status[6]
(Percentages)

| Office | Status before the Reform | | | |
	Landlord	Owner-farmer	Part-tenant	Tenant
Mayor, vice-mayor, treasurer	57	20	16	7
Councillor	39	22	28	9

[6] Table xxii derives from a study of the holders of public office in

But even if Mayors and councillors were often former landlords, they no longer formed a ruling stratum by virtue of their
authority as landlords. If ex-landlords were heavily over-
represented, this was because as a result of their wealth they had
received higher education and could claim to be better fitted in
knowledge and experience than former tenants or part-tenants.
Ability was a much more important pre-requisite for office after
than before the war, and it was no longer possible to be elected
simply on the grounds of one's family's traditional standing or
wealth. Since it was generally speaking only members of the
upper strata who were able to develop those abilities, they
naturally predominated among the office holders, and in a
situation in which political interests were defined in local hamlet terms rather than in class terms, it was still possible for them
to promote their own interests under the guise of pursuing their
hamlet's interest.

However, this kind of sleight-of-hand was no longer so easy
after the dissolution of the landlord system. The attitudes of the
voters had changed too, and they were no longer willing to bow
submissively to authority and accept the compromises reached
by the 'powerful men'. In those villages where the class tension
developed in the course of the land reform had led to the formation of Farmers' Unions there were 'movements for the democratization of village politics' and strong criticism of the 'rule by
powerful men' which had replaced rule by the landlords. Even
in other villages councillors were under much stronger pressure
from their constituents to promote their hamlet's interest and
the process of reaching acceptable compromises became more
difficult. The change in attitudes can be seen in the fact that
village authorities found it increasingly difficult to operate the
system of compulsory food deliveries which was carried over
from the war period. Village politics were no longer something
remote and the business of members of a superior landlord
class; it was something with which the ordinary villager was
concerned and in which he was involved. Those who held office

---

ninety villages from every part of Japan conducted in 1953 by the National
Central Agricultural Committee. Information on pre-reform status is
lacking for 2 per cent. of members of the Councils. See Chapter VI of Tōbata
Seiichi, ed., *Zukai Nihon no nōgyō*, 1954 (Shunjū-sha).

knew that they could only continue to do so if they provided real benefits for their electors.

Nevertheless these burgeoning trends of change in village politics did not develop satisfactorily. With the post-war extension of the compulsory education period, towns and villages had to devote the major part of their slender financial resources to the building of new middle schools. As we have already seen, the financial strength of local governments was not such as to permit them to formulate any positive policies. Again, with the completion of the land reform, the Farmers' Unions lost their immediate campaign objective and began to disintegrate; the awakening sense of class interest was once again submerged in the sense of hamlet community. And we have also seen already how the financial limitations of local governments forced greater reliance on the self-government activity of the hamlets which further prevented the development of a proper appreciation of the function of local government.

The Political Structure of the New Towns and Villages

Until the recent amalgamations most rural areas were included in town or village administrations. And for most towns and villages, consequently, local politics meant the politics of agriculture. With the amalgamations the situation has changed considerably, since rural areas of considerable size now come within the boundaries of cities. Whereas before the amalgamation 63 per cent. of the total population of Japan lived in towns and villages, the present proportion has fallen to 45 per cent. Consequently, it is no longer possible to discuss the political structure of rural areas solely in terms of the politics of towns and villages. City administrations must come into the picture too. Equally an understanding of the politics of towns and villages requires full attention to the commercial and manufacturing elements found in their central settlements. The power structure of rural areas, in other words, has become much more complicated. One effect has been to reduce the total number of local government councillors. For example, a village with a population of some 3,000 people might formerly have had a Council of sixteen members. Now amalgamated with

TABLE XXIII

Councillors by Occupation before
and after Amalgamations: 1955

New administrative unit (Number in sample)	Occupation of Councillors (%)			
	In new units		In same area before amalgamations	
	Farmers, foresters, fishermen	Others	Farmers, foresters, fishermen	Others
Cities (314)	45.3	54.7	67.1	32.9
Towns (914)	70.1	29.7	75.3	24.7
Villages (341)	84.9	15.1	87.4	12.6
Total (1569)	67.5	32.5	74.2	25.8

three or four other such villages into a town of, say, 12,000 to 15,000 inhabitants, the total number of Council members would be twenty-six representing a big proportionate reduction. Moreover, among the reduced number of councillors the proportion representing rural areas is likely to decrease. This tendency is particularly marked, as Table XXIII shows, in cities with very large commercial or manufacturing centres. In the towns and villages farmers still predominate among members of the Council, but if one takes into account the fact that members from the commercial centre are generally more influential, even a small drop in the proportion of farmer representatives may have a considerable effect on local politics. In the new cities the very sharp decrease shows that in these new mixed areas it will be hard for agricultural interests to get a fair hearing.[7]

The non-farmer members of these Councils are for the most

[7] At present the qualifications which a district must meet to be designated a city are that the population should be over 50,000, that 60 per cent. of the households should be in the central urban area, that 60 per cent. of the population should be engaged in urban pursuits, and that what are defined by local prefectural by-laws as typical urban facilities should be present. Until 1954, however, the minimum population qualification was 30,000 which made the birth of large numbers of new cities possible. According to the by-laws of most prefectures, towns must have a minimum population of 5,000. Table XXIII is based on a sample study conducted in August, 1955, by the National Association of Agricultural Committees (Zenkoku Nōgyō Kaigisho). See Hoshino Mitsuo, Nihon no chihō-jichi: jūmin-jichi to hoshu-kakushin no taiketsu, 1958 (Tōkyō Keizai Shimpōsha).

part shopkeepers and owners of small businesses, but among them the operators of construction and timber concerns very frequently have a source of strength in rural areas inasmuch as they offer part-time employment for poorer farmers. Such men are frequently at loggerheads with the Agricultural Co-operatives and, organized as a Chamber of Commerce, they are likely to promote the mercantile interests of the urban centre and prevent too much spending in the rural areas. When there is a factory of some size in the district it is likely to feel that it has a right to get its money's worth out of its property tax contribution to municipal finances, and to seek to get representatives of the firm elected to the Council. These are also likely to try to cut down on spending in rural areas. It is true that the largest proportion of funds spent under the heading industrial and economic affairs is pre-empted as counterpart funds for subsidies given by the Ministry of Agriculture, and consequently spent on agriculture, but generally speaking, in most of the local administrations newly created by the amalgamations the tendency in agricultural policy has been towards retrenchment.[8]

Similarly an increasing proportion of Mayors have been non-farmers. Even if village Mayors have never commonly been actual cultivators, this is a big change from the days when, as landlords, they could at least officially declare their occupation to be farming. Certainly few city Mayors are now farmers. This means that for most rural people the Mayor has become a somewhat remote figure. Gone are the days when it was always possible for a group of farmers to go along with their hamlet's councillor and plead personally with the Mayor to do something about their problems. The Mayor, particularly if he is a city Mayor or a town Mayor, is now somebody only to be approached by formal petitions through the Council.

Similarly, there has been a change in the village office. With the increasing volume of administrative duties delegated from

[8] On local politics after the amalgamations, see Fukutake Tadashi, ed., *Gappei chōson no jittai*, 1958 (Tōkyō-daigaku Shuppankai); Yamaoka Eiichi, ed., *San'in nōson no shakai-kōzō*, 1959 (Tōkyō-daigaku Shuppankai); Satō Tomoo, ed., *Chihō toshi*, 1961 (Tōkyō-daigaku Shuppankai); *Nōson no kenryoku-kōzō*, 1959, edited and published by Kokusai Kirisuto-kyō Daigaku, Shakai-kagaku Kenkyūjo.

the central government and with a wider area to cover, the new and enlarged municipal offices have been changed in structure, and given a new rationalized departmental system in which powers and responsibilities are more narrowly and clearly defined. In the former village offices, although there had been similar divisions, duties overlapped a good deal, and although there might have been inefficiencies, at least there was easy contact between officials and residents. A village office was a place where one could easily enough go in behind the counter for an extended chat. Now, however, this personal atmosphere of the 'village office' has given way to the impersonality of the 'municipal bureau'—especially if it is a city municipal bureau. In both the good and the bad senses of the term, the municipal offices have been bureaucratized.

In such changing circumstances the role of members of the Council has also changed. Now that several hamlets have to pool their votes in order to elect a single member, it is much less easy to control votes than it was in the days when most hamlets could elect a representative of their own. The result is that candidates, although of course they rely for a solid basis of votes on their own hamlet, need generally to have the backing of, or at least a record of activity in, some association of the kind that was formerly organized on a village-wide basis—an Agricultural Co-operative, for instance, or a Forestry Co-operative. They must, in other words, be men of a higher political calibre, but in effect they remain the representatives of regional interests, even though the regions now correspond to the former village areas, rather than to a single hamlet.

Their major functions are, firstly, collectively as rural area representatives to defend rural interests against the town interests and secondly, as local representatives, to defend the interests of their area—their pre-amalgamation village. In the newer cities rural interests very often come off second best, but everywhere the compromise balancing of local interests gives rise to troublesome problems.

The new local government units may have been able to build a fine block of municipal offices from money loaned by the state treasury, in order to put up a brave display of the benefits of the new regime, but with constant conflict over the division between districts of the meagre financial resources available, positive forward-looking policies are ruled out. It is no wonder that in such circumstances the dream of attracting industry for regional development should seem so alluring.

These councillors do, however, have an important function as intermediaries between the hamlets and their residents on the one hand and the now remote Mayor and bureaucratized municipal offices on the other. Hamlets send their headmen to a councillor urging him to press their claims for a subsidy for local projects, and if the subsidy is granted, he will justly be able to claim the credit. Later he may play a part in organizing the collection of the counterpart subscriptions, and he may be needed to see to it that the village office does its part in pushing the work ahead. It is through these mediating functions that the Council member becomes a local district boss.[9]

In other words, the basic principles of local government politics have changed little. It is still regional interests which are represented, not those of functionally differentiated strata. These regional bosses are, of course, of conservative leanings. The majority of them have no overt political affiliation, but in fact are closely connected with the conservative party which is centrally in power. Because their main concern is with the extraction of subsidies for the benefit of the particular region they represent, and because their ability to do so depends on their influence—the breadth of their 'face'—they naturally form connexions with politicians at the higher levels—members of the prefectural and national assemblies.

Nevertheless, there are some new features of politics in the post-amalgamation local governments which one would hardly have found anywhere in the old. The first results from the fact that the voting situation has become more fluid since hamlets are no longer able to exercise the same control over their votes. It has consequently become possible for new types of local councillors to appear, men whose support comes from, for instance, a youth organization whose members are scattered over a wide area. Such men can act in relative freedom from hamlet or other regional interests, and generally they are men

[9] See Shima Yasuhiko, 'Chihō-jichi to minshushugi' in *Gendai no chihō-jichi*, (*Kōza chihō-jichitai*, Vol. II) 1960 (San ichi Shobō)).

of a rather different mentality and outlook from the typical conservative boss.

Secondly, in those of the new cities and towns which contain numbers of organized workers, there have appeared a few councillors belonging to left-wing parties. Again, the trade unions which hitherto paid little attention to local government, have recently revised their opinion of its importance, and formed regional union committees specially concerned with local government matters. Another new phenomenon, in towns and villages which contain large numbers of people in regular wage or salary employment, is the occasional formation of 'employees alliances'. Their motive is protest against the fact that they seem to pay a disproportionately large part of the taxes for, and receive a disproportionately small part of the benefits of, local government activity. As such they represent an attack on the principle that global interests of local residential districts should be the prior consideration. It has happened in the new cities, too, with the expansion of the municipal office, that officials have formed their own union and affiliated to the federation of local government workers.[10]

If these two trends were to coalesce, the way would be opened for a worker-peasant alliance within the framework of local government. However, the way ahead is by no means easy. As a formal slogan the worker-peasant alliance sounds easy enough, but hitherto there have been few instances of successful achievement. There may have been momentary co-operation prompted by some particular incident, but it is rare for such alliances to last long.[11]

The reasons are, firstly, that it is hard for new leaders to emerge from the farmer's side, or if they do emerge they are always likely to be converted into old style bosses. The young men of the calibre to make new-style leaders usually have their

[10] For an example of youth group activity, see Namie Ken, *Asu no nōson o tsukuru senkyo*, 1958 (Nōsangyoson Bunka-kyōkai). On the employees alliance, see Gotō Kazuo, 'Kyūyosha dōmeikai no seiritsu to sono jōken', in the 2nd Annual Volume of the Sonraku-shakai Kenkyūkai, *Nōchi-kaikaku to nōmin-undō*, 1955 (Jichōsha). See also Kimura Kihachiro and Tomaru Yasusuke, eds., *Chihō-jichitai to jūmin* (*Kōza Chihō-jichitai*, Vol. V) 1961 (Sanichi Shobō).

[11] See Matsushita Keiichi, *Gendai Nihon no seijiteki-kōsei*, 1962 (Tōkyō-daigaku Shuppankai).

own farm. Many of them are preoccupied with trying out new ideas such as co-operative management on their farms, and so have little time left to get into local government politics. Moreover as the income differential between agriculture and other industries increases, able young men are increasingly unwilling to stay on the farm, and consequently the hopes of finding new leaders grow more and more dim. In these circumstances if a young man does attempt to take part in local government politics, the chances are that, finding few kindred spirits, he will receive a tough initiation from the old style bosses, and eventually succumb to harsh reality and himself move in a conservative direction. He may intellectually appreciate the importance of alliance with the workers, but the difference in occupation makes this intellectual appreciation take second place to the realities of his situation.

From the workers' side, secondly, an important reason is that the unions, although they have begun to show a little interest, are still not very positively concerned with local government. The fact is that full-time workers are not very concerned about the district they live in, while those who are part-time workers and still draw some income from agriculture are given a certain security by the land they own and tend to be lukewarm towards union activities. The most insecure, the casual daily labourers, are less likely to be organized by the unions than by the owners of local construction firms. Where there are large factories in the area and a good number of workers on the city Council they tend, in terms of city politics, to think of their firm's interests first. They, who from the point of view of income levels represent a labour aristocracy, seem not to have much appreciation of the troubles of farmers in their own city let alone the inclination to help them.[12]

Thus, at present, local government remains largely in the hands of local political bosses whether from the villages or from

[12] For examples of union representatives from big firms acting, as members of city Councils, largely in the interests of their firm, see Nihon Jimbun-kagakkai, ed., *Kindai kōkōgyō to chiiki shakai no tenkai*, 1955 (Tōkyō-daigaku Shuppankai); ibid., *Gijutsu-kakushin no shakaiteki eikyō*, 1963 (Tōkyō-daigaku Shuppankai); and Matsuura Kōsaku and Hamajima Akira, eds., *Nihon shihon-shugi to sonraku-kōzō: Chin-rōdō kengyōka no shakaiteki eikyō*, 1963 (Seishin shobō).

the town areas. It is because of this, and because it is possible for a small number of people to settle matters, that 30 per cent. of the Mayors of towns and villages are elected unopposed. It is because of this too that in elections for town and village Councils, although there are only 30 per cent. more candidates than seats, voting ratios reach more than 90 per cent. This high level of voting is not a reflection of a deep concern with local government matters; it is better seen as an index of the strength of the local bosses and of their ability to mobilize the votes of their respective districts. It is the overwhelming strength of these conservative independents in local government which produces parliamentary majorities for the Liberal-Democratic Party, and which produces the Socialist Party's 'inverted pyramid'— the phenomenon of diminishing representation the lower one goes in the local government scale, from one-third of the seats in the national Diet to a much smaller level in prefectural assemblies and almost no representation at all in local municipalities.

CHAPTER XII

NATIONAL POLITICS AND THE VILLAGES

National Politics and the Political Behaviour of Farmers

It would be little exaggeration to say that in Japanese villages before the war only landlords played any part in national politics. Under the old Constitution, in any case, sovereign power did not lie with the people, and as for the ordinary farmer, his part in the system was simply to be ruled. When the Constitution was first granted the mass of farmers did not even have the vote, and even when the suffrage was later extended one could hardly say that the majority of farmers exercised their right to vote according to their own self-conscious and self-determined will. Again for those seats in the House of Peers reserved for representatives of the highest taxpayers, only a small handful of very large landlords had the right to vote.

We have seen how local government tended to be landlord-dominated. So too in the national Diet, founded a year later than the local government system, the landlords, and especially those with the biggest estates, at first exercised considerable power. In the first two decades of the parliamentary system, around the beginning of the century when Japanese industrial capitalism was barely established, the landlords were nationally, too, a political force comparable to that of the capitalists. In fact a good number of the more powerful landlords worked their way through the ranks of the district assemblies and prefectural assemblies to enter the Diet.

In the second decade of this century, with the development of monopoly forces in Japanese capitalism, the influence of the landlords became increasingly circumscribed. But this did not affect the need for politicians to keep close liaison with the landlords who controlled the village vote. Both of the big Japanese parties sought to consolidate their electoral support by forging links with landlords. Every village had its powerful landlord, affiliated to the Seiyūkai or to the Minseitō, either as a member or as a sympathizer in close personal relations with politicians at the prefectural and parliamentary level. The combination constituted a formidable political force. So much so that, as, in the 1920's, Japanese politics moved into a phase closely resembling that of the classic two-party parliamentary system, and as rivalry between the two large conservative parties became increasingly intense, national rivalries were transferred to the villages and rival landlord leaders were allied into opposing factions.[1]

These political developments had little effect on the average farmer. He simply voted for the candidate supported by the landlord with whom he had the closest connexions. As for the parliamentary politicians, they had no need to make any direct appeal to the farmers as such; it was enough for their election if they could mobilize the support of landlords. One cannot leave out of the picture the fact that, with the formation of Farmers' Unions, farmers' votes were given, though in very small numbers, to the candidates of the proletarian parties. But in the total picture of Japanese politics these were very minor parties indeed, and in a quantitative sense—whatever its qualitative significance—farmers' support for the proletarian parties was insignificant in relation to the general political role of farmers.

The era of party politics ended, finally dissolved in the wartime regime. At this point the whole of the farming populace was incorporated into a political organization for the first time —into the Imperial Rule Assistance system. This only meant, however, that they were integrated into a national network for the downward transmission of orders; it meant, in other words, that everyone including the landlords were firmly relegated to the status of the ruled. Hence, even in their capacity as electors,

[1] See Imanishi Kinji, *Mura to ningen*, 1952 (Shin-hyōronsha), and my own chapter on village landlords and politics in *Nihon sonraku no shakai-kōzō*, 1959 (Tōkyō-daigaku Shuppankai).

the vast majority of farmers never were able to play an independent role right up to the end of the war.

In the post-war regime, the people were now declared to be
sovereign. The farmers too were counted in the ranks of the
sovereign people, and they ceased to be mere voting machines
manipulated by the landlords, for tenancy relationships no
longer gave the landlords the influence wherewith to direct
their tenants' votes. Their votes were not perhaps completely
freed from the influences exerted by the social pressures of the
hamlet and consequently by the richer 'powerful men' and
village politicians who dominated hamlet opinion, but these
influences did allow, and work upon, realistic judgments of
advantage—that a vote for such-and-such a candidate would
be in the interests of the hamlet or of the village. At least they
no longer voted for any man just because he was backed by
their landlord; they needed to be persuaded that there were
advantages to be gained for their locality.

However, these new voting patterns do, in their final effect,
give support to the conservative parties. At present, when the
left-wing parties, of negligible importance before the war, have
succeeded in securing a third of the Diet seats, the vast majority
of rural votes go to form a powerful basis of support for the
majority conservative party which holds the other two-thirds.
If one divides the prefectures of Japan into agricultural and
industrial prefectures according to the proportion of their
working population employed in agriculture, the agricultural
prefectures returned an overwhelming proportion of conservative Diet members. One can interpret this as peasant conservatism causing the farmers to distrust a left-wing party, their
instincts of petty proprietorship making them shun what they
see as parties of the property-less workers. However, one should
not overlook the mechanisms which lie behind these voting
patterns.

Local government, which is of the most intimate concern to
farmers, is supported by equalization tax rebates and subsidies
from prefectural and central governments. Similarly, local
government loans cannot be floated at will; permission is
necessary and for the most part these loans depend on central
government funds. A slight change in the assessment basis for

the equalization tax rebate can have a very large effect on local government funds. The size of the grants or subsidies received determines the funds available for industrial and economic development. Without loan issues it is difficult to go ahead with the building of schools and municipal offices. For these reasons Mayors and influential members of the Council must maintain close connexions with members of the prefectural assembly and the latter's ultimate patrons, members of the national Diet. And it goes without saying that these Diet members have to be members of the government party if they are to have any influence.

It is by utilizing these connexions that towns and villages get their municipal offices and their schools built and keep their roads and their bridges in good repair. These are looked on as benefits received through the efforts of the locally elected Diet members. And it is by pointing out that the Diet members who have worked so hard for local interests can be relied on to continue to do their best in future that the local politicians can mobilize support for them in elections. At the same time it is through these connexions with Diet members and the benefits they bring that Mayors and influential councillors can demonstrate the strength of their own influence, and so ensure their own re-election.[2]

However, Diet members cannot be absolutely certain of enough votes for election simply by acting as brokers in this kind of petition politics. In an electoral system where constituencies elect between three and six members and where there are only two major parties, candidates of the dominant party must face competition from other candidates of their own party. If their role as mediators in the petitioning process is not enough to secure the loyalty of town and village Mayors and influential councillors they must play a full patron's role, finding some way of lending their support to their clients in their own elections and contributing in some degree to their election expenses. And if,

---

[2] For a schematization of relationships between Diet members and local politicians, see the relevant chapter in Isoda Susumu, ed., *Sonraku-kōzō no kenkyū*, 1955 (Tōkyō-daigaku Shuppankai), p. 277. See also a book by the author of that chapter, Ishida Takeshi, *Kindai Nihon seiji-kōzō no kenkyū*, 1956 (Miraisha).

further, the hold which these local politicians have over the farmers' vote is less complete than that formerly enjoyed by the landlords, and if the voters are much more sensitively aware than they used to be of where their own material interests might lie, they must seek to retain the loyalties of even lower levels of local politicians, making contributions to their campaigns in town and village Council elections, and generally nursing their constituencies by all the means available to them.

Thus Diet members create their own Support Societies, organizing them around a nucleus of prominent local politicians and spreading the net to embrace men of lesser influence. When they return to their constituencies they hold meetings of their Support Society and give parties to feast their members. They make donations to local societies, subscribe to local festivals, send their secretaries to act as tourist guides when parties of farmers come up to the capital, send wreaths to the funerals of local politicians and help their sons to get jobs—in these little everyday matters no effort must be spared. Needless to say, the expense of thus nursing a constituency is of no mean order.

In return for all these favours the Diet member's lesser followers in the villages reinforce the Mayor and the influential local politicians in explaining to the farmers just how much their patron is devoted to local interests. Sometimes, perhaps, the propaganda work will be assisted by the occasional drinking party. And when it comes to elections this network of local bosses, large and small, will be mobilized into full activity. Election expenses, as a consequence, are likely far to exceed the legal allowance.

And whence, one might ask, come these funds for elections and for nursing constituencies between elections? The obvious and simple answer is that the Liberal-Democratic Party itself, and also individually the leaders of factions within the Party, extract money from the big capitalist firms. This is the mechanism through which the conservative party is able to afford the expenses of retaining power. The process is perpetuated by its ability, through its individual Diet members, to keep the local interests of the farmers primed with the benefits of petition politics, while in the field of government activity proper, they requite these financial contributions by promoting policies attuned to the interests of monopoly capital. As long as the farmers are kept happy with the lollipops of local benefits, they fail to perceive the richer fare which is served up to the capitalists. Nor do they become conscious of the fact that these benefits, provided under the neutral guise of services to the whole community, by no means in fact benefit every member of the community.

It should be added, of course, that farmers today are not satisfied simply with local benefits. In matters of national policy, too, they show a sharp hard-headedness where their own interests are directly involved. The determination of rice prices is an example in point. Under the present food control system this is a matter of very great concern to the Agricultural Co-operatives, the majority of which depend for a good deal of their income on handling charges for the rice they collect on behalf of the government. Through the system of National Co-operative Federations the farmers exercise a good deal of political influence. The Co-operatives are the farmers' pressure group, and their affiliated association, the Farmers' Political Alliance (*Nōmin Seiji Remmei*) represents for Diet members a reservoir of votes which they cannot ignore.

In their pressure group activities, the Agricultural Co-operatives—partly because they are basically economic organizations—are generally on the defensive. In order to protect the farm economy and consequently to strengthen the foundations of the co-operatives themselves, they seek to raise the price of rice, but they do not attempt to go further and press for policies which will ensure the future development and stability of agriculture. At the village co-operative level, the officials themselves are generally elected on a hamlet-representation basis, and since the Co-operative's Director is generally a conservative village politician it is inevitable that the officers of the National Federations should also have conservative connexions. Moreover, the kind of connexions which they forge with members of the government party under the necessity of negotiating from a defensive position prevent them from developing more positive pressure group action.[3]

[3] On the subject of Agricultural Co-operatives, see the analysis in Ishida Takeshi, *Gendai soshiki-ron*, 1961 (Iwanami Shoten).

The only possible substitutes are Farmers' Unions as explicitly political organizations. But as we have already seen, since the end of the land reform the Farmers' Unions in the villages have either dissolved or lapsed into dormancy. The left-wing parties still have as supporting organizations a national system of Farmers' Unions, but at the local level they remain inactive. One reason for this is the lack of organizational power in the left-wing parties, but another reason is the lack on the part of farmers, caught up as they are in the political system described above, of any consciousness of the need for creating such organizations.

Hence, national policies are not designed to promote the farmer's welfare. Since the farmers are an important source of electoral support the Liberal-Democratic Party always seeks in its policies to present an appearance of giving agriculture every consideration. In particular, as househeads have lost their authority in the family and ceased to be able to control the votes of their children, with a consequent tendency for votes of the younger generation even in rural areas to go to the left-wing parties, the Party has recently been at great pains to speak of the need for modernizing agriculture and to stress its determination not to sacrifice the farmers' interests. Nevertheless national policies are in essence always attuned to the interests of big business and when they speak of consideration for agriculture and for farmers there is always the proviso: in so far as this does not clash with business interests or hinder their development.

The Growth of the Economy and Agricultural Policy

As stated at the beginning of this book agriculture was the springboard for the development of Japan's capitalist economy. But agriculture itself never found the road of escape from a system of minuscule family holdings.

The Japanese Government's initial attempt to deal with the situation of excessively small holdings was its policy of improving agricultural techniques, largely relying on landlord leadership. But for all these production-oriented policies designed to diffuse improved seeds, encourage the use of more fertilizer, or improve cultivation techniques, it was impossible to keep the farm economy developing at a rate comparable with that of the industrial sector. It was inevitable that the stagnation of agriculture and rural areas should become an overt problem, posed in the form of 'the conflict between town and village'. When, in the agricultural depression which followed the First World War, the impoverishment of the villages and the desperate plight of the farm economy became even more pronounced, the Japanese Government embarked on a policy of subsidization. On the one hand, subsidies were designed to prevent the strains of the tenancy system from becoming critical by allowing tenants to buy their own land. On the other, they were used for the direct protection of the small family farm system, and linked to plans for 'rehabilitation through self-help', the campaign to encourage, among other things, the development of a more diversified type of farming.[4]

During the Second World War these policies were forced to give way to an overwhelming emphasis on food production, and this emphasis was continued through the food scarcity of the post-war period. At the same time the earlier moves towards extension of the owner-farmer system were crystallized under Occupation pressure into the land reform.

The basic emphasis of agricultural policy on increasing food production later weakened as the food supply improved. As a result, from about 1953 onwards, agricultural policy began to lose its sense of direction. As the capitalist industrial sector moved from its phase of reconstruction to its phase of rapid growth, simultaneously the need arose for a change in policies which hitherto had concentrated on increased production of staple grains, and in 1956 the Government announced its Integrated Programme for the Construction of New Villages. However, this went little further than proclaiming the importance of selecting the most suitable crops for local conditions, and hardly represented a turning point in agricultural policy.

That turning point—and it was a sharp one—came when the Japanese economy began to grow at an unusual rate and the gulf between agriculture and other industries was rapidly

[4] See Ouchi Tsutomu, *Nihon nōgyō no zaiseigaku*, 1950 (Tōkyō-daigaku Shuppankai) and also Ouchi Tsutomu, ed., *Nōgyōshi*, 1960 (Tōyō Keizai Shimpōsha).

widened. In 1959 the Government established a Commission of Inquiry into the Basic Problems of Agriculture, Forestry and Fisheries and in the light of its Report the Basic Law of Agriculture was passed in 1961. The preamble of this Law states that 'It is a duty springing from our concern for the public welfare, and a necessary complement to the mission of agriculture and of agriculturalists in our society, to ensure that those disadvantages resulting from the natural economic and social limitations of agriculture are corrected, to promote the modernization and rationalization of agriculture while respecting the free will and initiative of those engaged in it, and to ensure that the nation's farmers can enjoy a healthy and cultured livelihood not inferior to that of other members of the population.' The purpose of the law is defined as being 'To indicate clearly the new directions which agriculture must take and to establish the objectives of policies relating to agriculture.'[5]

Under the new law the Government began its so-called Agrarian Structure Improvement Programme. Its basic intentions were to change the constitution of Japanese agriculture which was seen as having been brought to a dead end of stagnation by the excessively small size of holdings. An agricultural industry which could not withstand foreign competition had also become an obstacle for development to the capitalist economy, and the improvement of the agrarian structure, if it could be done cheaply enough, was now in the interests of big business too. The aim of the programme was to adjust the basic production system, providing subsidies and credits for the facilities necessary to modernize management. To give a simplified example in terms of rice production, the plan envisages fields of 0.3 hectares in size, mechanically cultivated by tractors, and it is hoped that on this basis agricultural incomes could compete with those in other industries.

In the ten years starting in 1961, the Government expects to bring within the scope of this programme some 3,100 towns and villages outside of the areas expected to be most affected by industrialization and urbanization. In some of these administrative areas it is intended to establish pilot districts over a period

[5] The Report of the Commission of Inquiry was published under the title: *Nōgyō no kihon-mondai to kihon-taisaku*, 1960 (Nōrin-tōkei Kyōkai).

of three years which will act as models. The scale of expenditure for the average village is expected, for general village projects, to amount to a 50 per cent. subsidy for assisted projects totalling 90,000,000 yen with loans available for projects costing a further 20,000,000 yen. Even for the smaller pilot areas selected for specially close guidance and assistance the totals are only 50 per cent. assistance for projects to the value of 60,000,000 and loan assistance of projects to the value of 15,000,000. The sums may seem large, but they do not amount to a very great deal per farm, and the recipients will have to bear the cost of loan repayments for half the value of the assisted and the whole of the value of the other projects.

The question is whether these measures will achieve their intended objective of improving the structure of Japanese agriculture. The Commission of Inquiry took as its objective the equalization of incomes and envisaged the establishment of viable farming units which would engage in a large measure of co-operation, on the assumption of a large movement of population out of agriculture into other industries. However, the actual plans contain no provision for helping part-time farmers to move out of agriculture nor are any clear guide-lines laid down for improving the profitability of the individual farm. And there is the danger that uniform administrative guidance will stifle the independent initiatives of the farmers themselves. So long as the road ahead after the project works are completed is by no means clear, it is doubtful if the farmers will feel sufficiently enthusiastic to shoulder considerable loan burdens. At present it hardly seems that the Structural Improvement Programme is going to do much to improve the health of Japanese agriculture.[6]

These moves cannot simply be dismissed, as they frequently are by some critics, as 'the policy of wiping out the poor farmer'. Even if part-time farmers with tiny holdings did farm co-operatively or collectivize, little progress would be achieved; what is necessary is that the poor part-time farmers should be, not wiped out, but made able to transfer to some other occupation without hardship or insecurity. Real structural improve-

[6] See Kondō Yasuo, *et al.*, *Kōzō-kaizen: Sono ito to genjitsu* (*Nihon nōgyō nempō*, Vol. XI), 1962 (Ochanomizu Shobō).

ment will be impossible unless this is achieved parallel with an increasing development of co-operation among the remaining farmers. It is because the Structural Improvement Programme contains no provisions for aiding migration that it is open to criticism as a 'wiping out' operation.

Another related aspect of these problems which deserves consideration is regional development. The growth of the economy not only increased differentials between different branches of industry, but also at the same time widened the gap between the unindustrialized regions and those where industry is highly concentrated.

In 1950 the Government announced its Policy for Integrated Development of National Resources which concentrated on river development, but this ended up as an operation for distributing project subsidies as widely as possible, and achieved very little. Then, from about 1955, policy concentrated on regional development by the wider distribution of industry. In response to this a good many local governments made it a central feature of their development policy to attract industry and industrialize their region.[7]

The intention of local politicians, of course, is to increase tax revenue through the property and other taxes which the factories will pay, and this, they say, will be for the benefit of the whole community. For this reason cities and towns have drawn up special Industrial Development By-laws which provide, for instance, for exemption or reduction of business and property taxes for a fixed initial period, or which promise municipal help in the purchase and preparation of factory sites, the laying on of roads and water supplies at municipal expense, and so on. By these extremely beneficent measures they served the interests of businessmen and indulged in visions of a prosperous future.

However, it is questionable whether these visions will materialize. These measures will necessarily entail to a greater or lesser extent the conversion of farmland, but will there be

[7] For an example of one of these integral development plans involving riverine development, see Nihon Jimbun-kagakkai, ed., *Kitakami-gawa: Sangyō-kaihatsu to shakai hendō*, 1960 (Tōkyō-daigaku Shuppankai), and for an example of attempts to attract industry, see Nihon Jimbun-kagakkai, ed., *Kindai-sangyō to chiiki-shakai*, 1956 (Tōkyō-daigaku Shuppankai).

any compensating benefits for rural areas? In the first place, the very large initial expenditure needed to attract industry for these future tax benefits has to be borne by those at present living in the area. Among these inhabitants the farmers in particular have to see the funds allocated to agriculture out of the industrial and economic budget severely cut in order to cover this expenditure. Secondly, even if in the future, tax income from the factories swells the revenues of the municipality, there will be a corresponding reduction in the equalization tax rebate, and there will inevitably be extra expense to compensate for, or to prevent, damage from the factories to surrounding agricultural land. Also, the bigger the firm the more the local city or town government is forced to serve its interests and the more agriculture is likely to be neglected. Thirdly, the new factories are unlikely to absorb as much of the agricultural population as is expected. Even if there is an increase in employment, this is likely only to mean an increase in part-time farming with no substantial reduction in the number of farm households. Fourthly, even if it does become possible for some farmers to enlarge their holdings because others have left farming or reduced the size of theirs, the general rise in land prices as a result of the introduction of industry will affect agricultural land too and make the capital cost of enlarging their farms too high for the operation to be profitable.

Thus regional development is no answer to the problems of rural areas. Local industrialization is intended as a means for improving the welfare of the local inhabitants, but as long as emphasis is laid on the means the likelihood is that there will be an actual loss of the welfare which is supposed to be the end. Except for a small minority who can expect to gain, the consequences are likely to be serious for everybody, but especially for farmers. Hence, the current plans for regional development are unlikely to resolve the conflict between rural and urban areas; they are more likely to intensify it. The majority of small businesses in the area are also likely to be adversely affected when industry moves in, but for agriculture the disadvantages are likely to be decisive.

If neither the government's agricultural policy nor local industrial development offer prospects of a brighter future, what will become of agriculture and the villages? As long as present trends continue there is likely to be a progressive increase in part-time farming; no improvement in the basic structure of agriculture can be expected, and more and more villages will gradually decline into desolation. No one can be satisfied with this. It is essential that the Liberal-Democratic Party which controls agricultural policy should realize that its responsibility for the country's future lies in expending every effort to improve the agrarian structure and resolve the confusion between ends and means implicit in present policies for local industrialization. At present, policy is too much attuned to the interests of big business for it truly to appreciate these responsibilities. One might go even further. The fact is that in the logic of the Government's present economic development plans the objective of popular welfare does not occupy an important place.

The only thing which can force popular welfare into the position of a major objective and correct the present bias towards big business is, of course, the votes of the masses including the farmers. And if the farmers' vote is never likely to be used except in the ways described earlier, the future is indeed dark. Nevertheless it would be wrong to say that there is no hope. As industrialization does proceed on these lines, with all its accumulating contradictions doing further damage to agriculture, one can expect a change in the voting behaviour of the masses. These changes are likely to begin with the industrial population as it grows in size and becomes increasingly organized, but as one generation gives way to the next one may expect them to affect the farmers too.

FURTHER READING

On local and national politics, see:
Beardsley, Hall and Ward, *Village Japan.*
Dore, *Land reform.*
P. S. Dull, 'The senkyoya system in rural Japanese communities', University of Michigan, Center for Japanese Studies, *Occasional Papers*, 4, 1953.
P. S. Dull, 'The political structure of a Japanese village', *Far Eastern Quarterly*, 13, ii, Feb. 1954.
Y. Hoynden, *Cooperative movement in Japan*, Tokyo, Maruzen, 1958.
F. N. Kerling, 'Decision-making in Japan', *Social Forces*, 30, October 1951.

E. Norbeck, 'Common interest associations in rural Japan', in Smith and Beardsley, *Japanese culture.*

K. Steiner, 'The Japanese village and its government', *Far Eastern Quarterly*, 15, February 1956.

K. Steiner, *Local government in Japan*, Stanford, 1965.

S. S. Ulmer, 'Local autonomy in Japan since the Occupation', *Journal of Politics*, 19, February 1957.

R. E. Ward, 'The socio-political role of the buraku (hamlet) in Japan', *American Political Science Review*, 45, iv, December 1951.

R. E. Ward, 'Some observations on local autonomy at the village level in present-day Japan', *Far Eastern Quarterly*, 12, ii, February 1953.

R. E. Ward, ed., *Five studies in Japanese politics*, University of Michigan, Center for Japanese Studies, *Occasional Papers*, 6, 1957.

PART FIVE

VILLAGE CULTURE AND
THE FARMER'S MENTALITY

CHAPTER XIII

VILLAGE LIFE AND CULTURE

The Living Standards of Farm Families

WE have long had a stereotyped idea of the farm family as essentially poor and of village culture as backward with strong traces of feudalism.

Before the war, as a generalization this was by no means mistaken. According to a household budget survey carried out by the Cabinet Statistical Office before the Great Depression, in 1926–7, the average farm family's income was approximately 70 per cent. of that of salaried workers' households, and even 5 per cent. below the household income of manual workers, whose wages were so notoriously low that world-wide charges of dumping were universally directed at Japan. Since farm families were usually larger than other households, in *per capita* terms their income position was even less favourable. As for the distribution of their expenditure, as Table XXIV shows, a very high proportion was spent on food. It is only a slight exaggeration to say that all their energies were bent not on 'living' but on 'surviving'. If the sample of farmers is divided according to tenancy status one sees how especially impoverished were the tenants. For this same 1934–6 period the proportion of total income spent on food was 49.2 per cent. for owner farmers, 51.7 per cent. for those who owned part of their land, and 56.7 per cent. for tenants. These economic differentials served to maintain the status hierarchy in the villages, and at the same time the status hierarchy itself was a contributing factor in maintaining wide disparities of living levels between the landlords at the top and the tenants at the bottom of the hierarchy.[1]

TABLE XXIV

*Composition of Family Expenditure by Items, Rural
and Urban Families 1934/6—60*
(Percentages)

		Item				
Year	Type of family	Food	Clothing	Heating	Housing	Miscellaneous
1934/6	Farm households	50.5	9.3	4.9	6.3	29.0
	Urban worker households	36.1	11.6	4.9	16.7	30.7
1960	Farm households	43.5	11.3	4.7	13.9	26.7
	Urban worker households	38.4	12.6	4.9	9.8	34.3

This situation changed somewhat during the war. Farmers were in the strong position of being the actual producers of food, and the real income of farmers came to approach that of those engaged in other industries. Immediately after the war, in fact, it exceeded that of both the salaried and wage earning groups. However, this trend was soon reversed with the reconstruction of the capitalist sector and farm incomes again fell below those of non-farmers. In 1960 the average farm household income was 85 per cent. of that of white collar households and 117 per cent. of that of manual worker households, but in *per capita* terms these figures were respectively 65 per cent. and 89 per cent.; or, for the two groups taken together, 73 per cent.

Consequently, farmers are still badly off compared with urban households. However, in real terms, compared with the 1934–6 period agricultural income has increased by about 30 per cent. and total farm household income, including an even bigger increase in non-agricultural income, by about 55 per cent. With income half as high again as before the war, living levels have improved. Though they still lag behind urban workers in this respect, the Engel Index for farm families—the proportion of total income spent on food—stood in 1963 at 37.2 per cent.

As these figures would suggest, compared with the pre-war period when farmers had a real struggle against poverty and cultural aspirations were far beyond their reach, in consumption

[1] For a statistical analysis comparing the pre-war and post-war situations, see Nōrinshō, Nōrin-keizai-kyoku, Tōkei-chōsa-bu, Chōsei-ka, ed., *Nihon no nōgyō keizai: Sengo no seichō to kōzōteki henka*, 1957 (Tōyō-keizai Shimpōsha).

patterns too farm households have been urbanized. The great gulf in living levels between the poor tenant farmers and the landlords has disappeared, a considerable levelling has taken place. This levelling up is largely because their intensifying consumer demands have prompted farmers to supplement agricultural income by an increasing resort to part-time occupations outside agriculture. In terms of household expenditure per person those farm families with less than 0.3 hectares closely approach those with more than 2 hectares, while the lowest figure is registered by those with between 0.5 and 1.5 hectares. In present circumstances these middling groups cannot live from their agricultural income, but on the other hand the land they have is big enough and demands enough of their time to prevent them from concentrating on other work. At any rate, with the part-time farmers gaining a large non-agricultural income in the lead, rural consumption habits are taking on an increasingly urban form. The dissolution of the traditional status hierarchy and the spirit of competition operating within the hamlet, are helping to spread this trend to every household.

However, even if the Engel Index has declined to 37, the proportion of food expenditure devoted to staple grains remains at over 40 per cent. so that compared to urban workers with an Engel Index of 36 per cent. and only 25 per cent. of food expenditure going to staple grains, the farmers' standard of nutrition is still low. This means that their purchase of consumer durables is at the cost of a certain amount of financial strain. The diffusion of these goods in the countryside of course lags behind urban rates, but nevertheless the fact that television is now installed in 80 per cent. of farmhouses, and electric washing machines in every other farmhouse, represents a notable advance. The spread of television is particularly significant since it brings rural people into constant contact with urban culture through a medium which by its visual impact is bound to have a far greater effect on rural life than did the radio.[2]

Thus, with rural living levels already 50 per cent. higher than they were 10 years ago, there is no doubt that the farmers' patterns of life will continue to be more and more urbanized in

[2] These recent consumer statistics are drawn from Nōrin-tōkei Kyōkai, ed., *Zusetsu nōgyō nenji hōkoku, 1964*, 1965.

the future, and there is little doubt that the middle strata of farmers, unable to maintain their standards of living from their agricultural earnings, will take more and more to part-time work. It used to be said that 1½ hectares was the watershed; below that level full-time farming was impossible. Now, and not surprisingly, 2 hectares is coming to be spoken of as the cutting point. The days when farmers were prepared to suppress their desires for the good things of life, when their strength lay in their ability merely to 'exist', to be satisfied with the fact that even on a meagre piece of land careful tilling could ensure enough food for survival—these days are soon to end. When they are finally no more, then farmers can look forward to 'living' in a truly human sense. That new age is already beginning to dawn.

The Culture of Village Life

A man whose whole life is taken up with work and sleep has little to do with culture. The English word culture may be etymologically related to cultivation and it may indeed be the ability to cultivate the fields which distinguishes man from the animals, but the cultural life of the man who devotes all his time to cultivating the fields is likely to be lived at a very low level.

'He sets out in the morning with the stars above his head; he returns at night treading his moon-shadow.' The phrase may be something of an exaggeration, but it is nevertheless true that the waking hours of the farmer in feudal Japan began and ended with work. And the income he received from these long hours of toil was very small indeed. It was inevitable that the development of peasant culture should have been retarded. The only alleviation of the asperities of a hard working life was the occasional festival in the agricultural slack season, the Bon dances or the feast of the local village god. In the farmer's daily life, thrift was a supreme virtue and consumption an evil. Insecurity drove him to seek salvation in magical religions which promised benefits in the here-and-now; his customary agricultural practices did not even require him to be literate or numerate.

The Meiji Restoration brought a change. Education was

necessary for men who were to become useful conscripts or play their full part in capitalist factory production. By the early years of this century illiteracy had practically disappeared from the villages. The development of capitalism brought the commercial economy to the countryside and so changed the material culture. Living levels too were considerably improved in comparision with the Tokugawa period. However, the burden of the work needed to operate a family small holding did not diminish and compared with the towns the level of living too was still low, as we have pointed out in the last section. Village life remained dominated by the twin themes of diligence and thrift; from these there was escape only for the landlords.

Since the war the situation has changed. By international standards Japanese agriculture is still characterized by a highly intensive labour input, but it is no longer possible to perpetuate a situation in which improvements in living levels depend solely on the increase in unit yields achieved by ever more intensive manual labour. The time has passed when farmers were content to look on agriculture as their ancestral 'calling' and did not count the labour of family members in their costs of production. Though still on a small scale, mechanization has begun in the tilling process. Working hours have been shortened. Compared with the pre-war period (1934–6) the number of hours of labour devoted to rice production per unit area have decreased by 26 per cent; by 15 per cent. compared with ten years ago. Agriculture can no longer take the form of following empirical customary methods. A certain level of scientific techniques has become indispensable.[3]

As farmers become more conscious of the value of the hours they spend at work and as they acquire a respect for the rationality of science through their acquaintance with new agricultural techniques, so the culture of village life has changed. The old peasant logic which saw consumption as an evil and any-

[3] The decrease in working hours and the changing structure of the farmers' day can be seen in studies conducted by the Japanese Broadcasting Company (NHK) first in 1941 and then again recently. These studies indicate, on the basis of questionnaires, the average amount of time spent eating, sleeping, reading, etc. The movement towards urban patterns in the last twenty years is fairly clear. See NHK, Hōsō-bunka kenkyūjo, *Nihonjin no seikatsu-jikan*, 1963 (Nihon Hōsō Kyōkai).

thing more than the bare necessities of life as unjustifiable
luxury has ceased to be accepted. (And along with it has gone
the agrarian fundamentalism which will be discussed later.)
The pressure which set a limit to men's wants has been lifted
and now they seek actively to fulfil them. Farmers who once
accepted as perfectly natural the idea of stratified consumption
levels now think that every man is equally entitled to try to live
as well as he can. The farmer who once thought it perfectly
natural that the landlord should have a radio because he was
a landlord, and that such things were not for the likes of him,
nowadays, irrespective of whether he used to be owner-farmer
or tenant, will buy a television set as soon as he can afford it.
The dissolution of the *ie* system has made the present living
members of the family more important than the ancestors; the
old ethic which required one to endure meagre poverty in order
to increase the 'family property' through diligence and thrift, is
irreparably weakened.

Thus there has been a change in the basic material constituents of village life; in clothing, food and shelter. Farmers of
every stratum have a western style suit for Sunday best. The
jacket which was the mark of landlord status is so no longer.
Women go to beauty parlours just as their urban sisters do, and
western-style clothes have become normal. Food habits have
also changed, and bean-paste and soya sauce have ceased to be
the only condiments. Houses have improved, especially
kitchens. Where once the housewife spent long hours bending
over her stove fanning the flames into life, making constant
journeys from kitchen to well and back again with no thought
that things could be otherwise, there are now new stoves
installed, and at least a quarter of settlements now have piped
water, even if the facilities are only of a simplified kind.

Nor is the farmer's recreation any longer confined to the
seasonal festivities of the Bon dance, the shrine festival and the
occasional travelling theatre company; leisure has now become
a daily matter. Eighty-five per cent. of the population visit the
cinema at least once a year. A trip to the cinema in the local
town, more especially for the young men, has become a regular
event. Instead of setting off after the harvest for one of the
cheapest hostels at a hot-spring resort, a bag of rice under one

arm, bedding under the other, groups of farmers now hire coaches for day trips to pleasure resorts. And whereas it was only the older folk who went to the hot springs, nowadays everyone can go. A trip to the local town, too, partly for shopping, partly for pleasure, has become a commonplace.

As a result there has been a marked increase in the proportion of family budget expenditure classified under the heading 'culture and entertainment'. As far as school education goes, too, it has now become the normal thing for farmers' children to go on to high school after finishing the compulsory education period. The days when a primary school education was thought sufficient have long since passed. Nor are people indifferent to opportunities for adult education. The classes held in the local Citizens' Hall, and the activities of the home economics adviser, which form a part of the Agricultural Extension Service, have had their effect in raising cultural standards in the villages. However, human cultures are not changed overnight. Nor, indeed, has the economic improvement been such as to permit a dramatic and wholesale transformation. Hence there are certain imbalances in a picture of general improvement compared with the pre-war period. For instance, farmers are much more likely to buy themselves a suit for Sunday best than they are to improve their working clothes or their underclothes. They seem not to have given much attention to obtaining better bedding. The outside of the house which is visibly on display may be rebuilt, while the bedrooms remain untouched. Increased consumer wants can also mean cutting corners in food expenditure. In order to install a television set the family may postpone the purchase of desks for the children to do their home work. The Ministry of Education's recent surveys of academic achievement in primary and junior secondary schools have shown farmers' children to have the lowest average scores. The literacy survey conducted not long after the war produced similar results, and it seems that this position of relative inferiority is not likely soon to be changed.[4]

[4] See Ishiguro Osamu, *et al.*, eds., *Nihonjin no yomikaki nōryoku*, 1951 (Tōkyō-daigaku Shuppankai). Also relevant are: Uchiyama Masateru, *Atarashii nōminzō: sono ishiki, seikatsu, kyōiku*, 1954 (Nagano-ken Nōson Bunka Kyōkai) and Ota Takashi, *Nihon no nōson to kyōiku*, 1957 (Kokudo-sha).

Consequently, while recognizing that farmers are ceasing to 'exist' and beginning to 'live', one cannot be wholly optimistic about the future of village culture. Farmers have taken that first step towards awareness of the dignity of the individual which consists in counting the cost of family labour, but one cannot say that the awareness has yet gone very deep. Individuals can no longer be prevented from having desires of their own, but nevertheless the '*ie*' and the 'hamlet' which required the suppression of such individuality are still living concepts. Hence such desires are likely to express themselves in a warped form. The way in which vanity, the need to keep up appearances, have helped in the spread of television, has already been mentioned, and while there is much talk of simplifying the formal celebrations of weddings and funerals, the concern with the *ie*'s reputation, with what the hamlet will think, still often prevents the effective reduction of unnecessary waste.

The various movements which have sought to raise the cultural level of village life have not managed to break down this barrier. One reason for this is that they are forced to operate within the framework of political neutrality—and because of this limitation they are prevented from penetrating to the fundamental question of what it is that keeps that barrier intact.

CHAPTER XIV

CHANGING AND UNCHANGING ASPECTS OF THE FARMER'S MENTALITY

The Social Characteristics of the Farmer

IT is unnecessary to repeat that the personality of the typical farmer was moulded by the *ie* characterized by unilineal patriarchalism, and by the holistic community-like hamlet dominantly characterized by its status stratification.

We have already described how the *ie* required its members each to keep their proper place under the authoritarian direction of the household, resigning themselves to the suppression of personal desires unbecoming to their position. Thus was order within the *ie* preserved and its harmony guaranteed—a harmony not of liberated cheerfulness, but of smouldering reserve and the frustration of still incompletely repressed desires. In the same way the hamlet required the individual to submit to a customary order patterned by its stratification system. Here too independent individualism was repressed; harmony in the hamlet was preserved by each family keeping its proper place, conforming its behaviour to the need to maintain the status system, following the lead of the ruling stratum. 'The harmony of the hamlet' was no more attractive a slogan than 'harmony in the *ie*', but it was one capable of exerting considerable restraining power.

Thus the typical farmer was a man capable of being content with his lot and of integrating himself harmoniously in the group. The farmer's attitude to life may be summed up as being respectful of custom and obedient to authority.

Fear of disturbing the atmosphere of harmony means, in

effect, conformity with the majority. To go along with the crowd in the well-worn established patterns of traditional behaviour was thought always to be the safest course. This is why appearances and reputation—what people will think— was a dominant determinant of behaviour, and why adherence to custom conditioned the farmer's traditional conservatism. The emphasis on keeping one's proper station led equally to authoritarianism. To operate within a status system which had been evolved over long generations, to show compliance towards the authority of those above one and find some compensation for the accompanying sense of inferiority by lording it over those below, never to step in all one's comings and goings a foot beyond one's proper sphere—these were an important part of the social personality of the typical farmer.

However, these basic patterns inevitably underwent some change during the development of a capitalist society from the last century onwards. The permeation of the villages by the commercial economy taught the farmers too to make monetary calculations. As the formerly isolated self-sufficient village society came into increasingly frequent contact with the towns, the farmer's range of wants also expanded. The repercussions of economic change destroyed the stability of the village status system and brought fluctuations in the fortunes and 'standing' of families. For farmers still psychologically confined by the framework of the *ie* their chances of achieving their now expanded list of wants depended on improving their *ie*'s position —on redoubled efforts to raise its socio-economic standing within the status order.

Hence arose the spirit of selfishness, but in the holistic community of village society it could only be a latent selfishness. Although with the increase in productivity farming had become generally a matter of individual family enterprise with few elements of communal co-operation, the hamlet generally exercised communal control over the use of forest lands and water, so that complete independence and total indifference to one's neighbours was simply not possible. Consequently, the competition to rise in the status scale took on a covert form. Instead of growing into full-blown individualism, it became a stunted egotism.

Moreover despite these self-regarding ambitious efforts it was by no means easy to raise the family's standing. The size of the land holding of the family into which one was born set very severe limits to the effectiveness of one's efforts. Most could only grow resigned in the face of harsh realities. The conditions required to liberate the farmer from conformity and authoritarianism were not fulfilled.[1]

The changes in village society beginning with the post-war land reform have also had their effect on these characteristics of the farmer's social personality. With the dissolution of the status system, family egotism has been further stimulated, and with the breakdown of the community solidarity of the hamlet it has become more and more overt. As the constraints exercised by the hamlet community are weakened, the need for conformity diminishes. Departure from hamlet customs becomes easier. Again, with the disappearance of landlord dominance, the need for authoritarian behaviour largely disappears. The authority of the former landlord, once backed by the economic reality of a tenancy relation, no longer carries much weight when everyone is equally an owner-farmer.

Moreover, as we have seen in the last section, people are no longer so willing to be content with their lot, and the demand for a better life has become irresistibly stronger and more widely diffused. It is further reinforced by manifold urbanizing tendencies. As their need increases for cash to fulfil their growing wants, farmers inevitably become more profit-minded. Those whose farms are too small to satisfy their need for more cash begin to take side jobs and look for income outside of agriculture. This process of differentiation further weakens the constraints which the hamlet exercises on the individual, and as each separate group of farmers pursues its own particular interests co-ordinated action of the whole hamlet becomes difficult. The customary order inevitably changes, and this too weakens the spirit of conformity.

[1] On the question of the farmer's personality, see Fukutake Tadashi and Tsukamoto Tetsundo, *Nihon nōmin no shakaiteki seikaku*, 1954 (Yūhikaku), Ogura Takekazu, *Nōmin no shakaiteki seikaku*, 1954 (Nōmin Kyōiku Kyōkai), Ishiwata Sadao, *Nōmin wa hoshuteki ka*, 1955 (Shin-hyōronsha) and Nojiri Shigeo, ed., *Nōmin: sono seikaku to mirai-zō*, 1959 (Meibundō).

Nevertheless the egotism which has thus become overt does not develop into liberated individualism. Though crumbling, the *ie* system remains. As a community, the hamlet has not totally disintegrated. Egotism cannot exceed the bounds of family egotism and the parochial spirit of hamlet egotism—my hamlet against all comers—has not disappeared. Individualism does not develop because the family economy does not allow it, because productivity has not reached the levels at which an individual family can be independent of the hamlet. Apart from which, of course, personality characteristics formed under past conditions do not immediately respond when those conditions are to some extent changed. Even if the authority of superior status disappears, an authoritarian personality does not lose its pattern; even if the confining constraints of the hamlet are weakened, conformity does not disappear overnight. Rational individualism expressed in principled independent behaviour, the democratic spirit which permits rational co-operation with mutual respect for individual independence—these are things which the farmer has yet to learn.

This is why despite the progressively heterogeneous differentiation of the residents of the hamlet it preserves something of its holistic character and has not split up into differentiated functional groups. People still try to act on the principle that when any group is formed everyone in the hamlet should belong. Hence the fact that the Agricultural Co-operatives, though in effect dominated by a small group of farmers, continue formally to include every farming household; and hence also the reason why they can be incorporated into the governmental administrative system to such a degree that their independence is compromised.

One sees a similar phenomenon if one looks at the forms of production co-operation which are likely to become increasingly important in the future. There is a tendency, wherever conditions permit, for these co-operating groups to be formed on a hamlet basis, and, even where it is not possible that the co-operating group should coincide with the hamlet, they very frequently fail to take on a modern democratic form. Co-operation in the past, to repeat, depended on the smothering of individual interest and was possible only with authoritarian direction. Similar attitudes and assumptions survive today. Modern co-operation depends for its success on a rationalism which does not overlook even the slightest divergence of interest and on democratic management by members acting as independent individuals. But these have not yet become characteristics of the farmer's social personality.

Political Attitudes of the Farmer

It is sometimes said that the farmer has two souls. The one is the soul of the manual labourer which he is. The other is the soul of the petty bourgeois which, by virtue of his ownership of his land and farming tools, he also is. When he perceives himself as one who works by the sweat of his brow for an inadequate reward, as a member of the suppressed and exploited classes, he is a potential recruit for radical movements against the established order. But when he does not become conscious of his position in this way, the petty bourgeois in him smothers the worker and makes a conservative of him. Confined by the restraints of the *ie* system and of the hamlet community life, Japanese farmers have long preserved their conservative character. Their land is not for them a means of production, it is the 'family property'. To preserve the family property and continue the family 'calling' by unremitting manual toil was the fate assigned to them at birth. As long as life went on they did not offer resistance to political authority. The power of authority was looked on as something like the ravages of nature, something one could do nothing about. That it was the farmer's fate to be ruled admitted of no question.

This basic pattern of rural attitudes ought to have changed with the development of a capitalist economy since the Meiji Restoration, but this change was frustrated by the teachings of agrarian fundamentalism.[2]

Though in essence an anti-farmer ideology, it was offered as a solution for the psychological complexes of the farmer in a capitalist society, as a solace for his anguished soul. The agrarian fundamentalists taught that agriculture, left behind by the

[2] For a description of this agrarian fundamentalism, see Sakurai Takeo, *Nihon nōhon-shugi*, 1935 (Hakuyōsha).

development of industry, was the most natural and healthy of occupations. Whereas urban life led to the progressive degradation of man, agriculture, though at the base of the pyramid, was the support and foundation of the national society. This agrarian fundamentalism, landlord style, with its praise for those who could submit to poverty and endure heavy toil, delayed the farmer's political awakening. Apart from its momentary and partial ignition in the tenant union movement, for most of the pre-war period it is little exaggeration to say that the farmer's political consciousness was characterized by a blind lack of awareness.

The defeat at the end of the Second World War neutralized the effects of this indoctrination to the effect that 'agriculture is the foundation of the nation'. It lost its power to rationalize the fact that agriculture is an unprofitable business compared with others. Farmers begin to count the cost of unpaid family labour; they have come to expect that agriculture too should be an occupation capable of being pursued like any other for a profit. One no longer finds the old farmer mentality, the ability to restrain consumption in order to save and respond to hardship by working ever harder.[3]

In recent years in particular, during the period of abnormally rapid economic growth, as the income differential between agriculture and the other industries increases there is a growing sense among farmers that agriculture has reached a dead end. Those farmers with relatively big holdings have moved towards greater involvement in commercial production and strengthened their resolve to squeeze a profit out of their holdings which they regard no longer as the family property but as an instrument of production. This, they hope, will be their way out of the impasse. For those with less land, farming is something that simply provides a basic income which they will supplement from

[3] For surveys of farmers' attitudes in the post-war period, see Fukutake Tadashi and Tsukamoto Tetsundo, *Nihon nōmin no shakaiteki seikaku*, 1954 (Yūhikaku), Many other surveys have been carried out since, but none have been published in book form. The reader may refer, however, to Shimazaki Minoru, 'Nōmin no ishiki' in Fukutake Tadashi, ed., *Nihonjin no shakai-ishiki*, 1960 (San'ichi Shobō) and my essay, 'Sengo ni okeru nōmin ishiki no henyō' in Fukutake, *Nihon sonraku no shakai-kōzō*, 1959 (Tōkyō-daigaku Shuppankai).

elsewhere. In either case agriculture has ceased to be thought of as 'the family calling'.

As agriculture thus comes to be perceived as another occupation and a distinctly ill-rewarded one, one would naturally expect in these conditions a heightening of farmers' political consciousness. Since the dissolution of the landlord system, farmers have generally come to show some interest in politics, so that one might hence have expected that the farmer's radical soul would come to the fore. Nevertheless the villages are still spoken of as the solid bastion of the conservative party and the farmers' political attitudes are supposed to be chiefly characterized by a traditional apathy.

Until recently this was certainly the case. The sense that one was born to be ruled, nurtured over many centuries, is not one that is easily eradicated. However, one should not overlook at the same time the fact that in matters which touch on their immediate interests farmers in the post-war period have been by no means apathetic. They have been the reverse of the urban intellectuals, noted for their apathy concerning the politics of daily life and their intense interest only in national and international policy. In recent years, however, even on general political questions, it has become no longer possible to discuss the farmers' political attitudes in terms of such simple categories as traditional apathy.

Even today public opinion surveys in rural areas yield a fairly high proportion of 'don't know' responses on political questions, particularly from women. Nevertheless a fair proportion of farmers have come to hold political opinions, especially, since the enactment of the Basic Agricultural Law, on questions of agricultural policy. And they are intuitively aware of the fact that the policy of the present conservative party is geared to the interests of big business. They consequently have a sense of mistrust for national politics. Nevertheless the great majority of them when they come to vote support the conservative party. One might explain this in general terms on the grounds that as petty proprietors they are induced to avoid the radical parties which they see as exclusively workers' parties, and to support the government party for the practical reasons of local self-interest which were described in an earlier chapter.

However, in more detailed terms, this generalization needs to be analyzed into the following components. Firstly, the upper stratum of full-time farmers who intend to live by agriculture and improve the profitability of their farms support the Liberal-Democratic Party because they still see hope in its policies for an improvement in their agricultural prospects. In addition, these are the farmers who gain more than others from the kind of 'petition politics' which is concerned above all with the representation of local interests. By contrast, in those farm families which derived more of their incomes from outside than from inside agriculture, and where the main wage earner has a relatively secure occupation of a modern type, there is little positive interest in farming, and there may well be an inclination to vote for the radical parties as a result of contacts in the factory or office. As for the intermediate group of part-time farmers, the majority have not enough land to hope to make a profitable business out of agriculture, nor have they enough time to settle for an outside job. These are the most insecure, the most oppressed by the burden of the double job, and the least able to develop an interest in politics. In personality they tend to be the most traditionally conservative, precisely the stratum which can be categorized as showing the political apathy that is supposed to be typical of farmers. When they vote they are likely to be influenced by the realistic self-interest of the upper stratum of full-time farmers, and vote for the conservative party without having any clear sense of party allegiance. The other group of rural commuters who farm only to grow their own rice lack either the power or the will to draw this intermediate stratum towards support of the radical parties. They themselves as land-owning workers are no longer farmers; they are content with the relative stability of a way of life in which they can ensure their own food supply.

So much for the political attitudes of farmers in the present day and for the voting behaviour which springs from them. If the above picture is true one might expect that with the further development of Japanese society and economy, as this intermediate stratum is gradually forced to rely more and more on income from outside agriculture, and as the upper stratum of full-time farmers becomes progressively disillusioned with the prospects of improving their income from farming, there is a strong possibility of a radical change in the political attitude map. It is precisely then that one can expect the farmer's manual-worker soul to be awakened.

On the other hand it is likely to be some time before farmers' illusions about the possibilities of more profitable farming are dispelled, and the chances are that the intermediate stratum will for the most part follow the land-owning worker pattern, with very few of them leaving farming completely to become workers pure and simple. Moreover the left-wing parties have succeeded in making only a very weak impact on the farmer and their policies are highly formalistic and lacking in appeal. When they attack the Government's policy for improvement of the agrarian structure as 'wiping out the poor farmers' or talk of co-operative management as the solution to the problems of the disintegrating intermediate stratum, they can hardly expect to win the confidence of the farmers who vote for the Liberal-Democratic Party. The so-called 'poor farmers' of Japan by the standards of the advanced countries are far worse off than 'poor farmers'; even the upper stratum of farmers must co-operate if they are to have any future. When this is appreciated by farmers of the upper stratum themselves and when it becomes clear that the hopes of progress by individual management are illusory and if, at that time, the radical parties can offer concrete plans to substitute for that illusion, then and only then can one expect any new developments in the farmers' political attitudes.

FURTHER READING

On living levels, cultural life and attitudes, see:
Beardsley, Hall and Ward, *Village Japan.*
Cornell, *Matsunagi.*
Dore, *Land reform.*
Embree, *Suyemura.*
Norbeck, *Takashima.*
Raper, *Japanese village.*
Smith, *Kurusu.*
Agriculture, Forestry and Fisheries Productivity Conference, *Home-living improvement extension service in Japan* (*Agricultural development series,* 4), 1959.
Idem, *Farm household economy survey in Japan* (*Agricultural development series,* 13), 1960.

Japan FAO Association, *Agriculture at the cross-roads*, Tokyo, 1961.

Ministry of Agriculture and Forestry, *Annual report on the state of agriculture; 1961—*, Tokyo, 1963—

E. Norbeck, 'Postwar cultural change and continuity in northeastern Japan', *American Anthropologist*, 64, 1961.

T. Fukutake, 'Changes in the value system of Japanese farmers', *Sociologia Ruralis*, Vol. IV, No. 3/4, 1964.

INDEX

Affinal relationships, 61, 73–5, 76

Age groups, 102–3, 106

Age structure of population, 24, 37

Agrarian fundamentalism, 210, 217–18

Agrarian Structure Improvement Programme, 27, 197–9

Agricultural Associations, 7, 14, 172

Agricultural Co-operatives, 57, 92–3, 115, 121, 150, 183, 184, 194, 216

Agricultural Extension Service, 19, 211

Agricultural Land Adjustment Law, 17

Agricultural Practice Unions, 92–3, 94, 99, 101, 111, 115–16, 126, 135–6, 137; chiefs of, 121, 122, 150

Agricultural Study Groups, 19, 56, 113–14

Agriculture, improved techniques in, 3–4, 8, 20, 24, 34, 54, 195; strained by capitalism, 5; industry and, 5–6; smallness of holdings, 6–7, 11, 21, 31; not capitalist, 6; increased production in, 7–8, 16, 19–20, 24, 140, 144, 214; prices in, 7; stagnation in, 8, 22–3, 196, 197; feudalism in, 8–10, 13, 17, 18, 40–1, 42, 53, 84, 117, 205, 208; capitalism and, 8, 84, 195, 197; government policy towards, 17, 27, 194–9, 219–21; population employed in, 22–4; commercial, 25, 26, 57, 58, 59, 94, 141, 218, 220–1; families and, 26, 31–3, 45, 209, 218; prospects for, 201

Amalgamation of towns and villages, 26–7, 38, 88, 109, 117, 137, 150, 156–7, 160–2, 166–7, 173, 181–5

Ancestor-worship, 41, 53, 62, 66, 108

Ane-katoku, 43

Associations, functional, 94, 108–15; traditional, 95–108

Basic Law of Agriculture (1961), 27, 197, 219

Birth-rate, 34

Bosses in politics, 185–6, 187, 188, 193

Branch Citizens' Halls, 121–2, 123, 211

Branch families, 40, 42, 55, 62–7, 71–6, 98, 104, 138–9, 144

Brides, 32, 44, 49–51, 55, 56–7, 59, 73; 'young bride's school', 115 (*see* Daughters-in-law)

Bunke, 40, 42, 55–6, 64 (*see* Branch families)

Buraku, 88–9, 98, 109, 110, 118

Bureaucratization, 156, 184

Capitalism, growth of, 4–6, 13,

Library of Congress Cataloging in Publication Data
(For library cataloging purposes only)

Fukutake, Tadashi, date.
  Japanese rural society.

  (Cornell paperbacks)
  Translation of Nihon nōson shakai ron.
  Includes bibliographies.
  1. Villages—Japan. 2. Japan—Rural conditions.
I. Title.
[HN727.F813 1972]   309.1'52'04   72-4314
ISBN 0-8014-9127-4